Maps courtesy Wide World and UPI Newspictures

1961

Atlantic Ocean

MOROCCO 1956

TUNISIA 1956

ALGERIA

Mediterranean Sea

SPANISH SAHARA

SAHARAN DEPTS.

LIBYA 1951

EGYPT (U.A.R.) 1922

Red Sea

MAURITANIA

SENEGAL

MALI

NIGER

CHAD

SUDAN 1956

French SOMALILAND

ETHIOPIA

GUINEA 1958

U. VOLTA

1957

NIGERIA 1960

CAMEROON 1960

CENTRAL AFRICAN REP.

UGANDA

KENYA

SOMALIA 1960

SIERRA LEONE 1961

GHANA

DAHOMEY

Spanish GUINEA

REPUBLIC OF CONGO 1960

L. Victoria

LIBERIA 1847

IVORY COAST

TOGOLAND 1960

GABON

RUANDA-URUNDI

CONGO REPUBLIC

TANGANYIKA 1961

NYASALAND

ANGOLA

N. RHODESIA

MOZAMBIQUE

S. RHODESIA

SOUTH WEST AFRICA

BECHUANA-LAND

MALAGASY REP

Atlantic Ocean

UNION OF SOUTH AFRICA

1910

SWAZILAND

BASUTOLAND

Indian Ocean

THE NEW LEADERS OF AFRICA

* **THE NEW**

✳

LEADERS OF AFRICA

ROLF ITALIAANDER

Translated from the German by   JAMES MCGOVERN

✳

PRENTICE-HALL, INC.
ENGLEWOOD CLIFFS, N.J.

This book is dedicated to the memory of Diedrich Westermann, the Nestor of international Africanism, who continually inspired me to portray the Africans of today.

"The life histories that are related here have all one thing in common: radical change resulting from a meeting with European ways. That is the decisive factor today: the lives of individuals and communities flow together, but in every case inevitably along lines marked out by whites, and people's destinies depend on how they come to terms with this experience."

Diedrich Westermann
in "Africans Tell of Their Lives"

ACKNOWLEDGMENTS

※

This book could never have been written without the help of numerous individuals, scholarly institutes, and government offices, who made available to me biographies, speeches, reports, statistics, anecdotes, personal reminiscences, and photographs. I can't thank all of them here, and indeed some of the people who gave me information prefer not to be named. But the others I can thank. I am especially grateful to:

Dr. Abdel-Wahhab, Councillor of Embassy, Royal Moroccan Embassy, Bonn; Prof. Rom Landau, Stockton, California; Tunisian Embassy, Bonn; Dr. Wolfgang Berka, Royal Council, Libya; Press Division of the Embassy of the United Arab Republic, Bad Godesberg; Dr. Herbert von Veltheim, Cairo; Ministry of Information and Labor, Khartoum, Sudan; M. H. E. Misbah, Embassy of the Republic of the Sudan, Bonn; Dr. J. H. F. Otto, Addis Ababa, Ethiopia; the Press attaché of the Imperial Ethiopian Embassy, Bonn; M. Close, Information Officer, Department of Information, Nairobi, Kenya; Public Relations Department, Dar es Salaam, Tanganyika; Charles Ramanantsoa, Malagascay Republic, Tananarive; The editorial staff of *Asa Vao Vao*, Fianarantsoa, Madagascar; Information Office, Federation of Rhodesia and Nyasaland, Salisbury; Rhodesia-Nyasaland House, London; Press Section of the Embassy of the Union of South Africa, Bonn; *Africa South in Exile*, London; M. John Morrison, *Christian Action*, London; The Right Reverend Lord Bishop Dr. Ambrose Reeves, Johannesburg; M. R. Onckelinx, Office de l'Information et des Rélations Publiques pour le Congo Belge et le Ruanda-Urundi, Brussels; Dr. Adrian vanden Bossche, Director of the Congo Museum, Leopoldville, Congo; Graf J. F. de Liedekerke, Belgian Embassy, Bonn; M. A. Colard, Chef des Services Rédactionnels of *Pourquoi Pas?*, Brussels-Leopoldville; M. Bernard Fagg, Department of Antiquities, Jos, Nigeria; M. Sule Kolo, Nigeria House, London; Adolf Friedrich, Duke of Mecklenburg, Schloss Eutin; Office to the High Commissioner for Ghana, London; Mrs. Erica Powell, Government House, Accra, Ghana; Prof. Dr. K. H. Busia, Institute of Social Studies, The Hague; Press attaché of the Republic of Liberia, Bonn; Prof. R. T. Dempster, Tubman University, Monrovia, Liberia; Ingeborg Bauer, Hamburg; M. John Beer, London; Mr. Berman, British Information Service, Bonn; Mr. Alouine Diop, *Présence Africaine,* Paris; Prof. Michel Foucault, Institut Français, Hamburg; Mrs. Jan Guy, The Africa Bureau, London; Dr. Hertha Haas, Hamburg; M. L. Hirn, Le Chef du Service de Presse & d'Information, French Embassy, Bonn; International African Institute, London; Consul Philip W. Haley, British Consulate, Hamburg; Prof. A. E. Jensen, Frobenius Institute, Frankfort a/M.; Erich Lüth, Hamburg; Prof. Dr. J. Lukas, Director of the Seminar for African Languages, University of Hamburg; The Lutheran Church Bureau, Hannover-Herrenhausen, Dr. Piet Meertens, Koninklijke Nederlandse Akademie van Wetenschapen, Amsterdam; Dr. C. Nooteboom, Museum voor Land—en Volkenkunde, Rotterdam; Prof. I. I. Potekhin, Academie of Science, Moscow; Prof. Dr. E. L. Rapp, University of Mainz; University of London Institute of Education, Department of Education on Tropical Areas, London; Prof. Dr. E. Zechlin, Director of Historical Seminars at the University of Hamburg; Prof. Dr. P. Fried, Hope College, Holland, Michigan.

Thanks, too, to those publishing houses which have permitted me to quote from their books. Mrs. Nele Prufer and Hans-Ludwig Spegg, as they have done so often, rendered especially valuable service in proofreading my manuscript and sifting through my collection of materials.

Last but not least I would like to thank almost without exception the new leaders in Africa portrayed in this book, who either received me personally, or if I did not have the opportunity to meet them, corresponded with me or gave me information through their assistants, secretaries, or diplomatic representatives.

R. I.

The reader will find a detailed bibliography of the old and the new history of Africa in *Der Ruhelose Konh'nent* by Rolf Italiaander. The author is presently preparing a critical bibliography, especially concerned with contemporary African history, which will be published by the Department of History, Hope College, Holland, Michigan.

EMERGING AFRICA

✳

It seems to me to be a very fortunate coincidence that this edition should appear when I myself am in the United States as guest professor for African History and Civilization. The seminars I have conducted, and the lectures I have given in other colleges and universities in several American states, as well as my earlier sojourns in Great Britain and the Commonwealth countries, have shown me that our friends in both the United Kingdom and the United States have recently become especially interested in the questions posed by contemporary Africa.

Both countries are distinguished by their inestimable freedom of speech and deep joy in individual discussion, symbols of true democracy. Because of this I expect the appearance of this book in the United States and Great Britain to give rise to some spirited discussions—for it is a book designed to stimulate discussion about Africa.

It's possible that some Americans or Englishmen won't agree with one or another of the author's judgements—that they will have another point of view in certain instances. But as I have pointed out in many places in this book, it is a question here of a serious attempt to portray the personalities of contemporary African history. And how different are our estimates of historical personalities!

I would like my American and British readers—as are those in other countries—to be convinced that, after many study trips in

Africa during the past three decades, my principal aim is strengthening the ties of the Africans with the West. For just this reason some personal opinions, which may not conform to standard judgements, must be permitted. The African leaders will, I hope, also perceive from my numerous books on Africa that when the author occasionally criticizes one personality or another, or a system of government, he does so as one who is filled with great respect, even affection, for the new leaders in Africa and above all for the peoples of Africa, who have always allowed him to live among them as a brother.

I would like to express my warm thanks here to James Mc-Govern of The Pennsylvania State University for translating this work, and for having added some new information to bring it up-to-date. I would also like to thank the publishing house of Prentice-Hall, Inc., for giving me this opportunity to supplement my university lectures and courses in the English-speaking countries through publication of this book. America, like Great Britain, has a rich and valuable literature on Africa, and I consider myself fortunate to be able to count many of their African experts among my friends. Nevertheless, I hope that my work will fill some of the gaps in the American and English literature on Africa that is presently available.

This book is the result of nearly thirty years of travel and study in Africa. But as history is being made daily in Africa, and as the lives of the developing new leaders in Africa must perforce remain somewhat fragmentary for years to come, I was faced with this problem: which men should be considered, which ignored? There was only one solution: not to attempt to portray all of those who are in power today, but to make a representative selection. In this way, many heterogeneous personalities are brought close together. The constitutional monarch stands next to the nationalist rebel, who in turn is found next to the politician who is more obligated to the whites than to his brown or black countrymen.

This should not disturb us, but on the contrary should be welcomed, for it opens up the endlessly colorful play of historical forces, even when they are as yet inconclusive. We are here attempting to come to grips with a slice of contemporary history, by beginning first with Morocco and then making a clockwise tour of most of the other African countries.

An old colonialist once told me: "One can only love or hate the African, there's no other possibility." Perhaps some readers will think that I have displayed too much sympathy and friendliness for the African. Let me make this clear at the outset: honest accounts of careers, however short they may be, can only be written from the viewpoint of the friend or enemy. Any attempt at compromise can only result in a pallid book. Naturally, I have tried to be objective. However, some of my own subjective judgments have inevitably crept into this report, simply because I have come to know many of my "heroes" personally during the course of my life in Africa.

Whether or not men make history, or are merely the victims of uncontrollable circumstances, is still being argued. However that may be, individuals do play a decisive role in today's Africa. Even before the coming of the white man there were strong personalities here: kings, tribal chiefs, religious and military leaders. Although many of them resisted the white man, they were all ground down eventually. It was through the white man that Africa first became the continent of the shapeless, cowed, and submissive masses.

For three hundred years, the African masses found themselves under the yoke of the colonialists, who regarded them as little better than savages or semi-savages. As the colonial and imperialist era drew to a close, more and more countries began to produce individuals who, better than the masses, understood what had happened, how their peoples had been diverted from their normal historical development. They began to rebel, to form action groups, and with these—usually composed of only a small number of determined men—they at last brought the masses to revolt against their foreign conquerors. Many declarations of independence were not granted voluntarily by the colonial powers, but were wrested from them by the leaders of the African peoples themselves.

This book, therefore, is not only a portrayal of the new leaders in Africa, but also a contribution to the history of the creation of a cadre of qualified native leaders on this continent. And perhaps nothing characterizes the gigantic phenomenon that is Africa so much as the fact that one can already write a book about its new leaders.

I probably never would have written this book if I hadn't become convinced that the individual is the decisive motivating force of our time. As before in history, the new leaders find the world largely unprepared to accept their advanced theories and acts. Opposed to them are the masses, who are disturbed by these new men, and who would probably like nothing better than to divert them, to see them sink back into that obscurity from which they have recently emerged. However, those who possess real greatness, who stand under the protection of the Goddess of History, cannot be denied. And contemporary Africa has actually produced a number of unusually gifted men.

I would like here to recall a man who was himself born in Africa, whose work would have been inconceivable without the light of Africa, and who because of this fulfilled himself as both an African and a European: Albert Camus. He wrote: "I have constantly sought solely for ways to triumph over our dark Nihilism—not out of virtue or some strange pride of soul, but rather from an instinctive loyalty to that light in which I was born and in which men for thousands of years have learned to welcome life, in all its agony."

This light mentioned by Camus was the light of Africa. "I have few opinions," he wrote further, "but a single truth—when it is obvious—suffices for leading an existence. In any case, I have decided to speak out about the Individual."

I, too, have attempted "to speak out about the Individual." This book is not at all the work of a politician, but the work of a man who tries to feel, think, and act like a humanist.

R.I.

Department of History
Hope College
Holland, Michigan

TABLE OF CONTENTS

1

NEW MEN IN A NEW WORLD

❋

Imagine an eighteenth century man suddenly awakening after a long sleep to find himself in the modern world. Would he be able to orient himself, get about? Hardly likely. Quite possibly he would lose his mind or his will to live and ask nothing more than to resume his deep sleep, nevermore to be awakened.

Many Africans today find themselves in just such a situation. Most of them are making a journey through centuries. Yesterday they lived in the desert, the bush, or the primitive forest—today in modern cities. The surprising thing is not that so many of them slip and come to grief while making this leap from one time into another, but that so many of them do manage it successfully.

Before I present the new leaders in Africa, I would like to describe some personal experiences with contemporary Africans. As this book deals principally with statesmen and politicians, let's visit a government reception first.

A few weeks after Guinea, through the influence of Sékou Touré, voted for complete independence from France, I stopped in Conakry, its capital, and was invited to the first evening reception given by the new cabinet. The heat and humidity were enervating. I asked the office of the Minister of the Interior, Keita Fodeba, whom I had known earlier as a poet and ballet director, if I might come in a light tropical suit. His secretary gave me the Minister's best wishes, adding that "he had invited me, and not my suit." Guests could dress as they wished.

Shortly after dusk, the Minister of Public Works called for me at my hotel. Conakry lies on an island, connected for years to the mainland by a railroad and motor road, and we drove over to the outskirts of the city, past a row of splendid mansions with well-tended gardens. "Built by the French, but our ministers live in them now," my companion offered. We slowed down before one of these houses and parked in its front garden, among a great number of other automobiles.

It was a sultry tropical night, the sky full of stars. We walked through the villa's large and tastefully furnished rooms to the back garden, where the guests were standing about. Aside from cabinet officers, other high officials of the new government had been invited—and all of them were correctly dressed in dark suits. My light tropical suit made me feel ill-at-ease. Most of the men had brought their wives, some of them dressed in European, some in African styles.

Keita Fodeba came up, took me by the arm, and introduced me to several of the guests. President Sékou Touré greeted me warmly and introduced me to his wife. I was to meet her often later. Wherever she appeared, she was paid court to by both blacks and whites. She certainly deserved it! Once a secretary, and now "The First Lady of Guinea," she is both beautiful and charming.

Dinner began shortly after my arrival. A sheep was being roasted on a spit over an open fire. Keita Fodeba handed me a plate. "You're among Africans now, my friend," the Minister of the Interior said. "And here you have a good example of what barbarians we are. Isn't it true that they still think of us that way in Europe? We eat with our fingers, don't bother with knives and forks. Yes, we're still terrible barbarians." He laughed scornfully.

"The custom isn't unknown to me," I said. "In North Africa, I've often eaten this way. In the desert, too."

"But you're really a white African," he answered. Then, together, we tore off pieces of mutton. Delicious! When the dinner had ended, napkins and bowls filled with hot water and lemon juice were passed around.

During the meal, no one made me feel that I was the only white person present. Of course, there are Negro gatherings where a white man does feel a stranger. Such was not the case here.

The high point of the evening for me was a musical performance. Two handsome young Negroes appeared after champagne was served. One was dressed in blue jeans and a striped sailor's shirt, the other in a European lounge suit. The latter played a few solos on the guitar, then the other sang.

They were from the Minister of the Interior's ballet troupe, which has made foreign tours. As a finale, they sang together two war songs, a death chant, and a love song, which, I was assured, is one of the few love songs in Guinean folk music. Politics, plans for the future were forgotten.

When they had finished, I went up to the president of the Republic, thanked him for the enjoyable performance, and then wandered alone through the garden, observing this pleasant gathering of African officials of a young republic. I met Keita Fodeba when I returned, and he asked me how I had enjoyed myself.

"Very much," I said. "But once again, I see how much still remains to be done, on the human level."

Back in my hotel, as I spent a sleepless night on the balcony of my room, the same thought came back to me.

Things don't always go so harmoniously. As elsewhere, one can be surprised and disappointed in Africa. I was once shaken and depressed after a meeting with the president of Ghana, Dr. Kwame Nkrumah. To avoid misunderstanding, let me say that I consider him one of the most intelligent men in Africa today: he has real greatness.

Whenever I was with Nkrumah, he dispensed with formalities, called me by my first name, and was always most charming. He granted me many candid interviews in Accra and, during my last visit, my old respect for him increased. I made no secret of this, but soon discovered that my feelings were not shared by everyone.

I myself had an unpleasant experience in the photographic section of the Government Information Office, where Nkrumah had given orders that my film was to be developed. The official in charge told me frankly that he had no thought of helping me; he didn't like whites. I mentioned the president's orders. "He hates the whites, too," the official replied. "That's why we love him so much."

I was able to talk to several members of the opposition party. They all said: "Nkrumah's primary interest is advancing his own party." Dr. Busia, a prominent member of the opposition, has had to flee to Holland with his family. Other opposition leaders are in prison, or are watched day and night. Members of the opposition party, as well as Europeans and Americans, told me: "Nkrumah is a liar and a hypocrite. He's all things to all men—the born intriguer. Don't trust him."

Nkrumah spoke at the close of the All African People's Conference, and here I saw him in a completely different light. If I hadn't met him personally and had many pleasant talks with him, I never would have recognized him. His speech bristled with savage fanaticism, blind hate, and unrestrained attacks against everything of non-African origin.

I mentioned this episode to an English diplomat, who replied: "You've just seen the real Nkrumah. And all Negroes are like him. They don't understand ideals. When they talk about them, it's just pretense. They do it simply to curry favor with us. And why? Because they still need us. But when they don't need us any more, they'll become more overbearing, just as we once were in Africa."

Certainly, whoever reads the reports of the different committees of the All African People's Conference is in for a shock. A liberal Frenchman, sworn opponent of colonialism and imperialism, whispered to me during one of the sessions: "You know, I sometimes wonder if Albert Schweitzer, with his paternalism, and the South African nationalists, with their *apartheid,* aren't right after all."

Whoever tries to understand contemporary Africa is constantly torn between sympathy and hostility. But when one reflects on this, one comes to certain conclusions.

Men like Nkrumah have to act as they do at this time. There is no such thing in Africa as organic evolution, only revolution. For centuries Africa was asleep—and has now been awakened by a few rebels and leaders—children of their time. Certainly many Africans do not enjoy the experience of being suddenly thrust from the Middle Ages into the modern world; they would much prefer to continue their deep sleep. But with such people it is impossible for men like Nkrumah, or Tubman, the president of Liberia, to forge new African states. As good pyschologists, how do they solve this problem? Simply by constantly stirring up the masses, keeping them in a state of permanent revolution.

Many Africans, too, are not yet ready for democracy, but must be brought to accept it gradually. The colonial system under which they once lived was undemocratic, as was their own feudal system of kings and tribal chiefs. It is therefore logical for their leaders to sway between dictatorship and democracy, seeking to find through experimentation the right course to follow. Nkrumah himself, before Ghana was granted independence, confided to me his chief rule of thumb: the best way to learn to play the harp, is simply to sit down and play it, without worrying about mistakes or false notes.

This incident has nothing to do with the new leaders in Africa, but it did give me a vivid insight into what is going on there.

It happened during my last visit to Accra. My telegram from Timbuktu had been lost; no hotel room was reserved for me. To find lodging during the conference seemed impossible, but I tried at a hotel where I had often stayed previously. They remembered me, and gave me a room.

I recognized my bellboy from earlier visits. "Good evening, my boy," I said. "Nice to find you still here." He made no reply; the first Ghanian to be unfriendly to me.

As he unpacked my bags, I asked him why he was so distant; we had always gotten along so well. Going to the door, he stiffened and said, proudly, "I'm happy to see you again, sir. But I'm not so happy to see that you do not understand what has happened in our country."

Speechless, I asked him what he was talking about. "The last time you were here, sir," he said, "we were still a colonial people. Now we're free and independent. Before, I didn't mind when you called me *Boy*. But now, sir, I don't want you to call me *Boy*, but by my name, at least by my first name. It's Pius. And, believe me, sir, I'm doing you a favor by letting you call me Pius. For others, who don't know me, I'm Mister Pius."

With a slight bow, Mr. Pius withdrew.

And then there was the African who, while visiting me in Europe, explained why he desired independence for his country: the President of independent Guinea had been greeted in New York by a twenty-one gun salute, while the President of *his* country—because it belonged to the French Community—had only been greeted by twenty-one journalists. He kept coming back to this again and again.

One should keep these incidents in mind as we go on to portray the new leaders in Africa. One must try to understand that they stem partly from a huge inferiority complex, partly from that little learning which is a dangerous thing, partly from the fact that the African has only recently emerged from the jungle and primeval forest. Patience, tolerance are necessities—without them an understanding of what is taking place in Africa today is impossible. Above all, let us remember that the ways of life of the new nations in Africa are as different as the many races and religions in that huge continent. The peoples of Africa have really only one common bond; they have all been born under an African sun.

2

HASSAN II AND MOHAMMED V OF MOROCCO

*A Young Prince Succeeds His
Revered Father*

⁎

Mass demonstrations of grief took place in Rabat, capital of Morocco, on February 27, 1961, following the death of the young nation's beloved king, Mohammed V. Shortly after the untimely passing of the 51-year-old monarch, following minor nasal surgery, his son, Prince Moulay Hassan, 31, was proclaimed king as Hassan II.

Mohammed V, the founder of independent Morocco, was born Sidi Mohammed ben Moulay el Alaoui on August 10, 1909 in the old walled Arab city of Fez. Claiming direct descent from the Prophet Mohammed, he was a member of the Alouite dynasty, founded in 1660. Mohammed had never expected to be chosen Sultan. When his father, Moulay Youssef, died in 1927, the French passed over his two elder brothers and managed to have him elected by the Council of the Ulemas, the Moslem elders.

Mohammed V had two wives, who never appeared in public. No pictures of them were ever published; their birth dates and even their names were not made known. Of his six children by his two legal wives (he left an estimated 28 concubines) only the birth dates of his two sons were made public. Crown Prince Moulay Hassan, the present king, was born on July 9, 1929; Prince Moulay Abdullah on May 30, 1935. There are four royal princesses—the last born during Mohammed V's exile.

In Morocco, Mohammed V used to appear in a flowing *djel-*

labah and sandals, but when he received foreigners, or traveled abroad, he dressed in Western clothes—a small indication of why he represented a bridge between the old and the new in Morocco. He renounced the title of Sultan, because of its autocratic associations, and from August 1957 was called King (Arabic—*Malik*) because he wanted to be known as a modern ruler—"like the kings of European democracies"—and to underscore his break with the past.

Morocco was a free and sovereign state for eleven centuries, ruled alternately by Arab dynasties and indigenous Berbers. The French established their protectorate in 1912 and proceeded to introduce many needed reforms. Commerce grew, as did the cities. In 1917 Casablanca boasted 82,500 inhabitants; today it has 700,- 000. Rabat, the capital, has doubled its population in the last twenty years and will soon have more than 200,000 inhabitants. The total population of Morocco, thanks to European medicine and hygiene, now numbers around ten million.

The protectorate treaty of 1912 had two main objectives: military occupation, with the authority of French arms recognized everywhere, and guaranteeing the authority of the Sultan and his regime, so as to assure peace and order. This *pénétration pacifique* was completed by 1934. Mohammed V was the first Moroccan ruler whose authority was effectively established over all the many subject races of the country.

Largely because Mohammed V was a man of compromise, Morocco remained relatively peaceful until the Second World War. The French ruled, however, and not Moroccans. Mohammed V was obliged to sign the documents put before him by the French Resident General. In the 1930's, independence movements began to stir throughout Africa. During the war, the colonial peoples were promised eventual independence, if they would join the Allied cause.

A new generation grew up. Many young people learned to read and write, not only Arabic, but French and English. They traveled and studied abroad, and began to understand what was happening in their own country. The prosperity brought by Western methods, however, benefited the *colons* (French settlers) more than the Moroccans, with the exception of certain special groups like the Pashas.

During the war, Mohammed V, after a brief flirtation with Pétain, aligned himself with the Free French and the Allies. He repulsed, before the Allied landings, the efforts of Vichy to introduce the Nuremberg Racial Laws into Morocco, with the explanation that Jews and Moslems were equal under Moroccan law. He became friendly with President Roosevelt during the Casablanca Conference of 1943, and looked toward America for support in the eventual dissolution of the protectorate treaty. He and his people regarded Roosevelt's death as a great personal loss.

In 1941, the Atlantic Charter was proclaimed, and in 1945, the United Nations was founded. Morocco still waited in vain for its independence. In 1947, Mohammed V, prompted by the *Istiqlal* (Independence) Party, demanded freedom for his country for the first time in a public speech. Before, he had been a malleable friend of the French; now he was a declared enemy. The French tried to get rid of him; the first attempt, in 1951, failed, and the embittered *colons* adopted a more radical course.

On August 21, 1953, the *colons* won a great victory. Mohammed V was deposed and unceremoniously flown, with his family, to Corsica; later he was transferred to Madagascar. Sidi Mohammed ben Moulay Afra el Alaoui, an uncle of the exiled sultan, and a weak man who had never pretended to be a statesman or a politician, was named Regent.

The deposition of Mohammed V was soon revealed as a great mistake. The exiled sultan and his family were suddenly regarded by the Moroccan people as a symbol of the independence movement. All nationalist groups began to stir up the people against the French. In the next two years, French institutions and businesses underwent a sharp boycott. Here and there, it came to armed rebellion.

The French did manage, however, to win over a few leaders;

principally the Pasha of Marrakesh, Si Hadj Thami Glaoui el Mez-zouari. Over eighty years old, this Berber leader had cooperated with the French for decades and accumulated a princely fortune in the process. The French used him and his loyal Berbers to keep alive the old tensions between Arab and Berber.

The French policy seemed successful for a while, but at the crucial moment, El Glaoui defected. The Pasha of Marrakesh and the Berbers withdrew their support from the French and Sidi Mohammed ben Moulay Afra. The pasha even went so far as to tell an American observer that he wanted nothing more to do with the French. (In 1948, El Glaoui had confided to me that he and his family would one day have to pay a heavy price for his collaboration with the French.)

During the crisis, the Moroccan independence movement continued to advance its aims, refusing even to consider a settlement until the sultan was brought back from exile. The United States Government expressed its "strong misgivings" and "deep concern" at the sultan's deposition. François Mauriac wrote that Mohammed V had never been more powerful: "We hold his body prisoner, but he commands the hearts and souls of millions of Moroccans, who—and this is without precedent—would rather not pray, unless it be in his name."

As the rebellion gained momentum, and murder and rioting spread through the country, the French were forced to admit, after an attempt of two years to rule through the chiefs, that peace could only be restored by the return of Mohammed V and his family from Madagascar. The king's prophecy was fulfilled: "My deposition will not solve the Moroccan problem."

After an exile of twenty-seven months, the king and his family returned to Rabat in triumph. A few months later, after the formation of a national government, the French (on March 2, 1956) and the Spanish (on April 7, 1956) dissolved the protectorate treaty of 1912 and recognized the sovereignty and unity of Morocco.

The king's first task was to bring unity to a country whose territory, for the most part a French protectorate, had been governed by Spain in the north, with an international zone in Tangier. There is no doubt that he managed this in a remarkably short time.

Most difficult was the revival of the economy. French technicians, merchants, and settlers emigrated. The flight of capital began. The independent Moroccan government saw that there were not enough qualified Moroccans to fill all the newly available places. Aside from poverty, sickness, and unemployment, the fight against illiteracy had to be undertaken. The king discovered that Morocco had only twenty-eight native doctors. The country had a pitifully small number of skilled technicians and civil servants, not to mention diplomats. The few doctors and teachers were obliged to work in the foreign ministry. Suddenly there was a vacuum everywhere. The king must have asked himself if he and his people had not assumed too great a burden, too soon.

I asked the same question of many African leaders. They all expressed the sentiment that poverty in freedom was preferable to a slightly better life in slavery. It also became apparent—in Morocco and the other African countries—that one learns quickly when the will power is there.

The quick transformation of the country was in fact astounding. When one asked how it was possible, one always received the same reply: "God has helped us." Perhaps this answer is a reflection of the deep faith of Mohammed V, who used to withdraw several times each day to his private mosque for prayer and contemplation.

With Morocco independent, the king made a genuine effort to establish closer contact with his people. Always interested in education, he often visited schools, as well as handicraft workshops and factories. He asked questions wherever he went and took a special interest in the poverty-stricken small peasants—to whom he turned over much free land. He reigned as a constitutional monarch with democratic institutions, and paid a great deal of attention to the labor unions, which play the decisive role in social progress in the country today.

Mohammed V realized the necessity of bringing women into the active life of the nation, and letting them have some political responsibility. He himself prompted his eldest daughter, the

Princess Lalla Ayesha, to become president of a national welfare organization, and to introduce discussions of the Moroccan problem at international women's conferences. Mohammed V constantly made this appeal to the women of Morocco: "Guard the best in our traditions, but join them to modern progress."

Morocco lies in the furthest northwest corner of Africa. Mohammed V saw his country as the decisive link between the West and the Arab world, between the Mediterranean and the Atlantic, between Africa and Europe. And he knew that peace and prosperity are important not only for Morocco, but for all North Africa and the Near East.

Developments in Morocco entered a new phase in May 1960. The king dismissed the cabinet of M. Abdallah Ibrahim and on May 26 formed a broadly-based government with himself as prime minister, and his son, Moulay Hassan, as vice-premier, thus satisfying a long unfulfilled wish of the crown prince.

The former government had drawn its support from the National Union of Popular Forces (U.N.F.P.), which had broken away from the Istiqlal. It appeared to be taking a leftish course, and Moulay Hassan saw in this the end of the republic. He also considered Morocco not yet ready for democracy, in which view he was in complete agreement with his father. The king had observed the growing influence of Communism during his tour of the Near East. On February 23, the Istiqlal party newspaper alleged that leading members of the U.N.F.P. were involved in a plot to assassinate the crown prince. It is said that from then on, the crown prince put pressure on his father to take over active direction of the government.

In a broadcast to his people on May 23, 1960 the king declared that it was difficult, in view of the present political atmosphere, to form a government representing all political parties. He said: "In our anxiety to maintain political stability and national unity, we have preferred to take personal control and to direct the affairs of state through the intermediary of our crown prince. . . . In choosing the members of the government over which we shall preside and of which our crown prince will be vice-premier, we shall take into account only men's loyalty, integrity, and ability. The government will be responsible under our authority and in accordance with our directions, for carrying out the political, economic, and social program which we have drawn up.

"Our foreign policy will continue to be based on the principle of non-dependence. Our country will remain outside conflicts between blocs. She will aim at co-operation with all nations on a basis of equality and respect for sovereignty: the building up of the Arab Maghreb [i.e., North Africa] through the liberation of all its parts; the strengthening of our bonds with the Arab fraternity; co-operation with the independent states of Africa; and solidarity with its peoples who are struggling for their freedom. At home our government will spare no efforts to realize our national aspirations, the first of which is the evacuation of all foreign troops [i.e., French, Spanish and American] and the return of our stolen territories. It will also carry out the policy for which we have laid the foundations and drawn up the program, in order to complete our economic liberation, the struggle against unemployment, the modernization of agriculture, industrialization, and the training of cadres with a view to the Moroccanization of the administration, and to allow the nation to make progress in the social, cultural, and political fields."

Mohammed V concluded by promising to grant a constitution before the end of 1962. It would be drawn up "with the people's support," and "allow all members of the nation to take part, through their representatives, in the conduct of the country's affairs and to control the acts of the governments."

On May 29, 1960 came the first elections ever held in Morocco. They went off in an atmosphere of complete order, and between 70 and 75 per cent of the electorate cast ballots for members of the municipal and rural district councils. The Istiqlal won 45 per cent of the votes; the National Union of Popular Forces 30 per cent; and the rest were split up among candidates of the People's Movement, the Constitutional Democratic Party, the Independent

Liberals, and independents. The conservatives thus won a majority, but there is still no parliament in Morocco.

Even before he assumed leadership of the government, Mohammed V indicated the future course that Morocco would follow. In January–February 1960, he made a tour of the United Arab Republic, Saudi Arabia, Jordan, Kuwait, Iraq, and Lebanon. On January 19, he issued a joint communiqué with Nasser, in which they "proclaimed their complete support for the cause of the fighting Algerian people, as well as their endorsement of that people's right to total independence and self-determination on the basis of the unity of Algeria. . . . Their discussions also dealt with the Palestinian question and the right of the Arabs of Palestine to recover their usurped territory."

On January 31, 1960 the king flew to Iraq for discussions with Prime Minister Kassem. On February 3, a communiqué was issued stating that they had agreed to strengthen the Arab League by amending its constitution, to put through social reforms that would raise the living standards of the Arab peoples, and to consolidate their independence on the basis of Islamic ideals. They also agreed to support the Arab peoples in Mauritania in "their desire for reintegration with the Moroccan fatherland."

The policies of Mohammed V received strong support from his son, Crown Prince Moulay Hassan, now King Hassan II, who is one of the most dynamic representatives of the new youth of Morocco. Before his father's death he was Chief of Staff of the Royal Moroccan Armed Forces. His father, who was surprised to find himself chosen sultan in 1927, had not been trained for the job; Moulay Hassan has been.

Mohammed V had a school built for Moulay Hassan near the palace in Rabat, where he was educated with other young men of his age from all classes and all sections of Morocco. He learned French as a child. Specially selected teachers saw to it that he received a broad education. He is a trained pilot—and, like his father, an accomplished tennis player and horseman. He has been in large part responsible for the modernization of the Moroccan Armed Forces.

When Mohammed V travelled abroad, his son was completely responsible for government business. In July 1957, he was designated heir apparent, to strengthen the constitutional monarchy in Morocco.

The young monarch has already shown considerable skill in the rough and tumble of politics, but so far enjoys little of the instinctive respect his father commanded. As early as the first week of his reign he made it clear that he intended to rule with a strong central government and not to act merely as the symbolic head of the Kingdom. In an interview with French newspapermen shortly after his accession to the throne, Hassan said that he would combine his royal authorities with the duties of a premier. "In this period of uncertainty," he said, "of struggle against underdevelopment, of lack of trained cadres, the people need a man in whom they have confidence." His idea of government he said was "a team of responsible men grouped around a chief, capable of giving the powerful impetus necessary to lead the people in their fight for progress and against poverty." Sources close to the new king say that Hassan feels that an effective program for raising living standards must come before the establishment of a constitutional monarchy, which his father had promised and which the leftists demand.

A bachelor, who has spent much time during the past few years in the company of pretty French actress Etchika Choureau, Hassan will probably be obliged to marry a Moslem, because bachelorhood is not considered proper by Moroccans for the spiritual leader of the kingdom.

Immediately in the wake of Mohammed's death one thorny problem was solved for the young king, however. French military forces, stationed in Morocco for fifty years, withdrew on March 2, 1961, as agreed months earlier on the fifth anniversary of the country's independence, thus reinforcing the new regime of the young king. Spain, too, was gradually withdrawing her few remaining troops, and the United States had already evacuated the

Strategic Air Command base at Ben Slimane plus several radar sites, and has agreed to total withdrawal by 1963.

Mohammed V was accused of modernizing Morocco too slowly. But it must be remembered that the changes he introduced created difficulties and caused him to be regarded as a traitor to Islamic tradition by adherents of the old feudal system. He was a ruler forced to perform a balancing act between two entirely different eras. Hassan II, who personifies the new, self-confident Africa, independent of Europe, will probably have things easier.

3

FERHAT ABBAS OF ALGERIA

*A Pharmacist in the Alchemist's
Shop of Politics*

✳

During my recent travels through North Africa, I often asked who could be considered as representative of the independence movement in Algeria, that volatile land conquered by the French in 1830, officially a province of metropolitan France since 1848, and, since 1954, the scene of *la guerre sale,* the dirty war. Practically everyone I asked, including the president of Tunisia, Habib Bourguiba, named the same man: Dr. Ferhat Abbas, the premier of the self-proclaimed Provisional Government of the Algerian Republic.

It is one of the oddities of history that the political leader of the Algerian nationalists in a bloody war which has cost France about one and one-half billion dollars a year, should be a dour-looking, mild-mannered pharmacist who speaks better French than Arabic and once wrote: "We have discarded once and for all the nonsense and the chimeras in order to definitely align our future with that of the French work in our country."

Ferhat Abbas was born on October 24, 1899 in Taher, Algeria, the son of a *caid* (local governor) who became a Commander in the French Legion of Honor. He attended the college in Djidjelli and received his doctor's degree in pharmacy from the University of Algiers.

Even as a youth, Abbas was distressed by the political status of his people. He wrote newspaper articles, gave political and cultural talks, became president of the Algerian Moslem Students'

Association, and published a book in 1931, *Le Jeune Algérien.* After opening a drugstore in Sétif, in the province of Constantine, he was soon involved in local politics as a municipal counselor and became one of the leaders of the *Fédération des Elus Musulmans de Constantine,* which had been founded in 1930 by Dr. Ben Djelloul.

He was appointed editor-in-chief of the journal *L'Entente,* which supported the Blum-Violette program, the French socialists' first attempt at a policy of integration. At this time, Abbas was an *assimilationiste,* working towards the recognition of the status of Algerian Moslems and their integration into the country's political life. He wrote: "An Algerian fatherland does not exist; we are children of a new world, born of the French spirit and French efforts." In 1938, he founded the *Union Populaire Algérienne,* which was pro-French and had assimilationist tendencies, although committed to social reforms for Moslems.

Abbas was exempt from French military service, but enlisted in September 1939 and was sent to the front as a medic. After the fall of France, he returned to Algeria. The Vichy regime held out the promise of a reform of traditional colonial policies, but Abbas regarded their efforts as inadequate and quit the political scene in December 1940. A year later he returned and sent a manifesto on colonialism to Marshall Pétain.

On November 8, 1942, Allied troops landed in North Africa. General Giraud, commander of French forces, asked Moslem politicians for Algeria's support in the war effort. On December 22, 1942, Ferhat Abbas sent to the French authorities a *Message des Représentants Musulmans Algériens,* in which he asked for a conference to determine a new statute for Algeria; his appeal was not answered.

Six weeks later, Abbas composed the Manifesto of the Algerian People, which was signed by Moslem officials and *Oulémas* (leading Islamic theologians and scholars). Disappointed by earlier developments, they demanded an autonomous constitution, their own Algerian citizenship, and their own national flag.

On May 26, 1943, a new memorandum was handed to General

George Catroux, a confidant of de Gaulle. It dealt with the political, social, and economic problems of free Algerian citizens, religious and educational questions, and recommended the full participation of Algerian Moslems in the country's political life. The memorandum was greeted enthusiastically by the Algerian people; their dissatisfactions began to take alarming forms. General Catroux put its creator, Ferhat Abbas, under temporary arrest.

On December 12, 1943, General de Gaulle made known his thoughts on assimilation. But Abbas and his friends had waited in vain too long. Embittered, they now demanded Algerian independence from France. Abbas formed the *Amis du Manifeste de la Libérte,* and established a common front with the *Parti Populaire Algérien* (PPA) of Messali Hadj, who had been working for total independence from France since 1926, and the reform-minded *Oulémas.*

Savage rioting broke out in Sétif during the V-E Day celebrations. The cause was the appearance for the first time of an Algerian flag (green and white, with a red half-moon and a red star) and inflammatory nationalist banners. The bloody disorders took hold and spread. The French retaliated with artillery and air force bombing. One heard of several thousand dead and wounded; exact figures were forbidden by the censor. The French administration dissolved the *Amis du Manifeste,* Ferhat Abbas was once again arrested, and his newspaper—*Egalité*—banned.

Pardoned, the tenacious Abbas founded the Democratic Union of the Algerian Manifesto (UDMA) in April 1946. He still sought a liberal solution for the differences between French and Algerians. A few months later he, along with ten of his associates in the UDMA, was elected a deputy to the national assembly of the Fourth French Republic. On May 23, 1946, in Paris, Abbas submitted his program for a new Algeria. He came out against the French Union, in which—after all his fruitless efforts—he no longer had faith, and proposed a *Contre-Projet.*

In April 1948, Abbas was elected to the Algerian Assembly. Of its 120 seats, Abbas' party received only eight, because, as the French historian Charles André Julien noted, the elections were rigged to protect French sovereignty. But Abbas still held to his policy of moderate opposition. He described his position in these words: "I was born a moderate, I have lived as a moderate, and I will die a moderate." Nevertheless, his deep loyalty to the nationalist cause was never questioned. In order to play a more decisive role, he founded in September 1955, "The Committee of Sixty-one." But in the meantime, civil war had erupted.

The rebellion could just as well have begun after the "Massacre of Constantine" in 1945. That it did not, that Abbas and other nationalist leaders held off, is evidence of their patience.

On November 1, 1954, the day cited as the first of the Algerian war, bombs exploded simultaneously in thirty different parts of Algeria, and armed Algerian bands attacked French units. There had formerly been many nationalist parties and groups; now they joined together into the F.L.N. (Front de Libération Nationale). As the first warlike moves on the part of Algerians became known, men like Abbas warned against them and spoke of "almost criminal adventures."

Nine months later, Abbas still believed in a "genuine union of free people and nations," but put out his first tentative feelers toward the F.L.N.—"driven more by need than by inner enthusiasm," as one of his personal aides commented. The F.L.N. leaders, however, distrusted this moderate pharmacist. They limited him to pasting posters on walls at night with young recruits, and collecting funds. Abbas did not feel himself above this kind of work, and won the trust of the toughest revolutionaries. In March 1956, he announced that he had been following the wrong political line; everything which he had formerly written and done had been false and ineffectual.

The ranks of the F.L.N. were split between the so-called "hard ones" and the "weak ones." The former wanted to wage ruthless civil war; it was they who brought it on and still continue it. The French Ministry for Algerian Affairs has published a brochure: *Aspects Véritables de la Rébellion Algérienne.* It consists of one hundred and fifty pages of facsimiles of documents and over a hundred of the most revolting photographs ever published. One sees murdered men, women, and children, horribly mutilated and subjected to unspeakable bestialities. I have seen the same sort of photographs in the archives of the Kenya Government during the Mau-Mau uprising and in SS files. One cannot look at this book without feeling a deep depression over the depths to which man can sink. In all fairness, however, one must note that the Algerians have published the same sort of documents depicting French atrocities.

The F.L.N. realizes, however, that it can win no one to its cause through terrorism and cruelty. That is why it welcomes "the weak ones," like Abbas, especially in its dealings with foreign nations. Abbas was sent abroad as a spokesman for F.L.N. goals, and in recognition of his services, he was named a member of the seventeen-man revolutionary committee in October 1955, after he went into exile in Egypt. In August 1957, he was named as one of the nine members of the General Staff of the F.L.N. On September 18, 1958, Abbas announced the formation of a provisional government-in-exile of the Algerian Republic, with headquarters in Cairo (later transferred to Tunis); he himself is its premier. This government today is recognized by twenty nations —among them Red China and all the Arab lands.

In 1936, Ferhat Abbas wrote: "I have studied the country's history, read the works of the Koran scholars, searched through the mosques and cemeteries. Nowhere could I find a trace of an Algerian nation."

This sentence is thrown up to him today, and he is asked what gives him the right—in view of such sentiments—to fight for a free Algeria. To this he replies: "I am fighting because the European nations of today are the result of historical developments, not to mention the many African countries given boundaries for the first time by European powers, which has never been advanced as a reason for denying them sovereignty. Finally, we are the only Moslem country which has not received its freedom. It is our right as much as the others."

Men like Ferhat Abbas originally considered themselves to be Frenchmen of Moslem faith, and were proud of it. Abbas once said: *"La France, c'est moi."* How splendid that sounded coming from an Algerian. And thousands upon thousands of Moslem Algerians felt and acted like this pharmacist, son of an Algerian official in the French administration who had been decorated with the rosette and silver braid of the Legion of Honor.

It is common knowledge that Ferhat Abbas' native language is French. His upbringing and formal education were infused with the spirit of French culture and civilization. Like other North African nationalists, it was only later that he learned Arabic and studied Islamic culture. His wife, Marcelle Abbas, is a blonde of Alsatian origin; his son, Halim, was reared in France and speaks better French than Arabic.

Men like Abbas—and his name can stand here for millions—could have been the cornerstones of North African–European co-operation. They were ready to co-operate in a spirit of reason—with open hearts. Instead it was in their hearts that they were wounded—and shoved aside.

Ferhat Abbas has said that he wants to return to his drugstore when a solution is found for the Algerian problem. One can believe him. He abandoned his profession out of concern for his country—as did so many other Algerians. The bitter struggle could perhaps have been avoided if the radical rightists had not taken such a decisive role in determining the course of events. Admittedly, generations of *colons* have poured their sweat and talents into this land, and it is not only the *colons* who have benefited, but the land itself. But the *colons* must come to realize that land must be returned to its original owners, even when they did not work it formerly, when they now want to put it to use. It is not a simple question of ownership here; the present tensions have their roots in the rights of all nations to determine their own destinies. Algerians want to be respected as human beings. There are nine million of them in this country of 847,500 square miles —about four times the size of France itself—and only one million *colons*.

The United States has been caught on the horns of a dilemma in its policy towards Algeria. This was concisely expressed by Lorna Hahn, an American specialist in North African affairs, in a pamphlet she wrote for the American Committee on Africa, *War in Algeria: Is Confederation the Answer?*: "It has become increasingly difficult for the United States to retain its original position towards Algeria—a position which, although described as neutral, has been benevolent to France. By supplying France with money and military equipment to fight the Algerians, and by supporting her in the United Nations, it has strengthened the hand of anti-Western forces in North Africa who see no reason ever to hope for obtaining any real understanding of their problems from America. On humanitarian grounds alone, it is embarrassing that the leader of the free world has done nothing to stop the bloodshed and destruction which have continued more than three years. But taken from the standpoint of *realpolitik* on which foreign policies must be made, it is even more absurd to permit old friends and potential friends to pursue blindly a conflict which can only help the enemy of both—the Communists. The recent United States–British good offices mission between France and Tunisia, coupled with strong hints to France that she had better negotiate a settlement soon, suggests that the State Department realizes the seriousness of the present situation. It is to be hoped that the French government also realizes it, and takes the hint. The results would be beneficial to France, and to the entire free world."

Events are moving swiftly in Algeria. In mid-June 1960, de Gaulle rebuffed F.L.N. peace feelers at an inconclusive conference held in Mélun, near Paris. He demanded that the rebels "drop their knives" before negotiations could get underway. When he visited Algeria in December 1960, large numbers of city Moslems staged lengthy demonstrations, carrying pictures of Ferhat Abbas, shouting his name and F.L.N. slogans, and waving the forbidden rebel flag.

In the nation-wide referendum held in mid-January 1961, 75 per cent of the voters in metropolitan France approved de Gaulle's new plan to establish a provisional Algerian government, and later to offer Algeria self-determination. But in Algeria itself, 70 per cent of the city Moslems responded to the call of Abbas and the F.L.N. to boycott the referendum. The referendum showed that the hopes of the French right wing and the *colons* for an *Algérie Française* were breathing their last. It also showed that Abbas and the F.L.N. enjoyed more strength among Algerian Moslems than the French had assumed. To fulfill his plans for Algeria, de Gaulle must come to an agreement with Abbas and the F.L.N. But whatever the future holds for Algeria, the seven-year-old rebellion has shattered the *Présence Française* and taken a ghastly toll.

According to unofficial French figures, the war has already cost 250,000 casualties: French troops, 3,500 dead, 25,000 wounded; on the rebel side, 120,000 dead, 60,000 wounded or missing; among the Moslem civil population, 3,000 dead, 5,000 wounded, 7,000 missing. The provisional government of Ferhat Abbas has spoken of 600,000 casualties, which the French admit is possible, and which comprises five per cent of the Algerian population. *Le Monde,* at the end of 1959, estimated that the war had already cost France around 10 billion dollars. France has had to maintain an army of half a million in Algeria to combat about 150,000 nationalists who take these words of Abbas as their slogan: "We prefer ten million corpses to ten million slaves."

Ferhat Abbas, known inside and outside Algeria as a negotiator and peacemaker, once belonged to those who wanted to avoid violence. His efforts failing, he became a tragic hero. As such, at least, *le bon Papa de la Révolution,* as Algerian Moslems fondly call him, can be counted among the new leaders in Africa.

4

HABIB BOURGUIBA OF TUNISIA

An Enlightened Man
of Reason as President

✳

After a journey through central Africa in January 1956, I stopped in Tunis and asked if I might have an interview with the first president of the young Tunisian republic. Told that he was preoccupied with pressing governmental affairs, I attempted to contact him through friends.

Two days later my telephone rang; I was advised to be ready in half an hour to expose myself to Dr. Bourguiba. Punctually, thirty minutes after the call, a jeep driven by a Tunisian in black robes picked me up.

We sped through Tunis to the suburb of Belvedere and drew up before a white villa patrolled by armed guards. I was led through numerous rooms—more armed men carrying rifles and machine pistols—into a splendidly furnished room, its windows protected by iron bars. I had the uneasy feeling that I was being arrested. Then the president, Dr. Habib Bourguiba, appeared, dressed in an elegant blue double-breasted suit. He greeted me warmly and engaged me at once in a lively conversation, as though we were old friends. He had heard of my extensive travels through Africa, and asked for a minute description of them. I had come to interview him; he was interrogating me.

Three hours later, I made a move to leave. He insisted that we have a bite to eat. He clapped his hands; aides mysteriously appeared, bearing mountains of sandwiches and Tunisian pastry.

The aroma of peppermint filled the room. Later there was fruit, followed by coffee.

We talked of Europe, its youth, post-war experiences. Bourguiba's pro-Western, anti-Communist feelings were evident. I had heard that he was an intelligent and flexible man, but I had not been prepared for his deep understanding of world problems.

Bourguiba speaks excellent French. His bright eyes are set deep under a high forehead. His lips are thin, hard. He underscores his points with elegant gestures. His words, his movements reveal a man well above the average in will power and zest for life.

As we were sitting over coffee, a woman appeared. She was lighter than Bourguiba; typically French, I thought. *"Voici ma femme,"* the president said. Madame Mathilde Bourguiba did not stay with us long; she had only looked in to see how her husband was.

I was by now fairly tired after an unbroken conversation with this dynamic personality and relieved when—this time without being summoned—armed men once again appeared. They spoke in Arabic and seemed to be giving the president important news. Suddenly they all laughed. Bourguiba rose, shook my hand firmly, and thanked me for my visit. He had learned quite a few things, especially on this particular day. He wondered if I had read his book, *La Tunisie et la France, Vingt-cinq ans de lutte pour une coopération libre.* When I said that I had not, he had the book brought to him and wrote in it the following inscription: *À M. Rolf Italiaander en souvenir de notre entretien à Tunis avec ma vive sympathie et mes meilleurs voeux. Bourguiba.*

As he added the date, January 28, 1956, he exclaimed: *"Une date historique!"* Escorting me to the door, he gripped my sleeve and said, with a laugh: "If you should ever write anything about me, be sure to stress that you saw me today in excellent spirits and the best of health."

Back in my hotel, I wondered what this had been all about; it was hardly a normal visit with a head of state. That evening, at a reception given by the French High Commission, I did find out.

The atmosphere was tense. I finally asked some friends in the High Commission if anything was wrong. They looked at me as though I were a man from Mars. Didn't I know what had happened? Salah Ben Youssef, general secretary of the president's own party, the Néo-Destour, had tried to assassinate him. Others in the President's inner circle were to have been murdered. The worst of it was that Salah Ben Youssef had been able to flee. (He now lives in exile in Cairo as a "Pan-Arabic" politician, and has been condemned to death *in absentia.*)

"And how does the president feel?" I asked. "He is furious," I was told. "Imagine—traitors in his own official family. The poor man is supposed to have suffered a nervous breakdown. You'll never get to interview him now."

"But I spent practically the whole day with him," I protested. "He's in splendid shape. We had a stimulating and agreeable talk."

Several days later I learned that the president had had me brought to him precisely so that an objective foreigner could bear witness to his high spirits during this critical time.

Tunisia's population of almost four million is spread over 48,195 square miles. French military occupation resulted in the protectorate treaty of Kasr-es-Said on May 12, 1881. Habib Bourguiba's whole life had been devoted to the dissolution of that treaty.

He was born on August 3, 1903 in Monastir, Tunisia, the youngest of six brothers and two sisters. His father was an officer in the small army of the Bey of Tunis; Bourguiba, therefore, comes from the Tunisian middle class.

His oldest brother, married and living in Tunis, took the five-year-old Bourguiba into his home and saw to his education. He studied at the French *lycée* in Tunis, and also received a diploma in Arabic language and literature. Then the family sent this gifted young man to the Sorbonne, where he studied law and political science.

At the age of twenty-three, Bourguiba married a Frenchwoman

who bore him a son in April 1927; Habib Bourguiba, Jr. later became, in Paris, the first ambassador of the Tunisian Republic.

Bourguiba returned to Tunis in 1927, became a successful lawyer, and worked constantly for Tunisian independence. He founded the Néo-Destour (New Constitution) party in 1934, and during his struggles was arrested or forced to live in exile many times. Few North African politicians and statesmen have been imprisoned as often as this Tunisian lawyer. "How could you endure it?" I asked him. "You, who married a Frenchwoman, received a French education, and still have so much admiration for the *esprit français?*"

"It's true that the privations and strains, insults and humiliations were often more than a man could bear. But I was never without hope. My confidence remained unbroken. Because of this I was able to surmount all of these terrible obstacles."

Bourguiba's long struggle was not in vain. On March 20, 1956, the independence treaty was signed, and on April 14, 1956, as prime minister, he formed the first government of an independent Tunisia, at that time a monarchy. The Bey of Tunis, Sidi Mohammed al-Amin, was a pleasant, but weak man, interested in astrology and alchemy, but otherwise poorly educated. Bourguiba realized that dissident elements could form around the Bey, with the aim of overthrowing him and his Néo-Destour party. As a consistent rationalist, he also wanted to sever the last link with Islamic feudalism. On July 25, 1957, the constituent national assembly dissolved the monarchy and founded the first Republic of Tunisia, with Bourguiba as its president.

No one will be surprised if he holds the job for life; it was he who created an independent Tunisia and gave the new state a soul. His countrymen are right in saying: "Tunisians had forgotten that they were Tunisians. Bourguiba gave them pride and dignity, and he is now trying to awaken in them a sense of responsibility."

In numerous jails and places of exile, Dr. Habib Bourguiba formed his political philosophy, known as *Bourguibisme.*

What precisely is it? The official definition goes: "To deal with the enemy of today without ever forgetting that he could become the friend of tomorrow; if relations are broken off to make untiring attempts to establish them again; to turn to force only as a last resort, and then in full public view with flags flying; to build up the nation, but to rise above narrow nationalism and carry on the fight for freedom from a moral and ideological point of view; never to allow oneself to be diverted from the principle of independence, while taking note of its various stages of development and making the compromises that may become necessary. Once victory is achieved, to work freely together and forget past differences—these are the essential characteristics of the Tunisian revolution. This policy is given the name *Bourguibisme* above all because it can serve as a model. Tunisia's existence as a state is a test. Through the goals it has set for itself, the country has won respect and recognition that carries more weight than its meagre resources would lead one to expect." (From a brochure of the Government Information Office.)

There is no doubt that Habib Bourguiba is not only a revolutionary and reformer, but a clarifier and rationalist. He is a fanatic, but at the same time a man of good will, to whom friendship means more than enmity. One of his most remarkable characteristics seems to me to be his cultured and supple mind. *Bourguibisme* attests it. Another man would have broken off relations with France long ago after so many humiliations. Not Bourguiba. He has remained pro-Western, and would like nothing better than to see all of North Africa grouped into a pro-Western community, working with European industry and capital to develop the natural resources of North Africa and the Sahara. He has often taken firm stands against Communism and Nasser's "Pharaoh-like delusions of grandeur."

On that historic day when we talked together for so long, he reminded me of how small and poor his country was, of how its people were so few in numbers. But it had become great through the place it held in the hearts of the Mediterranean countries, rich in vital energy and its faith in progress. Bourguiba: "Our position between Western Europe, North Africa and the Near East gives us rights and duties. We will not turn away men of good will who offer us their spiritual or material help. We want to serve the cause of reconciliation between the Western and the Moslem worlds."

And relations with France? Bourguiba: "We hold no grudges and have no hatred of France, which had us under its tutelage for so long. We want to be friends with the French. We believe in justice and want to make our way with the weapons of reason and conviction." In recent years, the government of Habib Bourguiba has always gone out of its way to reach just agreements, despite the long chain of disappointments it has experienced.

And economic distress, which has worsened since independence? Bourguiba: "Our joy at winning independence has been impaired by our economic difficulties, and because of this, we must put an end to them. Everything, even certain traditions, must be subordinated to the achieving of this goal."

There are few statesmen who give one such a sense of the fusion of European and African traditions as does Bourguiba. He could be the cornerstone in European-African relations—and he would like to be. If one day he throws his support to Africa completely, one cannot blame him. His position is the same as that of so many other modern African leaders. He has said: "So long, for example, as no solution is found for the Algerian problem, those Moslem leaders who were originally moderate will become more radical in the course of events."

By early 1961 Bourguiba had emerged as the "honest broker" in the bitter Algerian situation. In February he met with de Gaulle for long discussions of not only French-Tunisian relations but the Algerian question as well. Following these discussions the two leaders announced their agreement that there exist "possibilities and hopes" for a "positive and rapid evolution in the lingering war of rebellion in Algeria." President Bourguiba's value as an honest broker arises from the fact that he knows intimately the positions of General de Gaulle and of the Algerian provisional government.

5

IDRIS I OF LIBYA

An Emir Who Became a King

❈

The former Italian colony of Libya owes its independence to the United Nations. It was a risky undertaking for the UN to bestow, in 1951, freedom and sovereignty on this "poorhouse of the world," whose 1,360,000 inhabitants and 679,358 square miles of territory (95 per cent of it worthless desert) suffered serious privations during the desert fighting of World War II. The UN dispatched teams of international experts to help put its "child" on its feet, and they are still working as advisers in all government ministries of the new kingdom.

The full name of the first king of Libya, Idris I, is Sayed Mohammed Idris-el-Awal el-Senussi. He was born on March 12, 1890 in Djaghaboub, an oasis in the southern portion of the Cyrenaica region, where the Senussi Order was founded by the king's Algerian-born grandfather, Shaikh al-Sayed Mohammed Ali ibn Senussi, "the Grand Senussi" (1788–1860). The Senussi, influenced by the Wahabis of Saudi Arabia, are an orthodox, almost ascetic Moslem order who were originally hostile to all Christians, especially Europeans. It was only in 1932 that the Italians were finally able to break their resistance, after two long, costly, and difficult wars.

The Italians and the Senussi tried at first to work together in a spirit of cooperation. In 1920, the thirty-year-old Idris was invited to visit King Victor Emmanuel in the Quirinal. But Fascism was coming to power, and the Senussi were asked to come to terms

with Mussolini's plans for a new Roman Empire. They felt betrayed, more so because they had avoided letting tensions with the
Italians come to a head. They turned from Italy, and sought counsel and arms from their Moslem neighbors.

After the occupation of Tripolitania and Cyrenaica in 1922,
Idris and his family went into exile in Egypt, where he remained
for twenty-one years. Here he sought the friendship of English
personalities, and from this time derive his contacts with the
British royal family. Idris today is on friendly terms with Queen
Elizabeth and Prince Philip; an inscribed photograph of Elizabeth
is the only one in the king's room. It was only natural for the
British, especially in view of the assistance given them by the
Senussi in World War II, to propose Idris as the first sovereign of
a new kingdom of Libya, after his return from Egyptian exile
in 1943.

Idris I was proclaimed king on December 2, 1950, and actually
ascended the throne on December 24, 1951. Tobruk is cooled by
sea breezes, and the king lives there most of the time; he has
another palace in El Beida, 140 miles east of Benghazi. On his
infrequent visits to the capital, Tripoli (pop. 140,000), he lives
in a palace built for the last Italian Governor General, Marshall
Italo Balbo. As the religion of the Senussi has been raised practically to the level of a state religion, and the king occasionally
favors Cyrenaicans in political matters, he has his enemies. After
a bomb attempt on his life in Tripoli in 1951, he has avoided the
capital.

The king has been married four times, but has no children. His
last wife is supposed to have had fourteen miscarriages. She was
a cousin of his, named Fatima, and did bear him a son, although
the infant died in a few hours despite the constant attendance of
three American doctors from Wheelus Field. In the meantime,
the king has married once again in Cairo—Alyal Lamloule,
daughter of an Egyptian Bedouin chief.

When his most recent marriage remained childless, the king
named his brother, Sayed Mohammed el-Rida el-Senussi, as heir
apparent; he died on July 25, 1955. The king then named his

brother's son as crown prince and heir apparent; he is more sociable and livelier than the king, and enjoys general popularity among the people.

The royal family numbers thirty-eight male members. Thirty-two of them are from another branch of the family, and one often hears of family tensions in Libya. Several princes have been exiled by the king; one of them, a nephew, was hanged in 1955 after he had personally assassinated an influential court favorite.

Idris I is one of the most retiring monarchs in the world. He became king through historical developments, not because he pursued the job. He therefore tries to discharge his duties in the best way he knows how. He is a king without worldly ambitions. Many Libyans consider him weak, and would like to replace this frail old gentleman with the crown prince.

Although seventy years old, Idris I gets up every morning at dawn to pray. He never begins work without first having read some verses from the Koran—in Arabic, as he knows no western language.

People have wondered why his likeness has vanished from Libyan stamps and bank notes in recent years. The king wanted this done; he did not want to become the center of a cult. He has also made it known that letters addressed to him can be sent without postage, and that any Libyan with a problem can come in and talk it over with him. He has transferred some of his palaces to the government; one houses the Military Academy, another the University of Benghazi.

The kingdom of Libya co-operates with all sections of the UN including UNESCO, but its membership in the UN was prevented by a Soviet veto. It sent representatives to the Bandung and Accra conferences and, as a Moslem nation, is a member of the Arab League and supports greater cooperation among Arab states. Libya is supported economically by Great Britain and the United States, both of which have air bases on its territory, and although it has opened diplomatic relations with the Soviet Union, resists Communist political infiltration.

The king has often said that he longs to see the Algerian conflict settled. In a speech from the throne in February 1960, Idris I promised the Algerian rebels material and moral support until the Algerian people win their freedom and independence. Because of his exile in Egypt and his marriage to an Egyptian, Idris I, and his government, feel great friendship towards Egypt and especially Gamal Abdel Nasser. Habib Bourguiba, the leading advocate of a North African federation, has said that he would like to see Libya join a community composed of Morocco, Algeria, and Tunisia.

Probably Libya, for the time being at least, will not align itself with either Egypt or Tunisia, in order to maintain and guard its strict neutrality, which the king seems to prefer. And perhaps neutrality is the best course for this very young, very poor nation.

6

GAMAL ABDEL NASSER OF EGYPT

A Cavalry Officer Makes World History

�֎

In January 1956, as Gamal Abdel Nasser was about to proclaim a new constitution for the young Egyptian republic, I received special permission to examine the exiled King Farouk's private rooms in the Abdin Palace. Admittedly, I was curious. Friends in Cairo had spoken so often of their contents, and their descriptions seemed to me unbelievable.

What did I actually find in the king's palace? A revolting mountain of trashy objects and pornography of the crudest, most primitive sort. The walls were hung with quite ordinary obscene drawings, and the private library contained a large collection of the most miserable pornographic books. Egypt lost nothing in this man. It was time for him, and his courtiers—who lived on graft and corruption—to vanish.

I underwent this depressing experience in the morning; that same afternoon I was President Nasser's guest at the proclamation of the new constitution. A huge tent had been built near the Abdin Palace; it was circled by soldiers and held thousands of people. Entry was by invitation only, and since Nasser could not invite all of his twenty-three million subjects, he welcomed representatives from all classes. I arrived early, and found a good seat in the honored guests' loge. Next to me sat the Soviet *Tass* correspondent, who occasionally interrupted the president's speech with hearty applause.

Around five, at the hour of sunset prayer, Nasser and his cabinet appeared through a side door. They removed their shoes, kneeled, and prayed. An awesome silence fell over the crowd; they, too, began to pray. It was a moving sight. I was only twenty feet from Nasser and could study his face very closely. He was not putting on a show for the masses; it was a sincere prayer on the part of a young statesman about to put a new constitution before his people.

The president commented upon the constitution personally. He spoke of the past, and presented a view of the future that it was possible for Egypt (386,198 sq. miles—96 per cent of it uninhabitable desert) to achieve through this revolutionary document.

After my Soviet neighbor had risen a few times to photograph Nasser at the closest possible range, I did the same. Looking through my view finder, I was dismayed. There was no longer any mildness, humbleness, or faith in Nasser's countenance. It was filled with ruthless fanaticism; his large hooked nose seemed larger to me; his mouth was hard, bitter—almost as though he were no longer capable of prayer.

Is this contradictory? Not really. Nasser is an ardent Moslem, just as he is an ardent Egyptian. His religious faith cannot be separated from him, nor he from it. We know that he would like to be the leader of all the Moslems in the world. It would almost appear that this cavalry officer became a politician and revolutionary for one reason: to become the president and eventually the undisputed ruler of one nation embracing all of Islam. Perhaps, gifted as he is with tremendous drive and will power, he has never entertained lesser notions, lesser goals. He would like to see his name ranked in Egyptian history next to that of the Prophet Mohammed, and no one else's. This is why Bourguiba spoke of "Pharaoh-like delusions of grandeur."

In private, Nasser is friendly, amiable, obliging, and polite. In public, he laughs a great deal, displaying his beautiful white teeth. Like Bourguiba he is flexible, and filled with overpowering energy. In Cairo, he is called "a man of fire and ice."

I met Nasser at embassy receptions in Cairo. I sensed his permanent mistrust of Europeans, and it became clear to me that he would never lose it. His political program gives evidence of this. He may make temporary treaties of compromise with the West, just as he has done with the East. But anyone who builds any hopes on him in the belief that he is not first and foremost an Arab is in for a disappointment.

It has been said that the president of this pivotal Arab land is a mixture of peasant, merchant, and soldier. This is not surprising. On his father's side, his ancestors were peasants; on his mother's, merchants. He carved out his own personal career as a soldier. And he became a soldier through conviction, as he has written in his *Philosophy of the Egyptian Revolution.* It was fortunate for him that he did take up a military career, for otherwise he would have remained just another small revolutionary, like dozens of others in the Arab lands.

Gamal Abdel Nasser was born on January 15, 1918, in Alexandria. He has described his own family, and his ancestors, as "children of the soil." They lived on the land and were mostly *fellahin,* small peasants, and settlers. His father, Abdel Nasser Hussein (b. 1888) could read and write—an exception in the family—and became an assistant postmaster, first in Cairo, then in Alexandria. Here he married, in 1917, Set Fatima, daughter of a rug merchant named Mohammed Hammad. Set Fatima died in 1926, leaving behind her three sons; the oldest was Gamal Abdel Nasser.

Nasser received his primary education in the village of Kathatba, later in Alexandria and Cairo, and was then admitted to the *Nahda el-Misria* Secondary School in Cairo. Today he is still proud of the fact that he—a poor boy from the country—graduated from this school (1936) with honors, although he had made himself unpopular with his anti-government views and actions.

A tall and extremely strong young man, Nasser wanted to enter the Royal Military Academy. But as a poor man's son, without personal means and with pronounced radical ideas, he was refused admittance and instead studied law for five months at Cairo's

Al-Azahr University. Suddenly there was a shortage of cadets at the Military Academy; Nasser applied again and this time was admitted. In March, 1937, at nineteen, he entered the Academy; by July, 1938, he was a lieutenant of infantry.

After graduation, he was posted to a cavalry battalion. In 1939, at the beginning of World War II, he was stationed in Alexandria, then in El Alamein, and finally for two years in the Sudan.

Nasser was not happy in Khartoum, capital of the Sudan. "It's easier to meet apes here than people," is supposed to have been one of his regular sayings. He was very pleased to be re-assignd to the General Staff School of the Military Academy in 1942, where he again won honors.

Georges Vaucher, the French author of *Gamal Abdel Nasser et Son Équipe,* took the trouble to find out which books Nasser had read in high school and later as a cadet at the Military Academy. In high school, he had read Egyptian and classical Arab works, as well as other works well beyond the comprehension of the average young Egyptian. As a cadet he read the following books, mostly in English: several volumes of Churchill's First World War memoirs; *Inside Europe* by John Gunther; the military studies of Liddell Hart; biographies of Emil Ludwig; biographies and autobiographies of Mustapha Kemal Ataturk, General George Gordon, Napoleon, Alexander the Great, Bismarck, Foch, Garibaldi, Hindenburg, Lawrence of Arabia, and Marlborough. As a captain at the Military Academy (1943–46) he read nearly all of the twenty-four volumes of the Encyclopedia Brittanica, numerous books on the First and Second World Wars, biographies of Kitchener, Mussolini, and Hitler. He studied all of von Clausewitz's military works, and innumerable writings on Egyptian and African problems, as well as on the war in the Far East, and even read Dale Carnegie's *How to Win Friends and Influence People.*

In his youth, Nasser was interested in poetry and the theater. At seventeen, he acted in a school play at the *Printania Theater*

(January 1935). And his role in his only appearance on the stage? Julius Caesar.

In 1944 in Cairo, Nasser married Tahia Kazem. He is the father of two daughters: Hoda (b. 1946); Mona (b. 1947), and three sons: Khalid (b. 1949); Abdel Hamid (b. 1951) and Abdel Hakim (b. 1955). Nasser willingly lets himself be photographed with his children, but his wife seldom appears in public. Even among friends, he almost never speaks of his wife.

Nasser took part in the war in Palestine as a captain. During a scouting mission in July 1948, he received a shoulder wound and was supposed to spend a month in a Gaza hospital. He left the hospital after only a few days to rejoin the combat troops in Fuluja, however. His bravery won him the nickname *The Tiger of Fuluja.*

Even as a second lieutenant at his first station, Nasser established close ties with fellow officers who shared his political views, and later strengthened them at the Military Academy and during the Israeli war. He himself founded and organized a group of young officers which eventually developed into the Free Officer's Committee, described in an official Egyptian document as: "against the old politics, against corruption in government, against foreign occupation and foreign economic domination."

Soon after Nasser became an instructor at the Military Academy in 1950, and was promoted to Lieutenant Colonel in May 1951, his comrades voted him president of the Free Officer's Committee, at the age of twenty-nine. He was in the first line of those who planned and led the Free Officer's bloodless revolt of July 23, 1952 which forced the abdication of Farouk and abolished the monarchy. For a time, he wielded power through General Mohammed Naguib, who was the first prime minister and president of the new republic, and is now under house arrest. Nasser himself became premier on April 17, 1954, at thirty-six. In June 1956, he was elected president of the Egyptian republic by 99.99 per cent of the popular vote (according to government figures). He survived such crises as the nationalization of the Suez Canal and the British-French-Israeli invasion and, following the merger of

Egypt and Syria, was elected president of the new United Arab Republic on February 21, 1958. Again according to official figures, he received 99.99 per cent of the Egyptian and 99.99 per cent of the Syrian vote.

Nasser sees in himself "the embodiment of Arab nationalism" and the "God-summoned liberator of all Arab peoples." His *Philosophy of the Egyptian Revolution,* a series of three articles which he wrote for a Cairo magazine in 1953, is one of the most self-revealing documents ever written by one of the new leaders in Africa.

In it, Nasser asks why the revolt of July 23 was "only a military mutiny and not a popular revolt, why was the army then, apart from other forces, destined to carry out this revolution?"

His answer: "Throughout my life I have had faith in militarism. The soldier's sole duty is to die on the frontiers of his country. Why then was our army compelled to act in the capital and not on the frontier?

"Once more, let me reiterate that the defeat in Palestine, the defective arms, the crisis of the Officers' Club election were not the real springs from which the current flowed. They may have accelerated the flood but they could never be the original source. Why then did this duty fall upon the army? . . . If the army does not move, we said to ourselves, who else will?"

Further on, Nasser wrote that in Palestine "we needed discipline but found chaos behind our lines. We needed unity but found dissensions. We needed action but found nothing but surrender and idleness. It was from this source and no other that the revolution derived its motto." That motto "Unity, Discipline, and Work," identifies Nasser as an entirely new type of Egyptian, and especially an entirely new type of Arab.

Also very revealing is Nasser's belief that Egypt is going through two revolutions, not one: "Every nation on earth undergoes two revolutions: One is political, in which it recovers its right for self-government from an imposed despot, or an aggressive army occupying its territory without its consent. The second revolution is social, in which the classes of society would struggle

against each other until justice for all countrymen has been gained
and conditions have become stable. . . . Political revolution demands, for its success, the unity of all national elements, their
fusion and mutual support, as well as self-denial for the sake of
the country as a whole.

"One of the first signs of social revolution is that values are
shaken and creeds are relaxed; fellow-countrymen struggle against
each other, individuals and classes. Corruption, suspicion, hatred
and selfishness dominate them. Between the anvil and the hammer
we now live in two revolutions; one demanding that we should
unite together, love one another and strain every nerve to reach
our goal; the other forces us, in spite of ourselves, to disperse and
give way to hatred, everyone thinking only of himself."

Nasser saw in the army the only possibility of avoiding anarchy:
"The situation demanded a homogeneous force. Its members
should have faith in each other and should have in their hands
such elements of material force as to ensure swift and decisive
action. Such conditions did not prevail except in the army."

In the third section of his *Philosophy of the Egyptian Revolution,* Nasser wrote of the sources of Arab strength: "The first
source is that we are a group of neighboring peoples joined together with such spiritual and material bonds as can ever join any
group of peoples. Our peoples have traits, components, and civilization, in whose atmosphere the three sacred and heavenly creeds
have originated. This cannot be altogether ignored in any effort at
reconstructing a stable world in which peace prevails.

"As for the second source, it is our territory itself and the position it has on the map of the world, that important strategic
situation which can be rightly considered the meeting-place, the
cross-road and the military corridor of the world.

"The third source is petroleum which is the vital nerve of civilization, without which all its means cannot possibly exist whether
huge works for production, modes of communication by land, sea
and air, weapons of war whether they are planes flying above the
clouds or submarines submerged under layers of water. All these,
without petroleum would become mere pieces of iron, rusty, mo-

tionless and lifeless." (It is worth noting that—at Nasser's urging —the economic council of the Arab League, in March 1960 in Cairo, agreed to the gradual development of an Arab common market; a special committee was appointed for this purpose.)

Nasser did not neglect to make known his thoughts on the relation of Arab Africa to the African continent itself: "We cannot look stupidly at a map of the world not realizing our place therein and the role determined to us by that place. Neither can we ignore that there is an Arab circle surrounding us and that this circle is as much a part of us as we are a part of it, that our history has been mixed with it and that its interests are linked with ours. These are actual facts and not mere words. Can we ignore that there is a continent of Africa in which fate has placed us and which is destined today to witness a terrible struggle for its future? This struggle will affect us whether we want or not.

"Can we ignore that there is a Moslem world with which we are tied by bonds which are not only forged by religious faith but also tightened by the facts of history? I said once that fate plays no jokes. It is not in vain that our country lies to the Southwest of Asia close to the Arab world, whose life is intermingled with ours. It is not in vain that our country lies in the Northeast of Africa, a position from which it gives upon the dark continent wherein rages today the most violent struggle between the white colonizers and black natives for the possession of its inexhaustible resources. . . . All these are fundamental facts, whose roots lie deeply in our life; whatever we do, we cannot forget them or run away from them.

"If we direct our attention to the continent of Africa, I would say, without exaggeration, that we cannot in any way stand aside, even if we wish to, away from the sanguinary and dreadful struggle now raging in the heart of Africa between five million whites and two hundred million Africans.

"We cannot do so for one principal and clear reason, namely that we are in Africa. The people of Africa will continue to look up to us, who guard the northern gate of the continent and who are its connecting link with the world outside. We cannot, under any condition, relinquish our responsibility in helping, in every way possible, in diffusing the light and civilization into the farthest parts of that virgin jungle. . . ."

The question of whether Nasser is an important figure in Africa outside of Egypt, whether the other peoples of this continent see in him a leader, must be answered with a definite yes. One sees his photograph not only in the market places of Libyan and Moroccan oases and towns next to the kings', but in Senegal, Ghana, and the Congo as well. In Dakar I noticed his photograph in a taxi, and asked the driver who it was. "The boss," he replied. "The boss of all of us!" During his state visit to India in March 1960, the Indian president, Prasad, described his Egyptian guest as "the symbol of the spirit of reawakening in the Arab world."

Nasser is not only the hope of many millions of Arabs, but—despite antagonists like Bourguiba and Abbas—the hope of millions of black Africans as well, for which Moslems admire him the most. They regard him today as the undisputed leader of world Islam. Nasser has given an order to organize a congress of all Moslem peoples, a plan discussed in Syrian religious circles in 1947. The yearly pilgrimage to Mecca would become a manifestation of all Moslems throughout the world and support the independence struggles of all peoples still under colonial domination. The Saudi Arabian government has made plans to reconstruct the environs of the Holy Kaaba (Arabic: *Bait Allah*—House of God) in Mecca so that over a half-million people can gather together for prayer at the same hour. Work was begun in 1956, and should be finished in 1962. The building costs of over twenty-five million dollars are to be borne not only by Saudi Arabia, but by other Moslem lands as well. Nasser has also ordered "religious attachés" to be stationed in all foreign missions of the UAR. They are to arrange marriage contracts, lead prayers in Moslem places, and take stands against anti-Moslem publications. Moslem offices are to be opened in Germany, England, Italy, Switzerland, and the United States.

In the last pages of his *Philosophy of the Egyptian Revolution* Nasser wrote: "My faith in the advantages that all Moslems can derive from a further strengthening of Islamic bonds deepened during my visit to Saudi Arabia with the Egyptian delegation. . . . As I stood before the Kaaba and saw with my own eyes the many parts of the world to which Islam has spread, the thought came to me that our conception of the pilgrimage must be changed. When one goes to the Kaaba, it should not simply be regarded as an entry card to Paradise, and also not as a means to purchase forgiveness for a turbulent life. The pilgrimage must be transformed into a great political force. The delegates of the Islamic states, their spiritual leaders, their scholars from all branches of learning, their writers, their leading industrialists, and not least of all, their youth, could assemble at this Islamic World Parliament in order to draw up their basic national policies and commit themselves to mutual cooperation until they next meet.

"They should meet one other in this spirit: reverential and humble, but strong; free from greedy overeagerness, but active; submissive before God, but powerful in the struggle against their difficulties and enemies: awaiting the after-life with longing, but firm in the resolve that they must assert their place in the sun in this life. . . . When my mind travels to the eight million Moslems in Indonesia, the fifty million in China, the millions in Malaya, Siam, and Burma, to the nearly one hundred million in Pakistan, and the more than one hundred million in the Far East, to the forty million in the Soviet Union and the other millions in the far places of the world, when I think of how these hundreds of millions of people are bound by a single common faith, then the tremendous possibilities become very clear to me that the mutual cooperation of all these Moslems can open."

It must be mentioned, however, that many Moslems throughout the world do not share these thoughts. Many people—in the Moslem world, too—fear the "Dictator of the Nile," the "Arab Hitler," the "Arab imperialist," or the "hot-headed young man from the Nile," as Khrushchev called him. Nasser himself has said that all of these epithets "leave him cold," and that he will call a permanent, yearly conference of Moslem peoples in Cairo if his plans for Mecca are not realized.

Nasser has written the following about Arab nationalism: "Yes, I am an Arab nationalist. The fact is, I entered the Egyptian revolution as an Egyptian patriot and Arab nationalist. . . . Arab nationalism means many things to me. Above all, it is a spiritual movement, the voluntary solidarity of all Arab peoples who share a common heritage of language, culture, and history. This is a feeling that comes from the heart. It derives from the Arab past, but can bring great practical benefits to the Arabs of today. Through military solidarity and voluntary cooperation in commerce, culture, and foreign affairs, each individual Arab nation can become stronger."

And concerning the meaning of his positive neutrality: "Many people find it hard to understand our policy of positive neutrality. Others attempt to destroy it through intrigue. I fear every association with foreign powers because I know Arab history and the Arab peoples. For hundreds of years they were habituated to regarding their governments with fear and suspicion as agents of foreign powers, as governments which took their orders from foreign embassies. I know that taking part in foreign alliances would isolate our own nationalist groups and leave leadership of the masses to Communists, or fanatics like the Moslem Brotherhood. When defense treaties become necessary in the Arab world, they should be negotiated by Arab lands. . . . And there is another compelling reason for my stand against the alliance of Arab lands with any of the great powers. Such alliances would open the door for the great powers to re-establish their dominance, and to re-impose colonialism and imperialism in the Arab lands."

Latent mistrust of the West is one of the unbreakable articles of faith shared by all of the numerous anti-colonialist and anti-imperialist movements. For them, colonialism and imperialism are inextricably bound up with the West.

The Lebanese philosopher, René Habachi of Beirut, has written in his *Notre Civilisation au Tournant:* "There is a gulf between East and West deeper than even our most anti-Western politicians are willing to admit. This gulf is not only political, but historical and cultural."

This throws a great deal of light on Nasser's pronouncements about Arab nationalism and positive neutrality. Both are designed to make the Arab think of his own historical and cultural values. The Arabs believe that the only way out of their present desperate situation is to return to the original sources from which their culture once flowed, and from which they can once again be nourished.

Seen from this point of view, Gamal Abdel Nasser is not so much the "new Pharaoh from the Nile," as a man who is fulfilling a historic mission.

7

IBRAHIM ABBUD OF THE SUDAN

The Field Marshal Directs a Putsch

✳

One day in Nairobi, Kenya, I was summoned to the office of the chief of police, who personally wanted to give me my visa for the Sudan. In a short time—January 1, 1956—the Sudan was to become independent, and relations with the British Commonwealth were as good as dissolved. The chief of police represented both Great Britain and the new Sudanese government which was soon to take office.

I had been waiting six months for the visa, and had just about given up all hope of getting it. People were very suspicious in those days. Unrest still reigned in the south of the Sudan. Refugees from the south—among them American and British missionaries —had told me of horrible atrocities. The chief of police said: "We have good and bad reports about you. But the good ones won out, so you'll get your visa. Anyway, we've met twice at parties." Finally, he said that he had asked me to his office to give me a little friendly advice. I was wearing a blue English club blazer with gold buttons, and he counseled me urgently to replace those gold buttons with dark ones before setting out on my trip. Since I wasn't an Englishman, there was no point in appearing in the Sudan dressed like one: it would be better for my safety. I took the chief of police's advice. When I arrived in the capital of Khartoum (pop. 80,000) I noticed that the preferred dress of the students at Gordon College, at least those who did not wear national costumes, was the blue English club blazer—with gold buttons.

The Egyptian revolution of July 1952 was bloodless. A document published by the rebel forces proudly declared: "No heads rolled in the sand, no blood was spilled. A king was deposed and escorted out of the country with all the honors that were once his due." The transfer of power in Khartoum on January 1, 1956 was even more dignified. But in the south Sudan there were barbaric clashes—rape, torture, murder, and acts of cannibalism right out of the darkest ages of this Dark Continent. It is still not clear whether the fighting was "only" a tribal war between north and south Sudanese, or whether it was a civil war instigated by the Egyptians or the British—or both—as a pretext for political intervention.

In November 1958, the government changed hands for a second time in the youthful history of this nation. Officers carried out a military putsch that deposed the democratic government. The rebels conducted themselves toward their opponents with all the chivalry of knights at a jousting tournament. Truly, the Sudanese are an astonishing people: "gentlemen by instinct" as the British in the Sudan called them.

Unlike so many other African lands, the Sudan has a place in recorded history. There were organized communities here in 5,000 B.C.; Egyptians expanded into the Sudan in 2,800 B.C. Islam spread down into the Sudan from Egypt, and for thousands of years there have been close ties between the two countries.

The Sudan was under joint Anglo-Egyptian rule from 1899 to 1953, when the original condominium was terminated. The British, fearing the strong influence of Egypt on the Sudan, preferred to see the country receive its complete independence on January 1, 1956.

In the Sudan (967,500 sq. miles—pop. 11,000,000) there is a general fear, especially since Nasser came to power, of aggressive actions on the part of Egypt. The Sudanese would like to see General Naguib, who has a Sudanese mother, released from house arrest, for they regard him as a man with considerable sympathy and understanding for Sudanese problems and anxieties. It is even possible that Naguib's supporters might try to install him as president, which would present Nasser with a dangerous opponent. Nasser dreams of a voluntary merger of Egypt and the Sudan, and is attempting by all possible means to win the Sudanese over.

Nevertheless, there have been tense moments between the two countries; for example, a border dispute in February 1958, and clashes over control of the Nile waters, which both countries regard as basic to their existence. In November 1959, these differences were finally settled in an agreement between the UAR and the Sudan, in which Nasser displayed a remarkable willingness to oblige. From the time the Aswan Dam begins to store water, the Sudan will receive eighteen and a half billion cubic metres; the UAR, fifty-five and a half billion cubic metres. In addition, Nasser committed himself to pay 15 million pounds as compensation for the resettlement of those 60–70 thousand Sudanese whose homes and land will be flooded by the construction of the Aswan Dam. The revolutionary government of General Abbud thus succeeded in reaching an important agreement with its larger northern neighbor where previous cabinets had failed.

The *coup d'état* in the Sudan took place at three o'clock in the morning of November 17, 1958. The army, led by its commander-in-chief, General Ibrahim Abbud, overthrew the democratic government of the pro-Western prime minister, Abdulla Khalil. The three most important cities were occupied; no shots were fired; no one was arrested. Cabinet officials were informed that the army had assumed the functions of the government in letters delivered to them by army officers. Abbud suspended the constitution and dissolved the parliament, declared a state of emergency, and banned all newspapers and printing presses.

In a radio broadcast at seven in the morning, the general explained: "You are no doubt aware of the state of degeneration, chaos and national instability which threatened the interests of the individual as well as of the community, and which extended to the machinery of the government and public utilities without exception. . . . As a natural reaction the Sudanese army and the security forces had no alternative but to take over in order to put an end to this chaos and restore peace and order for Sudanese and foreigners alike. Praise be to Allah that your loyal army has today . . . carried out a peaceful move which, it is hoped, will be the turning point towards stability and clean administration."

Abbud brought off his coup with the help of only twelve army officers. The world wondered who he was, and who was behind him. He had rarely appeared in public before, although he was known to be a close friend of Abdulla Khalil, the deposed prime minister. After dissolving parliament and all political parties, Abbud issued a decree in which he took upon himself the major powers of government: henceforth he would be not only commander-in-chief of the army, but prime minister and minister of defense. It soon became evident that he had not been supported either by Nasser or the Russians, and that he had brought off his own revolution without foreign assistance. Two days later, life in Khartoum returned to normal; this old army officer, held in general respect by the people, had carried the day.

On November 17, 1959, the first anniversary of his *coup d'état,* Abbud reviewed developments in his country and at the same time announced the goal of his program:

"The annihilation of that state of affairs was the only way out for the country's deliverance. . . . The army decided to take the initiative in this respect because while the people were unarmed and while they were divided into sectors and parties, it was united and cohesive. . . . I promised you in my first speech that our purpose was the correction of improper conditions, and was aware that that will not be accomplished in one year, since it entails the refabrication of society on a good strong foundation. Whenever I look back over my shoulder to ponder upon the efforts made by the Revolution in the course of one year, I feel great satisfaction. Our country was encountering an economic breakdown because the citizens dedicated their time not to production, but to partisan strife whose leaders exploited the people's faith and national devotion. The result was a budget deficit, an unfavorable balance of trade, unsold cotton, refrainment on the part of investors, whether national or foreign, negligence in government offices and an indefinite foreign policy. . . .

"I promised you in my first speech of the Revolution that we will remove the artificial strain which governed our relations with the United Arab Republic. . . . Moreover this does not conform with the national aspirations of the two peoples. . . . The moment the Revolutionary Government became convinced that the desired atmosphere was prepared, it sent to Cairo a delegation composed of its best men—a delegation motivated by hope and faith that a fair agreement would be reached. . . . These agreements have opened up before us extensive fields for organizing our trade, and for marketing our crops. Through them the Sudan will witness substantial economic prosperity, since we will be able to exploit our wealth of the Nile waters to the greatest possible extent. . . . We will start forthwith in taking the preliminary steps for the construction of our dams which are expected to convert millions of acres of uncultivated land into green plains as a part of our agricultural progress. . . . I am glad to announce to you that I formed last August a committee with unlimited functions under the chairmanship of the chief justice, with the purpose of making recommendations on the best ways for the citizenry to take part in the government of the country and play an effective role in developing their own affairs. It is hoped that this will ultimately pave the way for the constitutional setup which conforms with the nature of the Sudanese society. . . ."

General Ibrahim Abbud is a distinguished, conservative, straightforward man, short and thick-set, with a light skin and a large head, whose face often wears a grim and testy expression. In private, he is friendly and warm-hearted. He does not look at all like a dictator, but like a military man of the old school.

Abbud is married and has five children, with whom he plays affectionately in his free time. He carries out his official duties from army headquarters. As a man with no personal ambitions, he lives in Spartan simplicity. He is the born soldier. His manner and appearance are British, just as his uniform is modeled on that of a British general's down to the last button.

Abbud was born to a peasant family in Mohammed Gol, a small town in the eastern Sudan on the Red Sea, on October 26, 1900. He studied in the technical section of the Gordon Memorial College in Khartoum, and at seventeen entered the Military Academy; by July 1918 he was absorbed into the Egyptian army of occupation in the Sudan as a second lieutenant of engineers.

In 1925, he was transferred to the newly formed Sudanese army as a captain. He was assigned to England for further training, and learned English very well. He later travelled to England repeatedly as a member of military purchasing missions. During the Second World War he received many decorations for his part in the campaigns against the Italians in Eritrea, Ethiopia, and Libya. After the war, he was assigned to the staff of the English Camel Corps.

In March 1949, Abbud became the first native-born commander of the Sudan Service Corps; in 1952, the first Sudanese general staff officer in the headquarters of the Sudanese armed forces; in 1954, a major-general and deputy commander-in-chief of the Sudanese army; in 1956, commander-in-chief; and on January 6, 1957, a full general. On November 17, 1958, when the putsch took place, Abbud and his loyal old comrades created a twelve member Supreme Council of the Armed Forces, with Abbud as its president. This would be the country's highest constitutional authority, and delegated "all its legislative, juridical, and executive powers" to Abbud.

It is known that Abbud, in addition to his many other duties, takes an active interest in the business of the Foreign Ministry. For the putsch to be successful, it was crucial that the leaders of two influential religious sects pledge their faith in the officers to Abbud: Abel Rahman el Mahdi, leader of the Ansar Sect, and

Ali Mirghani, leader of the Khatimi Sect. Such religious sects are the principal guardians of Islamic tradition. They have been eliminated as a power factor in Tunisia and Egypt; it is difficult to predict how long they will remain influential in the Sudan.

I heard harsh words in the Sudan about the compulsory end of the democratic experiment. The old mistrust of soldiers as politicians works against General Abbud. And he is a military dictator, however benevolent. But in all fairness, it must be noted that many young African lands are not yet ready for democracy as we understand it in the West, and that Abbud has demonstrated his ability to create order, do away with corruption, organize the economy and increase production.

In a radio interview, Abbud explained: "We are soldiers and we would just as soon return to our barracks today as tomorrow. We will give up the power of government when all difficulties are solved. . . . We have harmed not a hair on any politician's head. But they would be well-advised to keep their peace. Perhaps in two years, we will call together independent political figures from all parts of the country—civilians, not military men —who can then assume the responsibilities of government."

As the Republic of the Sudan celebrated the fourth anniversary of its independence, President Abbud said: "In its original meaning, independence is responsibility, before it is a thing of pure pride. The real worth of independence can only be known when one assumes the responsibilities that come with it. . . . Independence can be celebrated when one works creatively to bring about a full renaissance that extends to all sections of the country and affects the life of every citizen. The achievement of this goal demands from the nation that it work together as one harmonious team to defeat poverty, hunger, illiteracy, and sickness, and to transform our dry deserts into green fields."

Since then, President Abbud has declared repeatedly that he would cooperate with all nations and accept economic assistance from all peoples, as long as it does not endanger the independence of the Sudan. How this concerns the Soviet Union remains unclear for the present, although Abbud—in an interview in the Cairo newspaper *Al Akhbar* that created a sensation—identified Communism as enemy number one. He went on to explain why this was so: "World Communism has concentrated its activities on Africa, and wants to envelop Africans in its imperialism, in order to rule them in the end."

The Soviet Union doubtless has a lively interest in the Sudan. The Soviets would like to see the country neutralized or brought into the Eastern bloc. Up to now, only Yugoslavia of the Eastern countries has maintained good trade relations with the Sudan. Great Britain does not want to give up its traditional ties, but to deepen them. The same holds true for Nasser and the UAR; even if the Sudan does not merge with the UAR in the near future, it will at least be expected to take part in Pan-Arab plans. All of these nations realize the truth of a saying I often heard in Khartoum: "Whoever has the Sudan, has Africa."

Exactly from this aspect, it is in the interest not only of the Sudan, but of the whole free world, that General Abbud truly becomes the "Saviour of the Fatherland." It remains to be seen how long he can hold on. But that is also hard to predict of the other new leaders in Africa, a continent where events are as fluid as the waters of the Congo or the Nile.

8

HAILE SELASSIE OF ETHIOPIA

An Absolute Monarch on the Throne of David

❋

I first saw Haile Selassie in 1936 at the League of Nations in Geneva, where I was living at the time as a student. He was a delicate, almost brittle man, with a dark complexion, piercing eyes, and an unusual beard. Several times I caught sight of him under a large umbrella, and I thought that this small but strikingly energetic figure was about to vanish beneath it.

Twenty years later, I saw him again in his capital of Addis Ababa (pop. 400,000). He had aged, but he still looked vigourous, agile, tough, and unyielding. But he was much more aloof than he had been in Geneva. In Europe, it was possible to speak to him directly in French or English. In Ethiopia (pop. 15–20 million; 350,000 sq. miles) this is discouraged. I was obliged to speak to an aide, who translated my words into Amharic; the emperor answered in Amharic; and his replies were translated into English and French by the aide. I found this difficult to comprehend, since I knew that the emperor speaks perfect French and English. But Ethiopian friends assured me that he employs this system to "preserve his dignity and give himself a chance to reflect on his answers."

In addition, the emperor requires even foreign diplomats to bow to him from the waist. Women are obliged to make several conventional curtseys. No one is permitted to turn his back on the emperor. Everyone granted the honor of a private audience is briefed beforehand on Ethiopian court protocol by a special master of ceremonies.

After Hassan II and Idris I, we encounter here another chief of state of royal blood, who occupies a throne that is one of the oldest in recorded history. The emperor of Ethiopia, therefore, is hardly one of the "new leaders in Africa." But as a reformer he belongs in this book as much as do the kings of Morocco and Libya.

Haile Selassie I is the 225th ruler in direct descent from Mene-lik I (David-King), son of King Solomon and the Queen of Sheba. Ethiopia, whose ruling class belongs to the Ethiopian Or-thodox (Coptic Christian) Church, regards itself as the oldest Christian nation on earth. Christianity was introduced around 300 A.D., and not centuries later by missionaries as in most other Afri-can lands. Also in sharp contrast, Ethiopia—until the five-year Italian occupation—was never under foreign domination and was never a colony or protectorate in its thousands of years of history.

Haile Selassie, under the name Lij Tafari Makonnen, was born on July 23, 1892 in Harar Province. His father was Ras (Prince) Makonnen, cousin and trusted general of the Emperor Menelik II. His mother died when he was three. From the age of five, he studied at a French Roman Catholic Mission school in Harar. At seven, he was taught French, and later English. Emperor Menelik II heard of this gifted youngster, and at the age of ten, he was brought to the Menelik School in Addis Ababa, an advanced school for the young elite.

At fourteen he was already governor of Garamoulatta in Harar Province, and by 1910 was chief of the provincial government of Harar. In 1911 he married Princess Menen, a granddaughter of the Negus (King) Michael von Wollo. The marriage produced six children, of which only two sons and a daughter survive.

Emperor Menelik II died in 1913, and was succeeded by a grandson, Lij Yasu, whose conversion to Islam touched off a bloody palace revolution and led to his deposition in 1916. The succession fell to one of Menelik II's daughters, the Empress Zaudita. She proved too old and incompetent to rule effectively and, in 1917, Haile Selassie was named regent and heir apparent. He survived numerous court intrigues and, after the empress' death, finally ascended the throne in a splendid ceremony on November 2, 1930 as Haile Selassie I, Emperor, Elect of God, Negusa Nagast (King of Kings), and Conquering Lion of the Tribe of Judah. The name Haile Selassie means "Power of the Trinity."

In July 1931, Haile Selassie—on his own initiative—gave Ethiopia its first written constitution. (He liberalized it in 1955 to provide for an elected national assembly.) He devoted himself to education and public health programs. Schools and hospitals were built, teachers and doctors trained. The emperor imported scores of foreign experts. In Ethiopia, whites worked for Africans, and not the other way around as in most other African countries. In the 1930's, Ethiopia had begun to develop into a modern state under the leadership of its emperor.

Then came Mussolini's invasion in October 1935, and the well-known events of the Ethiopians' gallant resistance, the emperor's flight in April 1936, and his futile appearances before the League of Nations. He lived in exile, first in Jerusalem, then in Bath, England. Almost five years to the day of his flight, he returned to Addis Ababa, on May 5, 1941 and helped organize the campaign in which British and Indian troops and Ethiopian guerrillas drove out the Italians.

At the end of the Second World War, the emperor began anew his tasks of reform. He rules firmly. Whether or not he is always right is for the Ethiopians themselves to judge. In any case, opposition is forbidden. In all circles of the capital one hears that the emperor—who has a complex, very suspicious character—is held in general fear. There is no area of public life in which he does not take a hand. He rules as an autocrat.

No one denies, however, that he is truly devout and tries to lead an exemplary Christian life. Each day he begins work with prayers. He attends church regularly, and makes certain that all Christian feast days are celebrated. The emperor is also "Defender of the Faith," and "undisputed head of the Ethiopian Church," which is regarded as a branch of the government. Direction of the welfare work of this church is one of his special cares. It is also indisputable that he is extraordinarily industrious. Other elements of his character are: stability, patience, and perseverance.

The emperor and empress live in the Guennette-Leul Place in Addis Ababa, cared for by a staff of over a hundred servants. It is known that their marriage is quite happy, and that the emperor is a doting father, grandfather, and great-grandfather. One of his favorite relaxations is playing with his grandchildren, and he is very interested in the education of the young, believing it to be "the surest guarantee of a better life."

Haile Selassie rises every morning at six, and refreshes himself with a glass of fruit juice. He is "half-vegetarian." After prayers in the palace chapel, he breakfasts with the empress. This is his biggest meal of the day; otherwise he eats little. Until audiences begin at nine, the emperor works in his library; he has little time for it during the rest of the day.

There are frequent meetings of the Crown Council, whose president is the emperor. The Crown Council is composed of princes of the royal family, important personages of the country—mostly nobles, and some members of the cabinet council. Afternoons are given over to receiving foreign visitors or making tours. The sovereign inspects hospitals, schools, and government offices. He has a healthy curiosity about everything, and worries about minor palace affairs that are "really none of his business," as some of his aides told me.

The emperor watches a motion picture practically every evening. Then he reads before going to bed at midnight. On weekends, he travels with members of his family to one of his country estates. He likes to ride and row, and sometimes hunts. The emperor has done a lot for sports in Ethiopia, and encourages sports activity among its youth.

The emperor's sons live in their own villas in Addis Ababa. The crown prince and heir to the throne, His Imperial Majesty Merid Azmatch Asfa Wossen Haile Selassie, was born on July 31, 1916. It was he who the leaders (members of the Imperial Bodyguard and young intellectuals) of the abortive revolt of December

1960 selected as their "figure-head emperor," and who proclaimed the formation of a rebel government over the state radio. Haile Selassie, on a state visit to Brazil when the revolt broke out, flew home, crushed it in three days, and subsequently forgave his son because he had acted "under duress." Asfa Wossen's own small son, Prince Sere Yakob Asfa Wossen, is next in line to the throne.

The emperor's second son, Prince Makonnen Haile Selassie, Duke of Harar, was born in 1923, and killed in an automobile accident in 1957, leaving behind him five sons. The Emperor's third son, Prince Sahle Selassie Haile Selassie was born in 1931, and educated in England at Wellington College and Cambridge. The emperor's first child, and only living daughter, is the Princess Tenagne Worq Haile Selassie; she is in her early forties and is married to the imperial viceroy in Eritrea.

It is almost impossible to obtain an objective estimate of Haile Selassie I in Addis Ababa, where he reigns as one of the last absolute monarchs in the world. There is little question that, thanks to his tenacity and extensive training, he has met with some success in his attempts to raise his people out of their medieval-barbaric condition (slavery was only abolished in 1944). In all areas, Ethiopia is making progress toward Western standards of culture and civilization. It is not the emperor's fault if there is still some regression to barbaric practices in remote provinces. As in all African lands, it takes time for reforms to reach all the people—especially those who live far from the capital.

The country's great tragedy is that practically its whole intellectual class was killed during the Italian war and occupation. There is a dearth of educated young people. In a square before the Royal Palace, one sees a bronze memorial which depicts the atrocities that took place during the Fascist occupation; it is a gift of Marshall Tito. This memorial is watched day and night by secret police, so that foreigners cannot photograph it. (In no African country is it so difficult to photograph the most harmless street scene. One is in constant fear that one's camera will be confiscated, which frequently happens.)

The emperor himself is certainly not pleased with Tito's gift. An indication of his desire to be just and objective is the fact that he personally never makes generalizations. Thousands of Italians still live in Ethiopia, and Eritrea—now federated with Ethiopia— and they are treated no better or worse than any other foreigners. When Allied troops entered Ethiopia in January 1941 to liberate the country, the emperor issued this proclamation: "Let us agree that all Italians, armed or unarmed, who fall into the hands of Ethiopian soldiers, should be treated with love and care—Don't let them feel the injustice of what they have done to our people. Show that you are soldiers of honor, with human hearts."

The frequently autocratic manner of Haile Selassie has occasioned criticism at home and abroad. But then it must be remembered that parliamentary democracy is a strange new thing in Africa. A weak emperor would never have been able to make as much out of Ethiopia as Haile Selassie has in the last decades; his accomplishment is worthy of respect.

One day in Addis Ababa I saw a pregnant woman on the steps of the Haile Selassie Hospital. Her labor pains had already begun. Her family wanted her admitted, but could not pay. The woman was turned away, which created a commotion. The emperor was driving by; he stopped and asked what was going on. I stood on the other side of the street, the only European present. The emperor fixed me with a brief, indignant glance. He seemed to have made up his mind about what to do, but I sensed that he hesitated to give a command because of my presence. But soon he did give an order. If the woman couldn't pay, she shouldn't be admitted. The law must be respected. The slogan "the law applies to everyone without exception" appears on billboards, and is frequently quoted in government offices.

Pensive, I left the scene, after a visit to those beasts who appear on the royal coat of arms, the lions, who—and this is hard to grasp—are housed near the hospital and have terrified more than one patient with their roaring. I wandered toward the center of the city. Suddenly an auto pulled up next to me. An officer got out and asked if he might accompany me for a little bit. He came immediately to the point. He had seen that I had witnessed the incident. Now I would think the emperor "an evil ruler," "a soulless tyrant."

"I have no right to judge," I replied. "I am only a guest here."

"You must understand the emperor," the officer said cordially. "He feels himself to be the tutor of every single Ethiopian. When he isn't strong, we'll have chaos again, just as we did before the time of our great emperor." Surely the officer had a point, considering how painful the incident was: for the pregnant woman, for the doctors, for the emperor himself.

Since then, a special hospital has been built for those without means. But also in the Haile Selassie Hospital—I have been told by a European doctor who works there—the emperor has lately taken to bringing in patients he has found in the streets and paying for their expenses out of his own personal funds.

For three thousand years, Ethiopia has been independent, and it is remarkable how Haile Selassie has known how to conduct international relations. The contradictions in his foreign policy mirror his conviction of the necessity for coexistence between East and West. Let us keep in mind that Ethiopia is an empire, ruled by an absolute monarch, and an ancient Christian land. Its whole structure is essentially oriented towards the West, and the emperor certainly maintains excellent relations with Western powers. Nevertheless, he carries on an active political line that reflects the basic philosophies of the Bandung Conference of 1955 and the Accra Conference of 1958, during which representatives from formerly dependent states met and laid the groundwork for Afro-Asian solidarity.

The emperor's friendly relations with Communist Yugoslavia are well-known. Marshall Tito has visited Ethiopia twice and was welcomed like a king. Yes, this emphatically Christian country has undertaken intensive relations with the Eastern bloc and the Soviet

Union itself. When I mentioned this to an Ethiopian minister, he replied: "Can one deny that a third of mankind is ruled by Communism, lives as Communists?"

From June 24 to August 24, 1959 the emperor travelled through the United Arab Republic, the Soviet Union, Czechoslovakia, Belgium, France, Portugal, and Yugoslavia. After his return, he gave a report to his people which is one of the most revealing documents published in Ethiopia since the end of the war.

Haile Selassie's greatest fear is the growing influence of the Moslem lands which are his neighbors. In 1957, the Ethiopian government accused Nasser of fomenting unrest in Ethiopia with the purpose of bringing down its Christian empire. But, in his report, the emperor said that he and Nasser had reconciled their differences.

Communist propaganda is very active in Ethiopia. Stalin had donated a hospital and a Soviet information center, and now the Christian emperor journeyed to Moscow and reported that his visit had been most rewarding. He reminded his people that the Soviet Union had been one of the few nations to deny recognition to the Italian occupation. He said that he had signed agreements that would strengthen the economic ties between the two countries and further their commercial and cultural relations. Ethiopia would receive from the Soviet Union a long-term loan of 400 million rubles that would assist in the financing of Ethiopia's five-year plan and other projects designed to develop the nation's economy and raise the living standards of its people.

As for Czechoslovakia, he noted that a history of friendly relations and assistance dated back to the Italian invasion, and that the Czechs "had demonstrated once again that a sincere and genuine friendship exists between our two countries." He was ready to accept technical and economic support from the present Czechoslovakian government, as he was from "our good friend Marshall Tito," for whom he had much praise.

The emperor went on to explain that though the nations he had visited had economic and political systems different from Ethiopia's, they existed to serve the special needs of those nations, were their own domestic concern only, and should not hinder the under-standing and cooperation of nations in important problems of mutual interest.

In a speech to the Foreign Policy Association during a visit to the United States, Haile Selassie declared that foreign policy was the cornerstone of a small nation's existence, which could not be defended by force of arms. Small nations had to find a reasonable middle ground if they were to survive. He said that because the small nations needed foreign assistance so desperately, they had become showplaces, where different nationalities could work and learn to get along with one another in peace, and that this was especially true of Ethiopia.

Haile Selassie, descendant of Biblical kings, has reached the Biblical three score and ten. He has managed to hold on through the many storms brought by the winds of change that are sweep-ing Africa, including the abortive Ethiopian revolt of December 1960. He may be a strange anachronism among the dynamic young leaders in Africa we shall shortly meet, but this intelligent, durable man does seem to grasp the challenges of the time. In opening the third conference of independent African states, held June 14–24, 1960 in Addis Ababa, he said:

"The bloodsheds and sufferings that we have witnessed during the past year in various parts of this continent are too vivid in our memory to require recital of the facts; they are tragic, and we must see to it that they do not recur. We must devise ways and means to arrest the senseless destruction of African lives. Africans have committed no sin, unless the pursuit of independence and freedom from colonial oppression is considered to be one. . . . We now have our destiny in our own hands, but we must never slacken in our determination never to allow new forms of colonialism, what-ever their guise, to take hold of us in a threat to our hard-won in-dependence."

9

TOM MBOYA OF KENYA

*A Young Union Leader Makes
the Most of His Opportunities*

⁂

My initial impression of Tom Mboya was not good. The first time I met him, at a meeting of young political activists in Nairobi, the capital of Kenya, his anti-British, and especially anti-white outbursts made me think he was just another one of those nationalist hotheads, of whom there are so many. He was wearing gray slacks and a white sports shirt, open at the throat, and he looked more like a professional sportsman than a politician with serious goals.

The next time I met him, during the Accra Conference, I found that I had underestimated him. Student friends from Achimota University brought us together. It was during a garden party given by Prime Minister Nkrumah of Ghana. Standing to one side of the large crowd of international guests was a well-groomed young man, smartly dressed in the English fashion, holding a glass of fruit juice in one hand.

"Is he lovesick?" I asked my student friends.

"He gives that impression," they replied. "But he has no time for love. He's married to Africa. On that big ring he wears is an engraving of his bride—Africa. He's like a panther. Always going off by himself, in order to return more furiously to the attack when he thinks the time is ripe. That's Tom Mboya."

"Now I recognize him," I said. "He's changed a great deal."

We renewed our acquaintance. I complimented him for the superb speech he had given—in faultless English—before the

64

Congress. His skillful handling of the Congress as its chairman had also impressed me. He was always direct and clear, coming right to the heart of the matter. I sensed at once his celebrated qualities of strategy, discipline and organization. My compliments did not impress him. I noticed that while he had nothing against me personally, he did have something against me on principle because I was white.

I brought the conversation around to Kenya's multiracial government.

"A farce!" Mboya replied, and it rang out like a shot.

I mentioned the Capricorn Society, which has taken the zebra as its symbol. The zebra's black and white stripes, in the society's view, signify that Africa can surmount her difficulties when black men and white men try to live among one another in peace.

"That's an obvious swindle," snarled the Panther. "A means to prolong white domination." His small, rather Asiatic eyes became smaller. He was implacable, especially during the closing session of the Congress. Exactly like Nkrumah, he repeatedly shouted into the assembly hall: "Europe is yesterday, Africa is tomorrow! . . . Hands off Africa! . . . Europeans get out of Africa! . . . Africans have had a belly full of Europeans!"

Once I encountered Mboya late at night, sitting with two Ghana cabinet officials in an outdoor dance pavilion. I danced the lively "Ghana high life" with one of the delegate's wives. The Ghanian officials were very cordial to me, and amused themselves over my sincere efforts to master their national dance. Mboya nodded to me curtly, and shot a contemptuous glance at the African woman who was dancing with me, a white man. He was sipping fruit juice again. He avoids alcohol, and does not smoke. This young fanatic permits himself only one pleasure: cowboy and mystery films.

The British Crown Colony of Kenya officially became part of the Empire in 1895. In its 224,960 square miles of lovely mountains, deep forests, and fertile green pastures, live some six million black Africans; 152 thousand Asians—mostly Indians and Goans; 33 thousand Arabs; and 57 thousand whites, mostly of British stock.

At the heart of Kenya's problems—and the recent Mau-Mau rebellion—is land. 12,700 square miles of the lush "white highlands," Kenya's finest farmland and source of its lucrative tea, coffee, sisal (hemp), and pyrethrum, were until very recently reserved for white European settlers only.

Tom Mboya was born in 1930 in the highlands of Kenya, in a worker's mud hut on the sisal plantation of a wealthy English farmer. He is not a Kikuyu, but belongs to the Luo tribe, the second largest in the country. His parents could neither read nor write. "I was born on the dark side of the street of life," he told me.

His father admired the white man, and perhaps feared him even more. He continually advised his son to get along with the whites, under any conditions. "Otherwise you're lost." At the same time Mboya's father had ambition. He wanted his son to become more than a poor plantation worker, and sent him to the Roman Catholic Kabaa mission, thirty-five miles from the plantation. Irish priests taught here under the most primitive conditions. There were not enough classrooms, blackboards, or books. The children wrote their ABC's in the sand, with their fingers. In this way, Tom Mboya also learned to read and write; he was nine years old.

From the mission station he went on to St. Mary's School, near Lake Victoria. Here he received his first English lessons. As a student he was not particularly outstanding; he preferred singing and debating. His teachers still remark today that he avoided violence as a boy. He never fought with his schoolmates. Even then, he admired great men. The student at the mission school wrote this about Napoleon: "the man who defied the whole world."

Later, at Holy Ghost College (high school) in Mangu, he studied history. His idols were Abraham Lincoln and Booker T. Washington. The missionaries developed a certain mistrust of him, because of his readings and historical interests. Did they already see in this young worker's son the future revolutionary?

Tom Mboya wanted to enter the priesthood, but the Church disappointed and embittered him. He found it "very weak on the colonial question." He later said, "The Church wants to preserve the status quo. I still consider myself a Catholic, but I'm skeptical about the Church." Mboya could not remain long at Holy Ghost College. His father, the poorly paid plantation worker, ran out of money. What to do next? Mboya took a free, three-year course in Nairobi to become a sanitation inspector.

During this time, he heard political speeches by the Kikuyu nationalist Jomo Kenyatta, who was later sentenced to hard labor as the leader of the Mau-Mau uprising. Kenyatta's fiery speeches awakened in Mboya political and social ambitions. "Very quickly I came to see how unjust it was, that I should receive ten pounds a month for my work, while my colleagues, the white inspectors, received five times that much for doing no more and no less than I did."

I was told of an incident that involved Mboya when he was working at the health office laboratory. He was alone in the lab when a white woman came in to have a bottle of milk examined. "Is nobody here?" she asked. "Madam, there must be something wrong with your eyesight," Mboya answered. The Englishwoman stomped out of the office, muttering disdainful remarks about this impertinent young Negro.

Soon Mboya had little time for his job, as he became more absorbed in politics. Jomo Kenyatta was still his model. The latter had gone to England in 1929, stayed for fifteen years, then spent two years in Moscow before returning to Kenya in 1947. His inflammatory speeches unquestionably had much to do with unleashing the Mau-Mau rebellion, although it is still unclear how much he was personally responsible for its terrorist activities.

Tom Mboya was a member of Kenyatta's Kenya African Union, but it has been proven that he had nothing to do with the Mau-Mau terrorism. When Kenyatta was arrested, Walter Odede became president of the K.A.U., and Odede made Tom Mboya the party's public relations officer. After Odede's arrest in 1953, Mboya became treasurer of the K.A.U., and collected funds for

Kenyatta's defense and liberation. Kenyatta himself is supposed to have met Mboya only once, and he was not overly impressed. Mboya, on the other hand, fought incessantly for the rehabilitation of Kenyatta. He never stopped giving assurances that Kenyatta was not to blame for the Mau-Mau terrorism, and demanded his release from prison.

Here are Mboya's thoughts about Mau-Mau: "For many, Kenya is identified with Mau-Mau. Mau-Mau was a reaction against all the social and economic wrongs of the Europeans against the Africans. While neither I nor any African leader has ever favored or condoned terrorism or violence as a political instrument, I want to make it clear that I protest equally the brutal repression and injustice employed in stamping it out. Literally thousands of blameless Africans who had nothing to do with Mau-Mau were herded like cattle into camps, their lives and families disrupted or destroyed. Cold figures can but partly convey the horror of Kenya's suffering at that time: as against a handful of Europeans who lost their lives, several thousands of Africans were killed. I repeat that I do not support or condone violence; but in the final analysis it is the European settler community which is responsible for the circumstances which evoked such a frightening response."

After all the leaders of the Kenya Africa Union had been arrested—a fate which Tom Mboya always managed to avoid—he became, at twenty-three, the only prominent nationalist still at liberty. He devoted himself to the Municipal Workers' Organization, which he affiliated with the big Kenya Federation of Labor. After the K.A.U. was banned in the summer of 1953, the Kenya Federation of Labor became the most important grouping of African nationalists, and Mboya got its top job: general secretary.

In 1954, a new constitution for Kenya, introduced by British Colonial Secretary Oliver Lyttelton, took effect. Despite all assurances, the Africans still received no authority. Of the six people's representatives in the cabinet, three were Europeans, two were Indians, and only one was African. Tom Mboya abandoned all further cooperation with the administration, and took up passive resistance. Even then his goal was: "One man, one vote, on a common roll."

Mboya wanted to put his time to good use during this hopeless period. Foreign trade unionists helped with money and advice. The International Confederation of Free Trade Unions sent him to a labor seminar in India, in 1954. He studied diligently in Calcutta, and made contacts with Indian and American union leaders. The following year, he won a scholarship to Oxford's Ruskin College, where he studied under G. D. H. Cole, Kenneth Robinson, Margery Perham, and read Harold Laski. After a year at Oxford, he made a lecture tour of America, strengthened his contacts with American labor leaders, and received $35,000 from the A.F.L.–C.I.O. for the construction of a new union headquarters in Nairobi. (In 1959, Howard University gave him an honorary Doctor of Laws degree.)

Back in Kenya, he became president of the Nairobi People's Council and a member of Kenya's Legislative Council, to which Africans were elected—not appointed—for the first time. Mboya won his campaign with convincing speeches. The Legislative Council had fifty-eight members, of whom eight were Africans. Mboya was not satisfied with this. He presented a petition to the Colonial Office in London, but his demands were turned down, and success did not come to him until four years later, during the Kenya Conference of 1960.

In a short work, *Kenya Faces the Future,* which he wrote for the American Committee on Africa in 1959, Tom Mboya gave an excellent presentation of the African case concerning Kenya: "It is unfortunate that information about the African stand on our ultimate objectives for Kenya, as well as our position toward the immigrant communities, has generally come from settler spokesmen or the European press. We, the African elected members, have been called, among other things, obdurate, intransigent, racialists, extremists, and agitators. I have particularly been singled out and made the target for abuse. The most recent form such attacks have taken is that we are inconsistent, and by implication, dishonest, and that I personally speak with two voices—a sweet one in London and an extremist one in Africa.

"Such charges would be more amusing if they did not intensify an already tense situation. As for the last charge of inconsistency, any examination of the position of the African members, and of my own, will show, particularly during the last two years, the consistency of the African position and the almost ludicrous inconsistency of the position of the Europeans and the British Government, particularly in reference to the contradictory British policy toward different African countries.

"As for our position on ultimate objectives, that has been clear and consistent throughout: the demand for the development of Kenya into a democracy with equal rights and opportunities regardless of race, color or creed.

"While demanding fifteen more seats for the African people in 1957, the African members did not demand the reduction of European or Asian seats; on the contrary, they indicated that the Asians too had a case. In a statement to the governor, and later to Mr. Lennox-Boyd, the African members explained that their proposal was based on the need for Africans to have effective representation. We explained that the distances to be covered, the population to be dealt with, and the problems to be tackled in an African constituency were such that the then existing representation could hardly be capable of effectively serving the people.

"To us these arguments were not only sound, but our decision to ask only for fifteen more seats instead of immediate proportional representation reflected our acknowledgement of the need to ensure continued confidence on the part of the immigrant communities and to engender an atmosphere of cooperation and collaboration. Whereas the Asian and Arab members immediately announced their unconditional support for an increase in African representation, the European leaders condemned the proposal as an attempt at domination and interpreted it as a racialist move.

"Our attitude on the 'white highlands' is that this is an anachronism which must go. We cannot see any hope of developing happy

European-African relations when our people have only to travel by train or bus from an overcrowded and often arid reserve to see vast areas of apparently unoccupied land and to be told that this is exclusively reserved for white settlers. It is politically unsound for an immigrant community—so small in number—to continue to maintain this exclusive reservation and expect that this will not be a source of friction and ill-feeling. In our view this exclusive reservation cannot be defended on moral, political, or economic grounds.

"Africans are not unaware of the economic significance of efficient, large-unit farming in the highlands, but we feel confident that a program of land reform is possible without much harm to the economic interests of the country. We are aware that this stand has been interpreted by some Europeans as a warning that should Africans secure a greater voice in the government, European land may be expropriated. It is inevitable that in a program of land reform some measures may require the surrender of part of the land now held by some of the very big land owners, but so long as this is justly and fairly compensated, we should in the interest of the country try to resolve this problem by a mutually agreed plan. We seek changes that will reflect justice and equity, but to be achieved peacefully and cooperatively.

"Despite provocative statements by Mr. Lennox-Boyd and the local press, since 1957 the African elected members avoided any action that could have resulted in a complete breakdown in attempts at discussion. On every occasion on which they met the Governor it was at their own request. They have written letters and published statements. In the Legislature, the African members have from time to time made motions on various African political problems. Support has come from the Asians, but never from the Europeans, except for Mr. Cooke, a European elected member. After calling for a round table conference for a number of months without success, African members introduced a motion in the Legislature which was defeated by a combination of European and government votes—except for Mr. Cooke who again voted with the non-Europeans. The African members went ahead a few weeks later to publish a further policy statement including proposals for constitutional reform. This reiterated their stand on the ultimate objective of a democracy and also their commitment to transitional development. The document was submitted to the Governor of Kenya and again to the Colonial Secretary.

"Four months elapsed without a word from the government, and despite the importance of the statement the European leaders remained silent. It was left for us to take the initiative again in September and October in a number of visits to Government House and ultimately in November, we read the despatch of the Colonial Secretary, Mr. Lennox-Boyd, rejecting the African members' demand for a round table conference. In the summary his position was: that a constitution for Kenya must be subject to agreement; that it must provide for continued participation of all races; that it must be designed to respect the interests of the minorities; and that it must provide for a move away from communal representation to non-racial representation.

"A study of the African members' June policy statement and constitutional proposals will show that in fact Mr. Lennox-Boyd's principles were all met. If there is any difference it is in matters of detail which can only be resolved at a round table conference. The African members' proposals provided for continued representation of the immigrant communities in the Legislature and also in the Council of Ministers. They asked for immediate discussions on the workability of a common voters' roll. They provided for constitutional guarantee of individual citizens' rights with provision for appeal to the Supreme Court. And they asked for a round table conference so as to ensure agreement.

"Does this approach on the part of African members suggest intransigence and a lack of appreciation of the fears and interests of the other groups?

"The foregoing outlines the record and position of the Africans in the last two years, a position condemned and viciously attacked by the settlers and their press. Perhaps the most incredible part of the current impasse is the fact that the Europeans, while opposing every proposal put forth by the Africans since 1957, have not put forward any alternatives themselves."

In this same work, Mboya discussed prospects for the future, and came out strongly for democracy: "It is my conviction that the mistaken leadership of the European Community and the policies of the British Government are not only responsible for the continuing political crisis, but and in effect have actually worked against their own self interest. . . .

"Many of the Europeans are still committed to special privilege and domination as a policy, even though they know this state cannot be maintained indefinitely. The European realizes that the current status must change, but he does not know precisely what will replace it, and wonders whether the Kenya Africans will be driven by a desire to be vindictive over past injustices. Nothing can stop the changes sweeping over the whole of Africa, including Kenya, a fact generally accepted by both Africans and non-Africans. In my opinion, a clear statement from the Colonial Office committing Kenya to a genuine democracy would strengthen the hands of the liberal elements in the European community leaving the fanatics to fight a losing battle. . . .

"Some Europeans, while admitting the eventual necessity of democracy complain that democracy in Kenya would mean a majority of Africans in every walk of life. But what else could it mean in a country with 6,000,000 Africans and only 200,000 non-Africans? This need not however be synonymous with tyranny, dictatorship or victimization of the non-Africans. What is important is the grant of citizenship rights, and here the non-Africans and the Africans have got to learn to talk of individuals instead of groups. So far, it is only the Africans who advocate the need for getting away from communal group identity to democratic individual citizenship. The European leaders have yet to start educating their community towards the acceptance of this idea.

"Multi-racialism or partnership provides the second alternative in our situation. This idea was not even mentioned at the recent Convention of European Associations, despite the fact that since 1954 it has been the predominant idea in European circles. Afri-

cans rejected the idea of partnership or multi-racial government
for Kenya, right from the time it was first introduced in Central
Africa in 1953 and later in the version of the Lyttelton Plan in
1954. Such a system has numerous defects. Its first object is to
preserve the position of the immigrant minority groups so ex-
cessively as to ensure that they remain in control of the government. In order to do this a special franchise is necessary which in
effect leads to the disenfranchisement of the bulk of the non-
Europeans. Multi-racialism or partnership cannot succeed. Witness
what is already happening in Central Africa.

"Having ruled out domination by Europeans, racialism by Africans and multi-racialism and partnership, we are left with only
one logical and reasonable and just alternative—and that is democracy. Such democracy would recognize the individual as against
the present groups. It would seek integration instead of partnership. It would accord individual citizenship rights and protections
instead of minority safeguards and group privileges. It would out-
law all forms of race discrimination instead of condoning this
under various pretexts, as at present in schools, land, medical
services and public places. It would guarantee individual property
rights and aim at an economic and social system just and equitable
in relation to our entire community. We would face our problems
in their proper order where they would cease to be African, European or Asian problems, but economic or social problems. This is
what we mean by democracy for Kenya. And it is democracy which
must prevail."

On February 21, 1960, a round-table conference of British and
Kenyan government officials, with delegates from the white and
Asian settlers, came to a close in London. It had lasted four weeks,
and was in danger many times of being broken off, because—
among other reasons—of the insistence of Peter Koinange, a
trusted lieutenant of Jomo Kenyatta's, of being included in the
discussions.

Despite the fact that the conference was boycotted for a week by the Africans, it was a success—thanks in large measure to the reasonable attitude of Tom Mboya, who led the fourteen-man African delegation with his colleague Ronald Ngaba. The European settlers were the only ones who were dissatisfied with its results. Llewellyn R. Briggs, a former R.A.F. Group Captain and leader of the extremist United Party, described the talks as: "a death blow to the European community in Kenya." Michael Blundell, leader of the liberal-minded whites and the multi-racial New Kenya Group, would have a hard time preventing his white supporters from taking a more radical course. Tom Mboya and his new Kenya Independence Movement were criticized as too moderate by Radio Moscow. Extremists within his own party criticized him.

The conference resulted in a new constitution for Kenya. More Africans would be taken into the cabinet council of the British governor, who would continue to rule. Africans would receive thirty-seven of the sixty-five seats in the legislature, and were promised several leading ministries. The franchise of Africans was expanded. Every citizen of Kenya who could read or write, had a steady job or earned at least $210 a year would have the right to vote. For the first time, it became certain that the European and Asian minority—even though still assured important representation in the Legislature—would eventually come under the rule of the black majority.

But, as the *Times* of London noted, the decisive question in Kenya was not constitutional change, but land reform. The conference took steps to draft legislation that would guarantee by law the equality and protection of property rights. This will inevitably lead to the dissolution of the old system of reserved lands for separate races. In the spring of 1960, six hundred farms were up for sale.

In his speech as the representative of all African peoples in Accra, Tom Mboya once again renounced violence. It remains to be seen if he remains true to the policy of passive resistance until Kenya gains its independence, which is inevitable in the foreseeable future. And one wonders how he will conduct himself when Kenya (in 1962? 1963? 1964?) becomes in fact independent.

On Mboya's return from London, twenty thousand Africans greeted him in Nairobi's African Stadium with the cry: *"Uhuru!"* (the Swahili word for freedom). The thirty-year-old union leader had not achieved his promised goal of immediate freedom and independence. Nevertheless, he had brought back with him important political concessions for his country.

Before long, Mboya will probably be offered a cabinet post. Whether or not he will ever become prime minister is hard to predict, for although he is admired, he is not loved. He has no close contact with his people, though he himself has risen out of its lowest class. A bachelor, he lives with his teen-age brother in a rented duplex in the suburbs of Nairobi. He is a lone wolf, has no intimate friends who would make any sacrifice for him, and prefers to keep his own counsel. Perhaps because of this he is the most implacable, self-assured, and frequently the most arrogant intellectual among the new leaders of Africa.

Tom Mboya himself feels that his future career, despite his many successes, is still undecided. He frequently remarks that after the release of Jomo Kenyatta he will withdraw and let Kenyatta assume sole leadership of the Kenyan nationalists. Many people regret Mboya's lack of sense of humor, for many Negro politicians make good use of humor. He is tough, dictatorial, and often acts like a demagogue.

On the other hand, he is for everything modern and Western. In contrast to many of his colleagues, he prefers America to the Soviet Union. "If he were only ten years older," one of his European supporters told me, "everything would be a lot easier. He still has a chip on his shoulder. His friend Nyerere of Tanganyika matured from a severe extremist into a moderate, and it did him and his country a lot of good." Whether or not that happens to Mboya, he still ranks among the most prolific young politicians in Africa today.

In the summer of 1960, a new crisis threatened to develop in Kenya. In April Jomo Kenyatta had been released from hard labor in prison, but placed under restricted detention at Lodwar, in the remote Northern Province of Kenya. Mboya and other African leaders clamored for his complete release. But the British governor, Sir Patrick Renison, refused. Describing Kenyatta as "the African leader of darkness and death," the governor said that "in the decision regarding his release from restriction, politics is not my concern. My concern is security . . . [and] from the security viewpoint I think that Jomo Kenyatta's return to political life in Kenya at the present time would be a disaster." The governor was of the opinion that Kenyatta's release would touch off more violence and hinder the political development of the colony, and announced measures to limit the freedom of movement of the Kikuyu tribe in the central province, the Rift Valley province, and Nairobi to prevent a situation from developing that could lead to a rebirth of the Mau-Mau movement.

African nationalist leaders founded a new party, on the Tanganyikan model, the Kenya Africa National Union (K.A.N.U.), which embraced all the nationalist groups. Kenyatta was elected president at a meeting on May 14–15, 1960 but this was later rescinded and the K.A.N.U. was granted official registration as a party on June 11, after James Samuel Gichuru had been elected president in Kenyatta's stead. The general secretary is Tom Mboya, whose own party, which was largely limited to the Nairobi area, merged with the new, larger party.

Gichuru said that his election did not "undermine the position of Kenyatta, who is the only acknowledged leader of the African people." Gichuru was born in 1914 in Thogoto in the Kiambu Reserve. Although a Kikuyu, he is a Christian, studied at Makerere College in Uganda, was a schoolmaster at a Roman Catholic secondary school, and was the first president of the Kenya Africa Union, but resigned when Kenyatta returned to Kenya in 1947. From June 1955 to the end of the emergency in January 1960, he was under a restriction order. He has developed into a political figure of growing importance, and is regarded by many as Tom Mboya's chief rival.

The K.A.N.U., in continuing to press for Kenyatta's release much more forcibly than did the numerous smaller parties which preceded it, threatens to boycott any further talks about a new constitution. It would seem that Kenyatta will play the same role in Kenya as did Nkrumah in Ghana or Banda in Nyasaland.

In February 1961 most of the 1,300,000 African voters in Kenya cast ballots for the first time in the first common-roll election. Although Kenyatta was still confined to his desert village, it seemed as if he were the chief black candidate. His name and photograph were displayed everywhere.

The election was bloodless and Mboya was not his usual provocative self. "Let us not become arrogant or racial," he said, "but humble and conscientious in taking on our new legitimate and rightful status." His Kenya African National Union won control of 18 seats. In his own Nairobi district, Mboya won 31,407 to 2,668 for his closest rival, a Kikuyu doctor. "When the African majority takes power," Mboya said, "a one-party government in the initial stages will be necessary for stability in Kenya. Danger would come not from traditions or tribalism, but from a struggle for power between the parties," he said. "Inevitably this would produce violence and instability."

Following the election, James Gichuru assessed the political future by saying "Europeans and Asians who wish to continue to live here and who will accept an African majority have nothing to fear. We hope they will cooperate fully with the Africans in the life of Kenya. Land titles will be honored and land reform will be for the benefit of the whole country," he said. Both Mboya and Gichuru expect future help from the United States and Britain and made it abundantly clear that if this aid was not sufficient they would not hesitate to turn to the Soviet Union.

10

JULIUS NYERERE OF TANGANYIKA

A Schoolteacher Turned Statesman

✳

Tanganyika, home of Mount Kilimanjaro and a German colony until World War I, is a United Nations trust territory administered by the British. It is as large as Germany and France combined, and its population is overwhelmingly Negro African. Ninety-eight per cent of its 9,832,000 natives belong to the Bantu tribe. Its 75,000 Asians are mostly small traders living in the capital, Dar es Salaam. Of its 24,000 white Europeans, only 4,000 are permanently established as land-owning settlers, and of these only half are British.

The absence of a white settler problem is the great difference between Tanganyika, and Kenya and Algeria. There has been less friction, not to mention outright rebellion, here than in other African lands. The white settler minority seems finally to have realized that it will be its advantage to come to terms with the native Africans.

Tanganyika is now self-governing, and will become sovereign and independent in December 1961. When it does, Julius Nyerere, a tall, thin, mustached figure is almost equally certain to become its prime minister. Once a fiery radical, he has matured into a moderate, and is considered by a great many people to be the most capable of the new leaders in Africa.

Julius Nyerere was born in 1918, the son of Nyerere Burito, a chief of the Zanaki, one of the smallest of Tanganyika's 113 tribes.

His father, who was already a chief at the time of the Germans, was polygamous and had twenty-six children.

At twelve, Nyerere was sent to the Musoma school. From 1934 on, he displayed an interest in Christianity, but it was not until 1943, when he was twenty-five, that he was baptized a Roman Catholic.

After primary school, which he completed in three instead of the normal four years, he attended an advanced school in Tabora in the Central Province. From 1943 to 1945, he studied at Makerere University in Kampala, the commercial center of Uganda, which was then the only university in existence between Egypt and South Africa. Nyerere graduated from the university with a diploma in education and returned to St. Mary's Mission School in Tabora as a teacher.

From 1949 to 1952, he studied history and economics at the University of Edinburgh and returned to Tanganyika with an M.A. He resumed his career as a teacher at the St. Francis School near Dar es Salaam, but gave more of his time to politics than he had up to then. (Nyerere: "I followed my conscience.") He established residence in Dar es Salaam, and made quite a show of his marriage to a girl from another tribe, in order to demonstrate that he was enlightened and no longer gave priority to tribal loyalties. He was much more "a militant nationalist," as he described himself. He joined the Opposition, but quickly gained general respect —from the administration, too—for his straightforwardness, sincerity, and integrity.

Nyerere made contact with the Tanganyika African Association, which was originally founded by British officials as a social organization for Africans. In 1953, he became its president. He worked out a new constitution for the association, which was accepted in July 1954. At the same time he gave it a new name, the Tanganyika African National Union (TANU), and as its representative in the Legislative Council became the leader of the entire Opposition.

A United Nations mission visited the trust territory of Tanganyika in 1954, and invited Nyerere to New York in February 1955.

He gave a speech, "My People's Hopes," before the Trusteeship Council of the UN and made a deep impression on the delegates. Back in Tanganyika, he traveled for months throughout the whole country in a Land Rover, spoke ardently against the policy of separate races and advocated a "Tanganyikan national conscience." In November 1956, he returned to New York and addressed the UN again, describing himself as an enthusiastic supporter of democracy and eloquently demanding independence for his country in the near future.

In December 1959, the British agreed to a government with an African legislative majority for a four-year period of transition. In the elections of August 30, 1960 to the Legislative Council, Nyerere's monolithic TANU won 70 of the 71 seats, and the British governor, Sir Richard Turnbull invited Nyerere to form a government, with himself as chief minister; a post in which he is the governor's principal adviser and leader of government business in the Legislative Assembly.

Nyerere is not as flamboyant as many of the African leaders who are his contemporaries, but his astute leadership and logical and subtle mind have brought him respect and influence that goes far beyond the borders of Tanganyika. As Chairman of PAFMECA (the Pan-African Freedom Movement for East and Central Africa), he has proposed a plan for an eventual self-governing, independent Federation of East Africa, to include Uganda, Kenya, Tanganyika, Zanzibar, Nyasaland, Northern Rhodesia, and Southern Rhodesia.

The British expert on African affairs, Colin Legum, applauded Nyerere's plan in "Doom and Promise" (*The Observer,* November 26, 1960): "The situation is not yet irretrievable, provided British policy is capable of making one of its imaginative leaps which have been a feature of our imperial history. Instead of pursuing a policy that would lead to the violent disintegration of the Central African Federation, Britain has an opportunity of gaining for the Commonwealth a much wider and stronger federation, with anything from six to eleven members and embracing 30 million Africans, 400,000 Europeans, and 300,000 Asians. . . .

"The starting point would be for Britain to back the idea of an East and Central Federation sponsored by . . . Julius Nyerere, and supported by prominent African and European leaders in Kenya, Zanzibar, Northern Rhodesia and Nyasaland, and by a number of prominent personalities in Uganda. . . .

"The choice before the British Government is to adopt this imaginative idea of a new, loose confederation or to continue its sterile policies of trying to rescue the doomed Federation in Central Africa. It cannot pursue both objectives, since they are fundamentally incompatible. Unless the British Government understands the essential difference between the two, it may jeopardize Mr. Nyerere's initiative and might bring disaster on Central Africa."

The Economist, in "A Federal Case," November 26, 1960, had this to say about Nyerere's plan: "If his plans for federation of a major proportion of the east and central African territories did come to fruition he would have created the kind of pan-African unit Dr. Nkrumah, an earlier African dreamer, has failed to create. If Mr. Nyerere were at its head, there could be a giant new east African state able to approach Nigeria in size, and to rival any other country on the African continent in sense of purpose; and, in the tempest of change, even the unlikely is by no means impossible."

Julius Nyerere has written a short work, *Barriers to Democracy,* from which colleagues of his like Tom Mboya often quote. The historian whose destiny it was to make history himself here attempted, among other things, to give an analysis of the non-African:

"If I were a non-African and had no better reason for supporting the African's desire for self-determination, I would nevertheless reason thus: This country is bound ultimately to be governed by the will of the Africans. There is nothing that we can do to prevent this inevitable outcome. The African knows this. Our duty, therefore, is to do everything that our education and experience enables us to do to see to it that this transition is carried out smoothly and good humoredly. We should willingly put our education and experience at the disposal of the African and if he accepts it we are bound to have an influence in the affairs of this country out of all proportion to our numbers. What is more, that influence shall be welcomed by the majority of the Africans themselves.

"I would ask myself why I am afraid of the African, since the African is not, or at any rate need not, be afraid of me. I might discover that I am not really afraid of the African, but rather of myself. I know that the African is struggling against a humiliation or an oppression or a something. I am somehow identified with this something which the African considers to be a humiliation. I therefore shudder at the thought of the African being in power where once he was the underdog. I might discover that I am afraid of a vagueness which like a fog is intangible and yet is capable of clogging the vision. In other words, I might discover my fears are largely unreal, and that in so far as they may be real I am likely to be the cause."

As elsewhere in Africa, there is a great lack of men and women in Tanganyika who can take over the positions held by whites up to now. There are today 1,300 British officials of the higher grades, and 1,500 of the middle grades in the country, as opposed to 300 African officials. Nyerere intends further cooperation with British officials, only under different conditions than those which previously prevailed. He has learned a lot from Nehru in this area.

"Tanganyika will need the services of British officials for a long time to come. In West Africa, the Colonial Office has followed a clear policy from the beginning, and trained native officials. But in Tanganyika things have developed so quickly that there are simply not enough natives available with the necessary training."

For years, Tom Mboya has agitated for "one man, one vote, on a common roll." But for the time being, the British in Kenya have no intention of granting his demands. In Tanganyika, too, the civil rights of Africans have not yet been newly defined. In the long run, it is naturally out of the question that voting rights should be

limited to only a privileged class. Nyerere asked the British governor, Sir Richard Turnbull, why this should be so at a meeting of
the Legislative Council. I often heard whites say that it would be
unbearable to give "those primitive Africans in the jungle and
rain forests, those troglodytes, the right to vote." Nyerere explained to the governor why it is really not so unbearable:

"Our struggle has become a struggle for the rights of man. . . .
We are struggling against a tiny minority which has established its
dominance over a large majority. . . . There are countries where a
man's civil rights are determined by the color of his skin. . . . In
Tanganyika we believe that only evil, Godless men would make
the color of a man's skin the criteria for granting him civil
rights. . . .

"There are other lands where civil rights are based on material
possessions or education. . . . We are struggling against this
method of determining who shall be given the right to vote. . . .
The educated man is not necessarily more honorable, patriotic, or
selfless than the un-educated man. . . . He is not necessarily wiser.
. . . He does not necessarily cause less trouble, and one can also
not say that he is less responsible for the sufferings of mankind. . . .

"When the law requires a university education or the possession
of a fat bank account before granting a man his civil rights, then
the law must be regarded as unjust and arbitrary. . . . Isn't it
absurd to make education or an income of seventy-five pounds a
year the qualifications for the right to vote? . . . Why should a
man, who has managed to get a certain amount of education, suddenly be thought of as a better citizen than his neighbor who is
still illiterate? And is the difference between seventy-five and
seventy-four pounds a year income so great, that it can be the difference between full civil rights and second-class citizenship?
. . . No, these arbitrary qualifications are laughable. . . . Nothing
can justify them."

For the present, Tanganyika has a "responsible government," in
which the British governor retains veto power. It has internal self-

government, but is not yet independent. Nyerere: "For me, self-government means the same thing as complete independence."

But Nyerere repeatedly stresses the unhappy harvest his people will reap when this happens. People in Tanganyika think of themselves too much as Africans, Europeans, or Asians. They must learn to think of themselves as Tanganyikans. Nyerere: "Unity is our best weapon." As for racial differences, he intends to see to it that civil rights are equated with the personal rights of individuals, and do not become the property of any one race. In any case, the identification of economic privileges with any one race must be done away with.

And democracy? Nyerere: "Democratic reforms are naturally well-suited to African conditions. For me the characteristics of democracy are: the freedom of the individual, including freedom to criticize the government, and the opportunity to change it without worrying about being murdered." Nyerere, the former schoolteacher, plans to integrate the schools, in which up to now pupils have been separated on the basis of race. In addition, he wants to industrialize the country and put its natural resources to work.

He has been cautioned that full independence, if it is received too early, can also bring chaos into the country. Nyerere's reply: "I know that our trouble will begin when we take over the government. Nevertheless, we have no fear of chaos, or Communism. Our slogan is no longer simply '*Uhuru!*' but '*Uhuru Na Kazi!*' (freedom and work). In this spirit, we will manage all of our problems, just like all the other African countries. And I will personally see to it that the transfer of power takes place peacefully. Violence is unnecessary and expensive. I have demonstrated that I know how to take a moderate course. I learned how to be a moderate through observing the inflexible behaviour of the Europeans."

11

FROM SIR ROY WELENSKY
TO HASTINGS KAMUTZU BANDA

Antagonists in a Central African Tinderbox

⁂

In Nyasaland, as in other African countries, I met representatives of youth groups. They resemble each other in many ways. They are all full of life, like to dance and listen to modern jazz. But the youth of Nyasaland struck me as being more puritanical than the youth of other African countries. Once I invited a group to a discussion. When I asked them what they would like to drink, they all answered: "Water!" I did a double take and repeated my question. No, they did not want beer, whisky, lemonade, or seltzer water—just plain water. They explained that they had pledged themselves to drink nothing but water until their country became independent: the white man had introduced whisky in order to weaken the African's resistance; they intended to remain healthy and strong for the fight for freedom. A small incident, perhaps, but it is another illustration of why the struggle for independence has become almost like a religion for many Africans.

It doesn't take very long to see that conditions are more unpleasant for the African in the Federation of Rhodesia and Nyasaland than in any country we have written about up to now—Kenya excepted. At the border, it is necessary to fill out an astonishing questionnaire. It is more complicated and all-inclusive than those of other African countries. For example, I had to write down my race after my name, and specify whether I was white, African, Asian, or mulatto.

Salisbury (pop. 250,000) is both the capital of Southern Rhodesia and of the Federation of Rhodesia and Nyasaland. The gleaming city center, with its two dozen skyscrapers, is reserved for Europeans. Africans work here during the day, but at night they must return to their own primitive, wretched quarters, the "African Townships," which are quite far from the city. The white suburbs have charm, and one sees behind dazzling tropical foliage many inviting villas built in the old-English style. The hotels are comfortable and old-fashioned. The dining rooms of the leading hotels breathe an air of the old colonial era. One dines by candlelight, to the sounds of a murmuring fountain and the violins of the salon orchestra playing Viennese waltzes or other "melodies from a happier time." The Negro "boys"—four to six of them at each table—wear white uniforms, with white gloves and colorful sashes, and serve the guests with great politeness. If one could forget that this was the middle of the twentieth century, and an especially critical period for the white man in Africa, one could enjoy this Gay Nineties atmosphere. But the realities are too pressing. One cannot invite a Negro cabinet official or an Indian businessman to lunch or dinner here. This is for "Europeans Only"— the sign that one sees everywhere in Salisbury.

It's no different in the pubs. Many stores forbid entrance to the African. Banks and post offices have separate entrances and windows for Africans. Even the public toilets are separated on the basis of race. The administration discussed a plan to build "comfort stations for all races" in Salisbury. The proposal brought forth a storm of protest from most of the whites. A great deal is made of the multiracial University College, but of the 165 students enrolled last semester, only twenty-five were Africans and one was Asian. There is also considerable discrimination in wages and salaries; whites receive from fourteen to eighteen times more than the Africans receive for similar work—only because they are white.

Conditions here have not yet become so bad as in the Union of South Africa. But one can observe tendencies that have a lot in common with *apartheid,* and flow from the same fountain of racism. The nationalist leader Dr. Hastings Banda has said: "Between the regimes of Rhodesia and South Africa there is no essential difference, only a difference of degree."

The Central African Federation of Rhodesia and Nyasaland (pop. 7,650,000—488,060 sq. miles) is more than five times the size of Great Britain, bigger than the Union of South Africa, and is composed of three federated territories. The largest is Northern Rhodesia (pop. 2,310,000—288,130 sq. miles), which produces about 17 per cent of the world's copper; followed by Southern Rhodesia (pop. 2,641,500—150,333 sq. miles); and Nyasaland (pop. 2,709,300—49,177 sq. miles). Southern Rhodesia is a self-governing British colony; the other two are protectorates supervised by the Colonial Office.

The overwhelming majority of the Federation's population is Negro African. There are 287,300 white Europeans, and 33,600 members of "other races," as they are described in official statistics (mostly Asians and mulattos). Some 207,000 whites live in Southern Rhodesia; 72,000 in Northern Rhodesia, and only 8,300 in Nayasaland. The problem is that the Europeans constitute only 3.7 per cent of the total population, and the blacks do not want to be ruled by this tiny white minority.

British influence in the Rhodesias goes back to Cecil Rhodes. He founded the British South Africa Company, which—and not the British Government—administered the Rhodesias from 1889 to 1914, when its charter was extended with the understanding that the electorate could decide its own fate within ten years. In 1923, a thin majority of Southern Rhodesia's voters chose to become a self-governing colony, and were annexed to the British crown. In 1924, Northern Rhodesia was annexed as a protectorate. Nyasaland, which had been opened up by British Protestant missionaries, had been made a protectorate in 1891.

In 1953, over the protests of the African delegates, and after much stormy debate and discussion, the British government established the new Federation of Rhodesia and Nyasaland. It has been a very shaky, controversial, and strife-torn federation ever since.

Sharply questioned by Hugh Gaitskell, leader of the opposition, in a debate in the House of Commons on July 22, 1959, about the composition of an Advisory Commission to review constitutional changes in the Federation, Prime Minister Macmillan declared: "The purpose of our policy is as soon as possible, and as rapidly as possible, to move towards self-government in Northern Rhodesia and Nyasaland. . . . If the government were to agree to tear up a federation experiment only seven years old, which was started with a good deal of good will on all sides and has made considerable progress, it would be guilty of an act of treachery towards the high ideals and purposes which they set for themselves."

After pointing out that the choice lay between "partnership or chaos," and noting the advances the African had made in industry and agriculture, the British prime minister concluded: "In Central Africa let us try to follow the same broad purpose that we have followed in the Commonwealth, with so far as possible a joint approach between our political forces here. Above all, let us eschew the temptation to make it a subject of party dispute . . . in our domestic struggles. Let us not prematurely judge the final decisions we shall have to take."

But the Federation has continued to be a subject of bitter dispute, both in Great Britain and between the contending factions in Africa itself. The leading advocate of maintaining this landlocked federation, which is twice the size of Texas, is its prime minister, Sir Roy Welensky. Even those who disagree with him admit that he is a forceful, remarkable figure. His father was a half-Jewish Polish immigrant who gave up a prosperous fur trade in the American Middle West to seek his fortune in the South African diamond rush; his mother was of Dutch ancestry. Sir Roy once wrote to a friend that though he didn't have a drop of English blood in his veins, he had 100 per cent faith in the British

Commonwealth, and thought that an impartial observer would have to admit that the Commonwealth had always been an instrument of good.

As a thirteenth child, Roy (Roland) Welensky was born on January 20, 1907, in Salisbury, where he attended English schools until he was fourteen. Then he went to work on farms and in the mines. At one time he was heavyweight boxing champion of Northern Rhodesia. He changed jobs often, working as a butcher, baker, clerk, and salesman.

In 1928, he quit professional boxing, became a locomotive engineer, and—after receiving a promotion—married Elizabeth Henderson; they have a son and a daughter. Sir Roy does not drink or smoke. His favorite relaxation is listening to his large record collection, which includes everything from opera to jazz. He has always been a voracious reader, and today still studies Marx, Mill, Jeremy Bentham and Shakespeare.

After being transferred to the important railway town of Broken Hill, still his home constituency, Roy Welensky rose to become the undisputed leader of the powerful white railwayman's union in Northern Rhodesia. His rapid success as a union organizer inevitably led him into politics.

He held cabinet posts in the Federation ever since its founding: minister of transport, minister of telegraphs and posts, and from July 1954, deputy prime minister. In 1956, he succeeded the elderly Lord Malvern, first prime minister of the Federation. During the coronation celebrations of 1953, Roy Welensky was made a Knight of the British Empire.

He was an early supporter of the federation concept, and still defends it vigorously. In a speech at Kitwe on March 10, 1959, he refuted as a "fallacious argument" the idea that the day of the white man in Central Africa was drawing to a close. Those who thought so "should prepare themselves for a rude shock." He wanted to see African nationalism, to which he was not blind, directed along constructive lines that would benefit all the people and "not in the interest of unbridled hatred and a desire to see a return of the dark days of Africa in the 19th century."

In a speech at Broken Hill on March 16, he declared: "The tragedy is, of course, that if we had not had a gutless Labour Government in office in the period that led up to federation, we would not be facing the difficulties that we are today."

In a later interview with a correspondent of the London *Daily Express,* Sir Roy declared that if the Labour Party were voted back into office and "carries out its implied threat of tearing up agreements between the British Government and the Federal Government" the Federation might choose to become an independent state. "This country is 100 per cent loyal to the Queen. There will be no initiative on our part to 'go it alone'; it will only be if we are forced into it."

Sir Roy's declared policy of "racial partnership" is viewed with suspicion by many of his personal supporters. The Africans, on the other hand, see in this "partnership" only a veiled attempt to keep them from political power. Many prominent Englishmen believe this, too, and are watching the swift course of events in the Federation with great anxiety.

Sir Roy Welensky's most formidable white opponent is Reginald Stephen Garfield Todd, the first missionary ever to become a prime minister. Todd was born on July 13, 1908 in Invercargill, New Zealand, where his grandfather had emigrated from Scotland. He left school at sixteen, went to work in the family brickyard, and at twenty-one began to study theology. He was ordained in the Church of Scotland in 1931, and for two years was pastor of the Church of Christ in Oamuru, New Zealand. Here he married and volunteered with his wife for missionary work in Africa.

The young couple lived and worked for some months at Fort Jameson in Northern Rhodesia, then transferred to Shabani, in the middle of the asbestos and chrome manufacturing region of South Rhodesia. Todd became superintendent of the New Zealand Mission, and for thirteen years he and his wife were the only Europeans living on a reserve of ten thousand Matabele and Mashona. His practical training in the brickyard stood him in good stead, for his duties were not all spiritual: the mission had to build houses and schools, lay out gardens, and teach crafts. The school built by Todd eventually was able to accommodate four thousand children up to the third year of high school.

There were few doctors in this remote province, so Todd spent a year at Witwatersrand University in the Union of South Africa. He learned enough medicine to heal skull fractures, deliver babies, set broken bones, and pull teeth. He also taught efficient farming methods to innumerable Africans, and taught them how to combat soil erosion, which is no longer a problem in this region because of him. This practical and universal man learned to understand the African, his problems and his way of thinking. He has said: "For years, Mrs. Todd and I knew the Africans in this country much better than the European settlers. We are convinced that we know and understand the Africans better than any other group of the inhabitants of the Federation. And we must admit that we love them."

Garfield Todd was also popular with the Europeans. When he decided, in 1946, to take an active role in politics, his white supporters elected him to parliament. He became prime minister of Southern Rhodesia in September 1953.

His administration had great plans for bettering the living conditions of the city-dwelling Africans. It drew up a law that would make it possible for Africans to have free land on the outskirts of the cities. Todd also attempted to raise the wages of the Africans, in order to prepare an end for the unjust social conditions. The first protests of the whites against him became audible. Todd was called a "traitor to the white minority." He replied: "The whites retain all their opportunities, but all peoples of the Federation must take part in the increasing prosperity regardless of race." The white minority was of a different opinion. The Dominion Party took up the fight against the Liberals and won. Todd had to step down as prime minister of Southern Rhodesia in February 1958. His successor was Sir Edgar Whitehead; Todd later became minister of labor and social welfare.

Garfield Todd is a good looking man, tall and slim. In Parliament he is an impressive—if rapid—speaker (the stenographers can seldom follow his 180 to 200 words a minute). Among his many positive qualities are simplicity and courage. He still worries about the development of better agricultural methods, and himself owns a noteworthy cattle-breeding farm. Even as prime minister he drove a tractor or helped out as a doctor when needed. Todd's point of view: "Only active, militant Christianity counts in Africa, the good deed actually done and not just recommended." This is why he is held in great respect by all Africans in the Federation.

In recent years, Todd has joined forces with Sir John Moffat in a new political grouping, the Central African Party, and he became its president in June 1959. At a party congress, the CAP admitted African politicians who had fallen into disfavor—among them six from the banned African National Congress—as delegates.

Garfield Todd has often come into conflict with Sir Roy Welensky. Todd has described the ruling classes' administration as "tyranny and the unscrupulous use of power." He demands the dissolution of all discriminatory practices in the Federation as well as the breaking down of all barriers to African economic and political development. Todd: "What we need is a raceless community, in which the white, the black, and every other citizen enjoys equal protection before the law and equal opportunity for development."

In the present situation, Sir Roy Welensky commands the greatest support among the whites in the Federation as a whole. They see in his policies the only way to hold on to their rights. In Nyasaland, Todd's party has little influence because the overwhelming majority of the Negroes follow the nationalist leader, Hastings Kamutzu Banda. The CAP's strongest support comes from Northern Rhodesia, where it receives votes from the whites as well as the Negroes. (I heard it put this way: Southern Rhodesia is white, Northern Rhodesia is gray, and Nyasaland is black.) Nevertheless, one can say that Garfield Todd is an important political factor throughout the whole federation, above all the hope of the realists. He himself prefers not to be classified as a liberal, but as a realist.

African politicians respect him for this and often seek his advice.

Todd sees further developments running a peaceful course for the present: "The white community will come to see, at least at the last minute, that our course is best for the Federation, and not the course of the *apartheid* fanatics of the Union of South Africa or their spiritual brothers in the Federation. Otherwise we'll have catastrophe."

The key figure in Northern Rhodesian politics is Harry Mwanga Nkumbula, president of the African National Congress, which has 500,000 members. Nkumbula campaigns vigorously for a legislature where Africans will have a majority, although he admits that the white minority is entitled to representation. He contends that Sir Roy Welensky and his United Federal Party have not implemented their declared policy of "racial partnership," would like to see the Federation dissolved, and Northern Rhodesia gain its independence with an elected African majority in the government.

Harry Nkumbula was born in 1916 in the remote village of Maala among the feared Baala tribesmen, of a family of well-to-do cattle ranchers. He attended Methodist Mission schools, worked as a medical missionary's houseboy, and later taught at mission schools. He won a government scholarship in 1944 to Makerere College in Uganda, then a secondary school for Africans, where he studied for two years. From 1946 to 1948, with the aid of a British grant, he studied at the London School of Economics.

In 1948, the African National Congress of Northern Rhodesia was founded by Godwin Lewanika. Nkumbula soon became its general secretary, and later its president, which he has remained for eleven years. Nkumbula represented the African National Congress in the Northern Rhodesian general elections of March 1959, and was re-elected to the Northern Rhodesian Legislature.

Harry Nkumbula, as president of the African National Congress, addressed the first All-African People's Congress in Accra in December 1958. He sent me the manuscript of his speech, and

I noted some of its main points. Nkumbula thought that the 300,000 whites of the Federation, in striving to maintain their supremacy over seven million Africans were fighting a losing battle. The influence of South African *apartheid* was becoming increasingly felt in the policies of the Northern Rhodesian administration. All hopes of the whites and Negroes living among one another in a stable, healthy atmosphere were being destroyed; they lived completely separated and had become a nightmare to one another. The constitution was completely immoral, the hopes of the idealists for a compromise had been turned aside, and the people of Northern Rhodesia now demanded self-government and independence within their own lifetimes.

In February 1961, Harry Nkumbula was a delegate to the Conference on Constitutional Reform for Northern Rhodesia in London. Back in Salisbury, Sir Roy Welensky bitterly attacked the Colonial Office, and said that "we ourselves are fully determined to preserve the Federation," and that "the vicious influence of African nationalism has apparently turned the bone marrow of many metropolitan countries to jelly."

In London, Nkumbula replied that the Prime Minister was trying to provoke the Africans and was "looking for trouble," and that "the moment he starts pulling the trigger, he will get trouble." Harry Mwanga Nkumbula added that the Prime Minister should be told that bullets "could not stop the desires of the Africans to achieve what they want to achieve."

The political leader of the Nyasalanders is unquestionably the most popular personality in the Federation. Hastings Kamutzu Banda was born in 1906 and, like Nkumbula, educated in a mission school. He adopted his first name from a missionary friend, John Hastings.

A precocious youth, he left his parents' home and the mission school to go wandering from town to town through thousands of miles of bush and jungle without benefit of a single identity paper. He eventually reached the Union of South Africa, settled in the gold fields near Johannesburg, did odd jobs at first, and then served for eight years as an interpreter. He had already learned English at the mission school, and now went to night school to educate himself further.

Banda then decided to go to America. He had saved fifty pounds, and the remainder of his travel expenses were provided by American Methodist missionaries. A decisive factor for his journey to America was a speech he heard by the famed Negro politician and educator, Dr. J. E. Kwegyir Aggrey, of Accra, who also influenced personalities like Kwame Nkrumah.

Like many African Negroes, Banda made his way forward rather quickly in the United States. The young man was undemanding, lived from hand to mouth, and earned a meager living through odd jobs before embarking on a remarkable academic career. He studied on a scholarship at Wilberforce College in Ohio, earned a Bachelor of Philosophy degree at the University of Chicago, and later a medical degree from Meharry Medical College in Nashville, Tennessee (one of his first patients was Kwame Nkrumah).

Before the outbreak of World War II, he emigrated to England, continued his medical studies in Edinburgh, earned his L.R.C.P. (Licentiate of the Royal College of Physicians), and practiced in Liverpool and North Shields during the second half of the war. After the war, he settled in London, and soon built up an excellent practice (of mostly white patients) in the Kilburn district, which brought him a great deal of money.

Banda still had time for politics. He corresponded with African leaders in Nyasaland, wrote handbills and pamphlets, and inspired the founding of the Nyasaland African National Congress Party. In 1955, he settled in Ghana as a doctor, where he remained for three years. He appeared as a politician for the first time in public at the first All-Africa People's Conference in Accra.

Everywhere he appeared, this small, temperamental man made a striking impression. When we whites spoke to him, he was at first distrustful and surly. When we convinced him that we were seriously interested in his activities, he became a stimulating conversationalist; a man with great fundamental knowledge and humor, who also employed mockery and ridicule and cutting cynicism. Sometimes he lost control of himself completely and broke into almost hysterical outbursts of rage: "You whites think of yourselves as riders on a black horse. But you whites are finished —here in Africa and everywhere else in the world. It's your own fault. You're being paid back now for crimes committed centuries ago. There's no more hope for you. Make your exits! Get out!"

I remember very clearly such a scene, for which a British colonial official was perhaps not entirely blameless. But we were very moved and sympathetic toward Banda when, afterwards, he formally excused himself for his outburst. He didn't mean it to be as bad as it sounded, but we nevertheless had to understand him and his friends. They had assembled here together for the first time in the history of Africa. Wasn't that a cause for unbounded joy? Could one reproach them if they sometimes gave way to frenzied outbursts in their jubilation at finally being able to talk to one another freely?

Soon after the congress, Banda returned to his native land. He had carefully prepared the way for his return with his brilliant showing at Accra. After forty years of self-imposed exile, he was received in triumph. Nyasalanders hailed him as "Christ reborn," "a new Messiah," "the ultimate Saviour and Liberator," kissed his hands, and even covered the automobile in which he was riding with kisses. He openly described himself as "the most extreme of the extremists."

Banda said: "Why am I such an extremist? Wasn't Oliver Cromwell an extremist? He was a fanatic! Even Churchill was an extremist. I, too, will fight fanatically for my homeland, even if they throw me in prison. Brothers and sisters, I am ready for anything. *Ufulu! Ufulu!* (Freedom! Freedom!). And when I'm dead, my spirit, my ashes will fight for freedom—and against the Federation. What's the purpose of this damned federation? So that they can send us, like animals, to live in reservations in our own country! I went to a mission school. And just because of that I say, distrust the missionaries, distrust the whites! We have to fill up the prisons—that's the only way to gain our freedom. To hell with the Federation!"

When British journalists asked to interview him, Banda screamed at them: "What do you want? I don't have to fawn on you. I think you're all a pack of liars! The truth is, we Nyasa-landers want to be masters in our own house again. If that's treason, then call me a traitor. Why did you want this federation? Because in England itself since 1945, you don't have much to say —the reactionary Tories were thrown out of office. Now they've all come into the Federation—Lord So and So and Duke This and That—and have twenty or fifty servants. These gentlemen have calculated falsely! We won't permit them for very much longer to live here as they can't live at home!"

On his return, Banda took immediate charge of the leadership of the Nyasaland African National Congress, with the avowed policy of separating Nyasaland from the Federation. By spring 1959, he had already been declared a "prohibited immigrant" by Northern and Southern Rhodesia. In March 1959—on the grounds of the declaration of a state of emergency—he was arrested and jailed, along with other N.A.N.C. leaders like his colleagues Chimpere and Chrisiza. He was taken to Southern Rhodesia, be-cause in Nyasaland itself he had become a martyr and repeated attempts were made to free him. In prison, he began to write his memoirs.

The state of emergency had been declared in Nyasaland on March 3, 1959, because of serious disturbances in which sup-porters of the N.A.N.C. and security forces clashed. By April 1, 52 people, all Africans, had lost their lives. The governor of Nyasaland, Sir Robert Armitage, in a White Paper published in London on March 23, described a plot on the part of the N.A.N.C. to seize power on "R-Day." He and other senior British officials were to be assassinated, other Europeans and Asians, including women and children, murdered, and a campaign of sabotage un-leashed.

On March 23, the British government appointed a commission, headed by Mr. Justice Devlin, to "inquire into the recent disturbances." The Devlin Report, of 150 pages, was issued on July 23. It came to the conclusion that the government had been justified in declaring a state of emergency because it "had either to act or abdicate," but that there was no evidence of a "murder plot," although the N.A.N.C. had adopted a policy of violence.

The Devlin Report also noted that "Nyasaland is—no doubt temporarily—a police state, where it is not safe for anyone to express approval of the policies of the Congress Party, to which before March 3, 1959, the vast majority of politically-minded Africans belonged, and where it is unwise to express any but the most restrained criticisms of government policy. . . ."

The Devlin Report touched off a great deal of discussion in England, and had an explosive effect on political developments in Nyasaland, and in the whole federation. On April 1, 1960, Banda was released from prison, and flew to London for new talks. He demanded immediate independence and equal voting rights for all, but despite his imprisonment displayed no bitterness towards Great Britain. Lord Home, Minister for Commonwealth Relations, explained that independence would have to be postponed for a few years, because Nyasaland was "the slum of Africa." A new party, the New Republic party, has splintered off from Banda's party and demands immediate dissolution of the Federation, as well as full independence.

There can be little doubt that the Federation was created principally to guarantee the rights of the whites in British Central Africa, and that the rights of the Africans were neglected. Prime Minister Macmillan visited the Federation in the spring of 1960 and saw the gravity of the situation. He organized the twenty-six member Monckton Commission to look into the Federation's problems and to recommend constitutional changes that might salvage it. In October 1960, the Commission reported: "The dislike of the Federation among Africans in the two Northern Territories [Northern Rhodesia and Nyasaland] is widespread, sincere, and of long standing. It is almost pathological. It is associated everywhere with a picture of Southern Rhodesia as a white man's country."

The Commission recommended replacing the Federation's central structure with a loose association of three semi-autonomous territories, equal representation in the legislatures for whites and Negroes, and the right of secession under certain circumstances.

The Federation's whites received the Monckton Commission's findings with disappointment and anger. Sir Roy Welensky declared: "This recommendation on secession is one which I and my colleagues of the Federal Government reject out of hand."

Dr. Banda, in a statement in Ghana on November 14, 1960, declared: "We want secession and nothing but secession. So far as we are concerned, the Federation is dead. All that remains now is to bury it. . . . We are not going to negotiate or compromise over anything."

As of this writing, the shaky federation still exists. On October 8, 1960 Salisbury experienced the most serious rioting it has ever known; seven Africans were shot dead, 170 were wounded, and twenty Europeans were injured by flying stones. It would appear that if the tiny white minority persists in trying to dominate the huge black majority, the Federation of Rhodesia and Nyasaland could turn into the same kind of witch's cauldron as is the Union of South Africa.

12

HENDRIK VERWOERD OF SOUTH AFRICA

Champion of the "White Superiority" Myth

✳

Discussion of the racial policies of the Union of South Africa becomes more passionate with each passing day. The whole world is asking itself with growing uneasiness about the eventual fate of the whites in the Union now that so many African nations have recently achieved independence. The defenders of *apartheid* are constantly looking for new reasons to justify their point of view. Their main argument comes down to this:

The country was unsettled and uncultivated when the Dutch sailing ships landed here in the middle of the 17th century. The Boers, as they later became known, took land from no one, consequently the African has absolutely no valid claim to the country. South Africa was a "no man's land," which became a "white man's country" because it was settled and built up by whites. Whether or not the country was actually settled will be for later, impartial historical research—not influenced by nationalism—to judge. But it can already be said with assurance that much of the old information does not jibe with the facts of the matter, but has been changed to serve the claims of the Boers. All this is really beside the point: this is African soil, an African country, and belongs to the Africans.

Arabs are said to have sailed round the Cape of Good Hope before the Portuguese. It is certain that Bartolomeu Diaz sailed round the Cape in 1488. In 1652, the Dutch East India Company sent the former ship's surgeon Jan van Riebeeck to the Cape to establish a permanent supply station. In the 18th century, the rapidly growing Dutch settlement spread out from the coastal areas. They are supposed to have occupied land that was unsettled, but also came into contact with Bantu tribesmen coming down from the north.

The first war between whites and Negroes was fought between 1779 and 1781. At that time, it was "a struggle for bare existence," as Alan Paton has noted. The author of *Cry, the Beloved Country* also commented that between blacks and whites, and more so between white men and black women, there could be no association other than that between master and servant, or enemy and enemy; the Boer could only consolidate his ruling position by holding himself "apart"; only in *apartheid* was there hope for his own future and that of his children and his race.

What is happening in South Africa today is a struggle that had its origins in the 18th century, when the first immigrants from Holland built an existence for themselves in this part of Africa. The present animosities between the South Africans of Dutch or British descent also date back to this time.

The British occupied the Cape in 1795. Fifteen thousand British settlers arrived in 1820. The British of the Cape Colony wanted to anglicize the Boers. English was made the official language, and the pound the official currency. The Boers resisted these moves, giving rise to a duality that has plagued South Africa ever since. The climax of this internal struggle was the Boer War (1899–1902).

In 1910 the Union became a sovereign, independent and self-governing state within the British Commonwealth, after Parliament passed the Act of Union in 1909. The Crown was represented by a governor-general. Hopes that this would lay aside the old animosities proved deceptive.

On March 15, 1961 the Union of South Africa withdrew from the British Commonwealth of Nations, severing the half-century-old tie on the issue of racial policy. Verwoerd had found the other Commonwealth ministers so unalterably opposed to his country's *apartheid* that during the Commonwealth Ministers Conference in London, he announced his decision to withdraw, effective on May 31, 1961, when the Union of South Africa became a republic. Verwoerd predicted that the step he had taken, which he asserted the other ministers had obliged him to take, marked the "beginning of the disintegration of the Commonwealth."

Aside from Ethiopia, the Union of South Africa is the only African state that has been sovereign for a considerable length of time. A few figures: The Union, excluding its mandated territory of South-West Africa, is 470,000 square miles in area. Its population of 14,507,000 is composed of the following groups: 9,606,000 Bantus; 3,100,000 whites; 1,360,000 coloureds (mulattoes); 441,000 Asians. Of the two official languages, 57.5 per cent speak *Afrikaans* and 39.4 per cent speak English. About 1.3 per cent of the whites use both languages in private. It is worth noting that the Negroes and coloureds represent almost four-fifths of the total population. It has been estimated that their birth rate is outdistancing the white's by three to one, and that there will be around 19 million Negroes and coloureds by the year 2,000.

This, in rough outline, is the historical background from which one of the most ardent white racial fanatics in Africa has emerged, a man who has made himself the pitiless champion of white dominance in Africa. Verwoerd's spiritual brothers are not only the radical whites of the Federation of Rhodesia and Nyasaland, but the settlers of Kenya and the *ultras* of Algeria.

Even before Dr. H. F. Verwoerd became prime minister he held a key position in the government. From 1950 to 1958, he was minister of native affairs in the Malan and Strijdom administrations. As no other man, he is responsible for the strictest *apartheid* policies. Verwoerd has become famous as "one of the sharpest minds as well as one of the country's most energetic and untiring leaders with a boundless capacity for work and discussion."

Hendrik Frensch Verwoerd was born on September 8, 1901, at

Ouderkerk, near Rotterdam, of Dutch parents. The Opposition has often needled him about his birth outside the Union—as "a South African by adoption without roots in the national soil." Many South Africans, however, were not born in the Union. He was not yet a year old when his parents emigrated to Brandford in the Orange Free State, where his father became active as a missionary for the Dutch Reformed Church. The Dutch journal *Zuid-Afrika*—which promotes good relations between the Netherlands and South Africa—wrote in regard to this that the nationalism of those who come from another country is frequently more conscious and ardent than that of those natives of the country to whom nationalism is largely a question of tradition.

As a youth, Verwoerd went to school in Brandford and Southern Rhodesia. He studied psychology at the University of Stellenbosch in Cape Province, and from 1924 to 1928 at the Universities of Hamburg, Leipzig and Berlin. It has been said that he had close relations with the Nazis during this time, and got his anti-semitism directly from Hitler's racial theories.

Verwoerd won his Ph.D., and later made frequent scholarly visits to psychological institutes and conventions in France, Holland, England and the United States. In 1928, he returned to South Africa as professor of applied psychology and sociology at the University of Stellenbosch. At twenty-seven, he took charge of the Department of Sociology and Social Services and built it up into one of the leading centers of its kind in this part of the Union. He was very active in developing research into social problems, and played a leading role in numerous projects. He worked in the Cape Town Organization for Housing; was co-director of a civic model housing scheme; an organizer of the National Congress on the Poor White Question (1934); and afterwards chairman of this congress' standing committee for two years.

In 1937, the nationalist *Afrikanders* founded a daily newspaper in Johannesburg, *Die Transvaler,* which was to present their political views. Verwoerd gave up his scholarly career to become its editor-in-chief, and held this position until he entered the Senate in 1948. There is no doubt that he developed *Die Transvaler* into an important instrument of the Union's white nationalists. The paper was anti-Negro and anti-British, and frequently pro-Nazi during the Second World War. German successes were celebrated as "a victory over British-Jewish liberalism." After the war, a lawsuit was brought against Verwoerd and he was accused of having made his newspaper "a tool of the Nazis."

Verwoerd also used his newspaper to fight the emigration of displaced German Jews into the Union. Even today permission to enter the Union is restricted as much as possible to "blond, blue-eyed Aryans of Protestant faith." Rabbi Dr. Ungar of Port Elizabeth has reported that the 100,000 or so Jews in the Union are frequently subjected to the same sort of racial defamation inflicted upon the Negroes and Asians. In any case, racial and color prejudices have created a very dangerous climate for them.

Verwoerd received important political posts one after another: he was appointed a member of the Rand Advisory Council of the National Party, and to its Chief Executive Committee in the Transvaal and other committees. As a senator he became leader of the House and one of the few senators to hold a cabinet post after he was given the Ministry of Native Affairs in 1950. He was elected a Member of Parliament from Heidelberg in the Transvaal in 1958. In Parliament, he soon distinguished himself as an effective speaker with a thorough knowledge of his subjects. Upon the death of his friend, Prime Minister Dr. J. G. Strijdom on August 24, 1958, Verwoerd was elected chairman of the National Party. The governor-general charged him with the formation of a new administration, and Verwoerd became prime minister.

Verwoerd is married to the former Elizabeth Schoombee; they have seven children, five sons and two daughters. In an official portrait, one reads that: "Dr. Verwoerd is happiest in his family circle, the center of which is his wife. . . . She was a teacher at a girl's school in Oudtshoorn, and later taught *Afrikaans* in the Department of Education at the University of Stellenbosch and at a Teachers' Training School at Paarl. . . . Mrs. Verwoerd has personally supervised the raising of her children and did not leave it to the servants. (Mrs. Verwoerd has often explained why: so that her children would not come into contact with the inferior Negroes.) But it is the father, who, with patience and gentleness, draws the thorn from the sole of one of his younger children's feet, or dresses the wound when a finger is jammed in a door. . . . The Prime Minister is a good cook. He loves to relax with his Frisian cattle on his small farm in eastern Transvaal, and there are few chores around the farm that he can't do himself. He does everything with the systematic care he devotes to his public duties. He is a hard worker. He takes a briefcase full of documents home with him and often works on them until two or three in the morning. He pays rigorous attention to the smallest details."

Physically, Verwoerd—who is 6 ft. 2 in. tall—is described as "a solid, powerfully built man of Teutonic appearance."

When Verwoerd became prime minister he gave a speech to the nation in which he set forth his political concepts. He said that he had been called upon to take over the duties of prime minister at a time when the nation was mourning the death of Dr. Strijdom. "I hope that I will faithfully follow his path and also that of his esteemed predecessors."

Verwoerd explained that "the government of a religious nation should seek its strength and power as much in the future as in that past which determines the destinies of nations. No one need doubt that I will constantly strive to preserve the democratic processes of our country."

His government would strive to preserve the bonds of friendship between the mother countries of the Union (Great Britain and the Netherlands) and between the Union and its neighbors. It would continue to assist the underdeveloped states by making available to them scientific knowledge coupled with the unique knowledge of African conditions possessed by the Union.

Verwoerd said that the racial policies of the Union would continue to be misunderstood. Above all, the "uninitiated" failed to understand that separation was motivated by the basic concept that only through separation could the weak be protected by the strong, and that only through separation could the minority feel safe. In other words, racial conflicts could be avoided only by a policy of complete segregation. But the segregation of racial groups, whether by territorial or social categories, did not mean suppression. It meant equal opportunity for all individuals or groups in relation to the various stages of development they had achieved. This could be planned or achieved for each individual only within his own racial community.

Verwoerd hopes for an improvement in the relations between *Afrikaans-* and English-speaking citizens of the Union. "It will always remain my goal to mete out equal justice to all groups. But above all, I will rejoice on that day when we are all united, as a single people with two languages, by a common patriotism, so that such political differences as may then arise will be the result of social and economic problems and not of different ways of thinking."

In his struggle to maintain white supremacy in the Union of South Africa, Verwoerd warns of the danger of Communism— especially since he and his followers are constantly being accused of encouraging Communism by their repressive measures. Verwoerd claims that the Western world will lose the psychological battle for Africa if it continues its present methods. In attempting to beat the Communists at their own game, the West is weakening the white man's prestige in Africa and its connections with the West.

Verwoerd: "They say, almost as though to justify themselves, that colonialism belongs to the past, that they are ready to guarantee 'self-determination,' and that they will oppose 'the oppressed countries' such as the Union of South Africa. The Western world would have been wiser to counter the vague, generalized attacks of the Communists with a clear and specific declaration of what the white man and the Union of South Africa have accomplished, are presently accomplishing, and are prepared to accomplish in future for Africa and the Negro. . . . Communism has a goal in

Africa: to arouse the black man over the white man's presence in Africa. And the Western world, which would like to win friends in Africa, possibly to build up adequate strength for a later conflict, is now beginning—probably without realizing it—to play the same game. It tries to surpass the Communists in attacks on the white man's prestige in Africa. The West is afraid to suggest that colonialism has done more good than harm. The Western nations do not know what they are doing when they apparently sympathize with the slanderers of South Africa. . . . When South Africa is attacked, many Western nations either stand aside or join in the attack. That supports and strengthens the propaganda of the opponents of the Western world and increases the chances for success of this dangerous line of thinking. South Africa is the only trustworthy friend that the Western world has in Africa. We are the only area on which the West can absolutely depend, the leading fortress in any possible East-West conflict."

It would be foolish to deny that many good points can be found in Verwoerd's innumerable political statements. However, like many fanatics, Verwoerd, in overdoing his good ideas, is being led by them into absurdity. He has become the victim of his extremist concepts and has isolated himself and his National Party, which he leads as *hoofleier* (director), not only in the Western and Eastern worlds but in his own country, where he was obliged to support his rule with the bayonet after the disturbances of early 1960. *The New York Times* commented that *apartheid* was leading the Union only into isolation and a never-ending struggle that nobody wanted.

Who can really be counted among Verwoerd's supporters? Four-fifths of the population, the Negroes and coloureds, are against him without exception. Of the whites, those of English ancestry are overwhelmingly against him; they comprise more than half the population in two provinces of the Union, Cape Province and Natal. Among the *Afrikanders,* he has—as a militant and intolerant member of the Dutch Reformed Church—all the Catholics against him. The *Afrikanders* prevail in the Orange Free State and the Transvaal, the former independent Boer Republic.

Statistics show that 57.5 per cent of the white population in the Union is *Afrikander*. At the last elections in 1958, 1,174,158 voters were qualified to determine the destiny of 14,507,000 people. A mere 647,468 votes put the National Party into power (it holds 103 of the 163 seats in Parliament). Thus one can deduce that 4.5 per cent of the population supports a policy which over 13 million people reject. Whether this minority is in a position to maintain a "republic of a thousand years," to create it and build it up, can well be doubted. This *Republik von tausend Jahren* is in fact discussed, and G. A. Wastermeyer devoted a book of poetry to it that is favorite reading for the *Afrikanders*.

The fundamental concepts of the "myth of the higher races," and the "myth of the superiority of the white man," in which Verwoerd as a member of the Dutch Reformed Church of the Union believes, are well known today throughout the world. They can lead not only the unfortunate people of South Africa into catastrophe, but perhaps the whole Western world, although the latter is unmistakably showing increasing disapproval of Verwoerd's "ghetto politics."

During his African journey of 1960, Prime Minister Macmillan addressed both houses of the Union Parliament on February 8. He said that Great Britain wanted to support and encourage South Africa, but made it very plain that Britain could not support *apartheid* "without being false to our own deep convictions."

Macmillan spoke of the awakening of national consciousness, and its growing strength. "Fifteen years ago this movement spread through Asia. Many countries there, of different races and civilization, pressed their claim to an independent national life. Today the same thing is happening in Africa. The most striking of all impressions I have formed since I left London a month ago is of the strength of this African national consciousness. In different places it may take different forms, but it is happening everywhere. The wind of change is blowing through the continent. . . .

"Let me be very frank with you, my friends. What governments and Parliaments in the United Kingdom have done since the war in according independence to India, Pakistan, Ceylon, Malaya, and Ghana, and what they will do for Nigeria and the other countries now nearing independence—all this, though we take full and sole responsibility for it, we do in the belief that it is the only way to establish the future of the Commonwealth and of the free world on sound foundations."

The South African prime minister, like members of Parliament, was disturbed by Macmillan's candid statement of policy. In a brief reply, Dr. Verwoerd said: "I am very pleased you were frank. We are people who are capable of listening with great pleasure to what other people have to say of us, even if they differ from us. We never presume to criticize the application of policies in areas for which you are responsible. But on an occasion like this, when we can be perfectly frank, we can say we differ from you. . . . I bid you Godspeed on your return—and may you find in Great Britain fewer problems to deal with than we, unfortunately, have here."

Later, Verwoerd held Macmillan, among others, responsible for the riots at Sharpeville and called him "a political opportunist." Verwoerd's closest political associates declared that Macmillan's remarks had encouraged the natives to deny obedience to the government. All of this contributed to Macmillan's failure to work out a compromise at the Commonwealth Prime Ministers Conference of March 1961, when he sought to retain South Africa as a member of the Commonwealth while at the same time publicly disapproving its *apartheid* policies.

Instead of adding still another description to the already huge body of literature on *apartheid,* I would like to set down here the report of a Negro who fled South Africa, which clearly and authentically describes the consequences of all the unholy concepts which Verwoerd propagated as minister of native affairs. I consider this to be all the more important because—what with the radical policies and strict censorship of the Union government—the voices of South African Negro politicians are seldom heard in the forums of the world.

At the All-African Peoples' Conference in Ghana in December, 1958, Ezekiel Mphahlele spoke as the delegation leader of the African National Congress (which has been banned in the Union since April 1960). He was formerly a teacher in the Union, and like hundreds of other teachers, objected to government policy in the field of education. For this, he was forbidden to teach. He left his homeland with great difficulty to become a lecturer at the University College of Nigeria in Ibadan. In the meantime he has become well-known as a writer and journalist, and as a collaborator with the Congress for Cultural Freedom. He addressed the plenary meeting of the All-African Peoples' Congress as the representative of the African National Congress, as well as the South African Indian Congress, the Coloured Peoples' Organization, the Congress of Democrats, and "a small group of Europeans whose hearts are in the right place." He had this to say about conditions in the Union:

"The Situation: In April 1952, the Nationalist regime celebrated the 300th anniversary of Jan van Riebeeck's arrival at the Cape of Good Hope. The majority of the non-whites declined to participate in the festivities, for the white man was celebrating three hundred years of robbery, political suppression, slave trading, and forced labor. . . . The constitution of the Union explicitly states that: (a) only men of European extraction can be members of Parliament; (b) only men of European extraction can hold public offices such as those of district attorney, court clerk, judge, captain, commissioner and superintendent of police (the highest rank a non-white can achieve in the police is sergeant); (c) only white persons can enter the Army, Navy, or Air Force. In time of war, non-whites can only serve as truck drivers or litter bearers. In municipal administrations, no non-European can act as a representative or have a vote in the town councils. The non-white groups must live outside the city limits and we were told that no hope existed of our ever being integrated into the city community. . . .

"Work: The Native Labour Regulation Act determines the areas in which we are permitted to live, and determines the wages for

Africans who must work in the mines and on farms. To do such work requires a contract, and every worker who breaks this contract—often he does not understand it at all—makes himself guilty of a criminal offense. According to the law, it is a criminal offense to participate in an industrial strike. . . . There are schools for mechanics, but the white unions do not permit garage owners to employ Africans as skilled labour. Because of this our mechanics must remain within their own local communities. The same holds true for shoemakers, plumbers, welders, cabinet makers and so forth. The professions of pharmacist, dentist, engineer, building contractor, all of those professions which require a long period of study, are not accessible to the African.

"*The Land:* Approximately 11 million Africans own 13 per cent of the land, the rest is owned by two and one-half million whites. The land which 'belongs' to the Africans in the Union is for the most part located on a reservation, in an area of concentrated population under tribal chiefs. Today it is quite natural for a city population of 100,000 or more Africans to be resettled in an area outside the city by an order signed by the Governor-General, where they will live for the rest of their lives as tenants of the city. In these ghettos the Africans cannot come and go as they choose. They can only build stores if they are permitted to, trade is restricted by innumerable controls, and the pass laws are arbitrarily applied. Any city which wants to expand its industrial or residential area can change the living areas of the Negroes by a decree. No tribe in the reservations has a guaranteed right to its land. Tribes of thousands of people can be resettled from one area to another, if a group of white farmers petitions the government to do so. . . .

"*Other Laws:* A law was passed against Communism in 1951. It was designed to establish a 'legal Communism.' In practice, it had nothing to do with international Communism. Although it also affects those who publicly represent Marxist, Leninist, or Stalinist theories, it is purely a government security measure. Many are labeled 'Communists' because they have at one time or another protested against government policies. . . . 'The Public

Safety Act' gives the government the opportunity to intervene in unforeseen incidents which arise in the course of insurrections and other expressions of political instability. . . . 'The Criminal Law Amendment Act' foresees a fine of 500 pounds sterling or a prison sentence of three years, or ten lashes in combination with one of the two preceding penalties, for anyone who protests against the law or supports a struggle against the law. . . . 'The Immorality Act' declares that marriages between whites and Negroes are illegal and sexual relations between the two races forbidden.

"*The Centers of Cheap Labour:* For the average white in our country, the population consists of three million whites and a native problem. . . . There are three centers of concentrated African labor in the Union: the European farms, where around three million Africans work under conditions that can almost be called slavery; industry, which is sustained by four million Africans in the city areas; and the gold, coal, and copper mines which employ a labour force of around 400,000 Africans. For a group of twenty workers on a farm, life is hell. They cannot change masters, because the conditions of their contracts are strict and the pass system makes freedom of movement and changing from bad work to better practically impossible. Whole families work on a farm from dawn to sunset for a ration of corn, flour, salt and—occasionally—meat. The children of these farm workers begin school in neighboring villages, but for the most part they only begin. Where there are farm schools, the white farmer often drops by in the middle of the day and picks up some of the children for farm work. . . . It is not very often that a Reverend Michael Scott appears to make known the conditions of forced labour, the whippings and the slavery which prevail on the European farms. . . . Not often does a Father Trevor Huddleston come to South Africa and let the cry of our people ring out beyond the boundaries of our country. . . . Corpses of Negroes are still found tied to trees on the European farms. Labourers are still dying of brutal beatings with rubber hoses. Labourers are still starving, and the police are still using torture to extract information from Africans. . . .

"*The City Areas:* The four million Africans in the cities of the

Union live in constant fear of the police. It is not unusual for the police, while searching for alcohol, to enter Mr. and Mrs. B's house at midnight, roust them out of bed, rummage through the bed, throw the mattress aside and tear the clothes out of the closets. Moreover, these Africans live in constant fear concerning their permits and passes. The pass looks like a book of autographs containing the signatures and stamps of various officials and permits one to be at certain places at certain times. It is a criminal offense to be caught without a pass, and the courts permit no excuses for it. At least 60 per cent of the Africans in prison have been found guilty of breaking the pass laws. When a policeman looks at your pass, he knows if you are breathing the right air or not. . . . The pass system serves to concentrate cheap labour where the government needs it most. That was what the United Nations meant when it reported that a system of forced labour exists in South Africa. . . . Formerly, only men over sixteen needed to carry a pass. Now African women are also forced to have them. Recently more than a thousand African women were jailed because they held a peaceful demonstration against the pass system."

Ezekiel Mphahlele then recalled the founding of the African National Congress in 1910 and that opposition to the passes had already begun in the 1920's. He made foreign capital equally responsible for conditions in the Union, for it had made it possible for the whites in the Union to modernize their military forces against a possible revolt of the non-whites. "I must say here that the European nations had almost as great a part in our suppression as the whites in the Union themselves." He emphasized that the African National Congress would never have been organized if it hadn't been for the constant discrimination against the Negro. Again, the Negroes united with the Indians because it became increasingly obvious that the policy of *apartheid* was directed against all coloured peoples. He expressed gratitude to the democratic element among the whites which had declared its solidarity with the guiding principles of the Congress. In 1952, there was a campaign against the unjust laws which led to the imprisonment of

Morocco's King Hassan II, in white robes, prays with Ferhat Abbas, Premier of the Algerian rebel government, following death of Mohammed V, Hassan's father.

Tunisian President Habib Bourguiba (left) consults with Ferhat Abbas, Algerian rebel government leader, at Rabat, Moroccan capital.

Emperor Haile Selassie I of Ethiopia and Yugoslavia's Marshal Tito shown during the latter's 1959 visit to Addis Ababa.

General Ibrahim Abbud, Prime Minister of the Sudan.

The late King Mohammed V of Morocco with Gamal Abdel Nasser of Egypt.

King Idris I of Libya with Queen Elizabeth II and Prince Philip during the British monarch's visit to Tobruk.

Tom Mboya, active young Kenya nationalist, uses loudspeaker-equipped buses during his campaigns in behalf of the Nairobi Peoples' Convention Party.

thousands. In June 1955, the four congresses of the coloured peoples held a meeting to achieve a charter for the freedom of the country. The African National Congress pleaded for a multiracial community and proposed the following ten points as an outline for the Charter for Freedom:

1. The people should govern.
2. All national groups should have equal rights.
3. The people should have a share in the prosperity of the country.
4. Land should be divided up among those who work it.
5. Everyone should be equal before the law.
6. Everyone should enjoy the fundamental rights of man in equal measure.
7. There should be work and security.
8. Everyone should have the opportunity to learn and access to culture.
9. There should be homes, security, and comfort.
10. Peace and friendship should rule.

Mphahlele concluded his report as follows: "The Police—as a result of the Congress of the People—searched the houses of African, Indian, and European political leaders on the morning of December 5, 1956. In a few days, 156 men and women were arrested and charged with high treason. Among them were 23 whites. . . . In view of such a terrifying mass of oppressive laws, the question asks itself: How can a peaceful solution be achieved? Unfortunately, I can hold out no hope: we are dealing with a modernized and subtle barbarism on the part of the whites in South Africa. The alternative is clear: either a multiracial government or mutual destruction.

"The present prime minister of South Africa, H. F. Verwoerd, who is a Nazi, is stirring up more anger among the oppressed, and there is more suffering to come. The way is being prepared for a second, much more brutal uprising of the African national-ists, which will be completely uncompromising in its vengeance on the whites. The elevation of other African states, like Ghana, Guinea, Nigeria, Somaliland, etc., contributes to the influencing of the course of events in South Africa to the advantage of the African. They give my people hope and encouragement."

Let's recall now the events of March 1960. What happened then in the Union was a result of Verwoerd's policies, just as Mphahlele had predicted when he was in a free country. In the preceding months, disturbing news had leaked out of the Union. Willem Maree, Verwoerd's successor as minister of native affairs, forbade all employees of the ministry to shake hands with natives while greeting them. A European, who was buried between two Negroes in a Capetown cemetery, was exhumed without the knowledge of his coloured widow and reburied in the section of the cemetery reserved for whites; the widow now cannot visit her husband's grave. In a country where thousands of liberal books are banned, *Man and Point of View* by Dr. Erich Holm was allowed to appear, in which Hitler is honored as "one of the greatest personalities of history," and Jews, liberals, and so forth attacked. On January 1, 1960, it was announced that coloured Africans and Indians would henceforth not be allowed to attend the Universities in Capetown, Witwatersrand, and Natal. Figures show how Christianity is disintegrating in the Union; there are 78 "official" churches, and 1,286 sects.

Even before Prime Minister Macmillan visited the Union, four prominent leaders in the struggle for racial equality wrote him a letter asking him to say nothing during his South African tour which would in any way indicate approval of the policy of *apartheid*. They were Alan Paton, president of the Liberal Party, the journalist Jordan Ngubane, vice-president of the Liberal Party, Albert Luthuli, president of the African National Congress, and G. Naicker, president of the Indian Congress Party of South Africa. The Dutch Foreign Minister Lunds publicly declared that the racial policies of South Africa were "incompatible with the prevailing concepts of justice in the Netherlands."

At this decisive moment, the Netherlands Government showed

no consideration for its traditional relations with the Union. Even the Queen Mother, Wilhelmina, expressed her disgust at the policy of *apartheid*. In a pastoral letter, the Catholic Bishops of Africa criticized the existence of racial barriers in the political, economic, and social life of the Union. The Catholics were advised to assist in the solution of racial problems according to Christian doctrine. In London, the leader of the Labour Party, Hugh Gaitskell, the conservative Lord Altrincham, the liberal M.P. Jeremy Thorp, and the Anglican clergyman Trevor Huddleston all took part in a boycott demonstration against South African goods. Characteristically, the British Fascist leader, Sir Oswald Mosley, staged a counter-demonstration.

Bloody conflict finally erupted on March 21, 1960, in front of the police station at Sharpeville, an African township south of Johannesburg. Police fired on a large crowd of Africans, killing 67 and wounding at least 200. This was quickly followed by strikes, and serious riots in other cities and towns. The government retaliated with a heavy hand, arrested thousands of Negroes, whites, and Indians, and banned the Pan-Africanist Congress and the African National Congress.

The pass laws touched off the trouble. The Pan-Africanist Congress had selected March 21 as the starting date for a non-violent campaign against the hated pass books; it recommended that Africans let themselves be arrested for not carrying a pass book; some burned them publicly, like Albert Luthuli, the most prominent native leader. But the protest was also directed against the Bantustan Plan, in which the government, acting on Verwoerd's wishes, would crowd all of the Union's Negroes into reservations, just as wildlife is concentrated in Kruger National Park. According to a government declaration, the Bantustans (Bantu States) would comprise 40 per cent of the total area of the Union. The people, however, were able to ascertain that this figure included the British High Commission Territories of Basutoland, Swaziland, and Bechuanaland, which did not come under the jurisdiction of

the Union of South Africa at all. The natives would be left with
only 18 per cent of actual South African soil—and let us recall
that they number almost four-fifths of the total population!

Despite world opinion's renewed criticism of the compulsory
pass laws, the Bantusan Plan, and *apartheid,* Verwoerd's administration continued to pursue its oppressive policies. "It is a
shocking thing for Europe and the free world to stand by help-
lessly and watch three million Europeans in Africa destroy themselves. But where fear and hate rule, there is no room for reason,"
commented the German journal *Die Welt.* On March 30, 1960,
the government proclaimed a state of emergency, and all troops,
including reservists, were ordered to be ready for mobilization.

The Anglican Bishop of Johannesburg, Dr. Ambrose Reeves,
left the country secretly on April 1 and went to Swaziland, and
later England, carrying with him many documents highly unfavorable to the government. Dr. Reeves—like Pandit Nehru—
accused the police of the Union of mass murder. Was their protest
in vain? Nothing succeeded in changing Verwoerd's policies. Not
the economic crisis, not the collapse of the Johannesburg Stock
Exchange, not the appeals of South African businessmen, not the
shaken confidence of investors, nor the judgement of the United
Nations Security Council.

On April 9, 1960, a wealthy English-speaking farmer, David
Pratt, wounded the Prime Minister with two pistol shots fired at
point-blank range during the opening ceremony of the Union
Exposition in Johannesburg. World opinion condemned the attempted assassination. It became clear, however, that it was a
desperate act, that of a man of good reputation who was interested
in religious questions, the missionary work of the Anglican
Church, and Indian philosophy.

The British press spoke once again of "Verwoerd's police
state," in which he, as its chief architect, had built "crime on
crime." In Africa, the demonstrations began to take on a revolutionary character. The Vatican, through *Osservatore Romano,*
repeated its protests against *apartheid,* and pointed to its recent
elevation of a Negro to the rank of cardinal as evidence of its

continued opposition to separating human beings on the basis of race.

The Anglican Archbishop of Capetown, Joost de Blank, declared that Verwoerd's policies had brought the Union to the brink of catastrophe and endangered the missionary successes of the Christian Church. Father Pire, winner of the Nobel Peace Prize, joined in the protests and wrote Verwoerd that "human consciousness was being insulted" in the Union. As for the prime minister himself, he began to recruit white immigrants from Kenya and the Belgian Congo to gain supporters for his policies.

Next to Verwoerd, his associates in the National Party are held equally responsible for developments in the Union. These are the men holding key positions:

Governor-General Charles Robberts Swart (b. 1895) was minister of justice for eleven years and was known as "the man with the whip" because of his severity. He pushed a bill through Parliament making flogging the punishment for certain offenses. When the Opposition sought to have the number of lashes reduced from fifteen to ten, Swart replied: "What are five strokes among friends?" As minister of justice he was responsible for prisoners, and developed a system that made it possible for white farmers to use them as forced laborers. The British called it a provocation when he was selected to be governor-general—the representative of the Crown. This was Verwoerd's idea, though Swart has always zealously fought to have the Union leave the Commonwealth and become a republic. When Swart kneeled before Queen Elizabeth in December 1959 and kissed her hand as the newly-appointed governor-general, the British press called it blasphemy; Swart's bitter anglophobia is too well known. As a boy, during the Boer War, he was imprisoned with his mother in a British internment camp, and he has never forgiven the British for it.

François Christiaan Erasmus (b. 1896) succeeded Swart as minister of justice. His power is greater than that of all the law courts put together. He can discredit anyone disagreeable to the government as "a Communist" without a trial, take away his freedom of movement or even his right to work. In Malan's cabinet, he was minister of defense. He organized the *skietkommandos*—units of young farmers who can be called on to go into action against the Negroes if the need arises.

Eric Hendrik Louw (b. 1890) is foreign minister. In essays and brochures, and in speeches to the UN, UNESCO, and other international forums, he defends *apartheid*. It is said of him that he was often in Berlin in the 1930's, and displayed a lively sympathy for the Hitler government's desire to recover the former German colonies. Dr. Theophilus Ebenhaezer Dönges (b. 1898) is minister of finance and economics. He was formerly an attorney and co-editor of the *Afrikaans* newspaper, *Die Burger*. Paul Sauer (b. 1898) is minister of lands and public works, and, like the others, an old supporter of Malan, Strijdom and Verwoerd.

The position of the natives was expressed in the comments made by Ezekiel Mphahlele in Accra. To give a long report on the political leaders of the natives would be premature, and could also endanger them. Relatively little is known of them because of the strict censorship. Only the leader of the banned African National Congress, Albert John Luthuli, enjoys a wide popularity and is so well-known that there can be no question of exposing him to special danger.

Before Luthuli became president of the African National Congress (ANC) at the end of 1952, the Ministry of Native Affairs handed him an ultimatum: either give up politics, or be deposed as chief. Luthuli refused to let himself be diverted. He explained that he had been a moderate for thirty years and that it had done no good; the natives had fewer rights than before. He therefore preferred to give up his position and assured income as chief, and hoped to achieve more in politics. The administration was greatly disappointed; up to then, Luthuli had been known as "a good native," the model of a "mission boy." Two Luthulis had already ruled the Zulu tribe, and one of his uncles was chief when Luthuli himself was growing up.

He was born in 1899. His Zulu tribe, the Amakholwa, was Christianized by Mr. Grout, an American of the Congregational Mission. His own father was an interpreter at the Mission. From childhood on, Christianity had a strong influence on Luthuli, and he still likes to quote from the Bible. After attending local mission schools, he taught for fifteen years at Adams College in Durban, a well-known American missionary high school. He became chief in 1935.

Luthuli neither drinks nor smokes. He has been a burning idealist since his youth and believed that Zulu tradition could be allied to Christianity. He was himself chief for seventeen years, and, in addition, personal advisor and associate of the Zulu Paramount Chief Mshiyeni. As chief, Luthuli had to deal not only with all social questions, but with political questions as well. He loved missionary work above everything else, but gradually came to see that it was being misused. In 1946, he became a member of the Native Representative Council and at the same time a member of the African National Congress; he no longer wanted to live on the edge of politics.

This devout Christian journeyed to India in 1938 as a delegate of the World Council of Churches. In 1948, he traveled through the United States on a lecture tour for the American Board Missions. In the ANC, which has over half a million members, he received increasingly important posts. When he was proposed as president in 1952, he published a pamphlet, *The Road to Freedom is Via the Cross.* But to Anthony Sampson, editor of the South African Negro monthly *Drum,* and author of the book about the Johannesburg treason trials *The Treason Cage,* Luthuli said these bitter words: "Our movement is based on Christian philosophy, but the Church is hostile to us."

After Luthuli showed that he was no longer a "good mission boy," the government began to take sharp measures against him. He was restricted to his home in Groutville, Natal. When the ban was lifted in 1954, he called a mass meeting in Sophiatown, near Johannesburg, in order to carry on his struggle from the broadest possible base. He was ready to become a martyr. Finally he—along with hundreds of other members of the Opposition, Indians, Whites, Moslems, Christians, and Socialists—was made a defendant in the marathon treason trial which has been going on in

South Africa since 1957. He used the trial as an opportunity for sharp attacks on the whole *apartheid* concept, but always maintained a noble appearance and manner. The London *Observer* commented that Luthuli had the bearing and the native-born dignity of an African aristocrat.

Following events in the other African countries, the Bantu youth turned to radical measures. Passive resistance on Ghandi's model, represented by Luthuli, no longer satisfied them. In April 1959, a radical group broke away from Luthuli's party and founded the Pan-Africanist Congress with about 40,000 members. A young intellectual, Robert Mangaliso Sobukwe (b. 1924), was elected president.

Sobukwe immediately took up the slogan: "Africa for the Africans!" After his arrest in April 1960, Sobukwe declared that his movement was striving to do away with white dominance in South Africa completely. He was put on trial along with 22 other P.A.C. members for inciting the campaign against the pass laws. He refused to plead guilty or not guilty on the ground that "the law under which we are charged is a law made exclusively for the White Man, and the officers administering the law are White Men. We do not see how justice can be done in the circumstances." He said that the purpose of the P.A.C. was "the establishment of a non-racial democracy in South Africa as well as throughout the whole of Africa. . . . We regard it as our historic role to contribute towards a United States of Africa from the Cape to Cairo, from Morocco to Madagascar. We stand for government of the African by the African and for the African." On May 4, 1960, Sobukwe was sentenced to three years in prison.

Luthuli's party now became more radical than it had been. "The whole civilized world and the Christian conscience is in a state of uproar." Luthuli called for a strike "as an answer to the government's appalling attacks on us and our leaders." In addition, he put forth the following proposals: 1. Abolition of the pass books. 2. Release of the leaders of African organizations. 3. Abrogation of the state of emergency. 4. Lifting of the ban on African political organizations.

Luthuli stressed once again that the African National Congress had nothing to do with Communism, of which it had been so slanderously accused. On the contrary, he warned of Communism, and added that extreme nationalism was a greater danger than Communism.

Now, as never before, the hour had come for the white Opposition to make itself heard. Sir de Villiers Graaf, of the United Party, the leader of the Opposition, said that "there should be a change of attitude by all South Africans to our non-Whites. . . . You cannot go on having a large section of the population with whom you have no contact, and whom you do not allow to have any say at all in respect of the Government which governs them."

Dr. Harry F. Oppenheimer, a former United Party M.P., and now a member of the Progressive Party which includes many leading bankers and industrialists, discussed the disturbances at length in his annual report to the shareholders of the Anglo-American Corporation, of which he is chairman; the corporation controls 90 per cent of the world's diamond production. Dr. Oppenheimer said that racial segregation was impractical and dangerous; something had to be done and quickly; the longer a solution was put off, the harder it would be to reach.

The Progressive Party stands for a multiracial society in which every civilized man, no matter what his color, would have the right to vote, be elected to Parliament, and above all share in the government. It wants to head off: "a revolution which lies over our future like a shadow, by realizing the revolution's aims and making it unnecessary."

The Liberal Party of Alan Paton tried to gain more influence, but Verwoerd's policies continued to dominate. H. I. Huizinga, in the *Nieuwe Rotterdamse Courant,* commented that the Negroes had the status of foreigners in their own country. In light of all this, it is all the more astonishing that Luthuli still maintains that:

"We don't want to drive the whites out of the country, and we don't want to marry their sisters. All that we want is to be treated honorably in our own country."

It is understandable that the *Afrikanders* want to remain in Africa. But it is incomprehensible why they have adopted policies that stand in such bald-faced contradiction to the policies of the Netherlands (from which they originated, and which granted independence to the Dutch East Indies in 1949) and Great Britain, which is granting sovereignty to more and more countries.

The original source of this is the religion of the *Afrikanders,* the overwhelming majority of whom belong to one of the three branches of the *Nederduits-Gereformeerde Kerk*—the Dutch Reformed Church. They believe themselves to be chosen by God to remain in South Africa, like the Jews in the Holy Land. Another contradiction: anti-Semites comparing their mission to that of the Jews. Laurens van der Post has written that the first book in *Afrikaans* sought to prove that the real Garden of Eden lay in the heart of Africa. He added that Africa today remains basically a land of the Old Testament that needs temples and prophets, a David for a Goliath, before it needs parliaments, politicians, and trade unions.

Father Trevor Huddleston is a man who has shown deep understanding—and concern—for the problems of the Negroes in South Africa, and especially the contradictions between Christianity and the day-to-day realities of what is actually happening there. From 1944 to 1956 (when he was declared a "prohibited immigrant") Father Huddleston worked in the Union as priest-in-charge of the Sophiatown and Orlando missions in Johannesburg, then as Provincial in South Africa of the Community of the Resurrection. In August 1960, the 48-year-old priest was elected Bishop of Masai in the new Anglican Church Province of East Africa.

In his book *Naught For Your Comfort,** Father Huddleston

* Doubleday, 1959.

quoted from a statement of the Commission for Current Problems of the Federated Dutch Reformed Church:

"Every nation and race will be able to perform the greatest service to God and the world if it keeps its own national attributes, received from God's own hand, pure with honor and gratitude. . . . Equality between natives, coloureds and Europeans includes a misappreciation of the fact that God, in His Providence, made people into different races and nations. . . . Those who are culturally and spiritually advanced have a mission to leadership and protection of the less advanced. . . ."

Huddleston called this "sub-Christian." "I say sub-Christian rather than Old Testament because I suppose that somewhere behind the obscure and murky twilight theology it represents that there are remembrances of the Gospel message. I cannot find them."

Father Huddleston remarked that he did not "wish to impugn the sincerity of the devotion of the Dutch Reformed missionary. I have no doubt that his first purpose in undertaking the work or responding to the vocation which is his is to preach the Gospel, to teach his flock to know and love and serve Almighty God. But it is always with the conviction that somehow in the eternal purposes of Providence the white race is to *lead* the black: the black race is to depend upon, to look up to, to *need* the white. *Baaskap,* they call it. 'Boss-ship'—'overlordship'—in spiritual as in material things, for ever and ever, amen."

When one mentions the astonishing number of different sects in the Union, one must add that this is a direct result of the vague and questionable position of the Christian Church in the Union. Huddleston: "Already, in the African community, we are watching the emergence of a sectarian Christianity based partly on African nationalism, partly on a revolt against the disciples of organised Christianity, partly on the terrible example of disunity shown by white 'churches' of many denominations."

The Anglican Archbishop of Capetown, Joost de Blank, asked the Dutch Reformed Church, after the riots of March 1960, to disassociate itself from the government's *apartheid* policies, or else the Anglican Church would no longer cooperate with it in the World Council of Churches. Describing *apartheid* as a "hideous doctrine," Archbishop de Blank said that unless it were repudiated, Christian faith in Africa would be the loser. "I would be happy to step down, if my removal from the scene would win the co-operation of the Dutch Reformed Church in condemning *apartheid*." Declaring that he took no thought for his own career, he said, "My only concern is the future of the Christian faith in Africa." Dutch Reformed clergymen and other Protestant leaders repudiated the Archbishop's stand, and attacked him savagely in the pulpit and the press.

Huddleston regards Verwoerd as a man who despises men. "For if you really believe in *apartheid* as Dr. Verwoerd believes in it, if you really believe in white supremacy . . . then you are not concerned with persons as persons, and you cease to be concerned with justice as justice."

But "the Church sleeps on. White Christianity is more concerned to retain its character as a law-abiding force than to express its abhorrence of such attacks on personal liberties." What did St. Paul say? "If one member suffer, all the members suffer with it."

Huddleston thinks that the extremes to which European foolishness and evil can go are so great that it is difficult to believe in a solution. He believes that "any doctrine based on racial or colour prejudice and enforced by the state is therefore an affront to human dignity and *ipso facto* an insult to God Himself." He regards the whole policy of *apartheid*, especially the Bantu Education Act, as an "education for servitude."

The Anglican priest has come under heavy attack for his views. But he says that when he fights for those denied human and legal rights in South Africa, he is also fighting against the spirit of Hitler's S.S., Siberia, Algeria, Indochina, and the Southern states of America. "In opposing the policies of the present government, therefore, I am not prepared to concede that any momentary good which might conceivably emerge from them is good. Nor am I prepared to concede that the motives which inspire such policies have any quality of goodness about them. For both the acts and the motives are inspired by a desire which is fundamentally evil and basically un-Christian; the desire to dominate in order to preserve a position of racial superiority and, in that process of domination, to destroy personal relationships, the foundation of love itself. That is anti-Christ."

During the tragic events of March 1960, one often heard talk of replacing Verwoerd and his administration with another *Afrikander* government. But could his successors, in point of fact, pursue a different course? Doubts are justified. History indicates that dictators and their supporters, above all statesmen and politicians of semi-totalitarian states, usually hold the same convictions. Alan Paton has often said that when the *Afrikanders* finally decide to regard the Africans as "people like you and me," the latter, after all the bitter disappointments they have experienced, will no longer be prepared to believe in love, but only in hate.

Hendrik Verwoerd is principally responsible for turning the Cape of Good Hope into the Cape of False Hopes. For years, he and his associates have vigorously protested against being compared to Hitler and his racial theories. But aren't there many parallels? Racial and church policies plunged Germany into a catastrophe which it may never be able to repair. Exactly the same situation prevails in the Union today. Of what use are the magnificent cities, the modern scientific institutes and factories, all the progress that the whites in the Union have unquestionably achieved, when 95 per cent of the population lives in constant fear, oppressed, enjoying no freedom, that freedom which the West is trying to champion throughout the world?

Hendrik Frensch Verwoerd has an assured place in the history of Africa. He will be remembered as the most formidable, implacable opponent of the Negro politicians and statesmen. But anyone who observes what is happening today realizes that the future belongs to them, not only because the majority of the world's coloured population is on their side, but also the progressive forces in the white world.

Verwoerd does not represent the new Africa, but the old Africa of colonialism, imperialism, feudalism, and unrestrained capitalism. He is trying to stop the clock, to check the "winds of change" that are sweeping the world. One of these days there will not only be "tears in Johannesburg" (Alan Paton), but night, deepest night with all its terrible fears and cruelties.

I don't mean to disavow the white race by pointing up the failures of some of its members, but only to bring it to self-understanding, so that things can be changed for the better. Alan Paton has said that abstract justice is a great and powerful thing, but that practical justice is still more powerful—it alone can guide the peoples of the world towards good.

13

MICHAEL SCOTT

The White Man Speaks for the Black Man

✳

Whoever reflects on the innumerable problems of the Union of South Africa may well despair. Everything appears hopeless. Up to now, at least, the opposition forces have had little influence. The comparison to Hitler's Germany comes to mind for several reasons. The English poet, Stephen Spender, in his autobiography *World Within World,* expressed what many feel: "Almost as terrible as the actions of the Nazis was the indifference of many people to these things, the lack of horror in the face of horror. This was more than a failure to read the signs of approaching war. It was a moral indifference among those not directly involved, although just such callousness had made Fascism possible among the Germans. Certain Germans, living in some square of a German city, could be reproached for not inquiring into the disappearance of neighbors who were Jews or Communists. But this attitude was equally reprehensible in people of other nations who allowed individuals, and whole groups, and finally even nations, to be crushed."

The Africans and their Asian allies will be justified, too, in reproaching the free world if it stands by and does nothing in the face of what is happening in South Africa. It should be remembered that the free world can only win prestige in African and Asian eyes if it takes a firm Christian and humanist stand. In the middle of the 1950's, esteem for the United States had sunk to a low point in Africa and Asia. But when the United States came out against the British-French intervention in Egypt during the Suez crisis of 1956, it was once again respected as "an anti-colonial power" in the whole colored world.

Father Trevor Huddleston is hated in the Union. But hated even more is his friend and model, the English missionary Michael Scott. Why? Because he is constantly protesting not only in England against South African conditions but in the forums of the whole world. There are those who regret Scott's expulsion from the Union. They would much rather have put him in jail for life, or, as one South African newspaper wrote, "broken him on the wheel." The Reverend Scott, however, wants nothing more than to see the rights of man respected in the Union. Michael Scott is neither an agitator, nor an intriguer. As a skeptic and pessimist, he simply calls an injustice an injustice, a crime a crime.

I had corresponded with him, but never actually met him until the All-African Peoples' Congress in Accra, Ghana. The delegates had been invited by Kwame Nkrumah, and they came from most of the African countries. In addition, observers attended the conference, for example: American Negroes, Russian Africa experts, and some independent friends of the African—anthropologists, ethnologists, historians. The delegates could take part in all of the sessions, while the observers were on occasion barred.

There were few whites present. But any white who wore a Congress pass on his jacket was everywhere treated with kindness, and there were no difficulties in making acquaintanceships—and even friendships—and collecting information of every kind. There was only one white man at the Congress who was permitted entrance to all the secret sessions. Strangely enough, he was the same man whom the delegates and the observers treated with reverence and the highest respect: Michael Scott. He was a man in his fifties, tall, slim, with an earnest, taciturn, almost ascetic face. He wore a light tropical suit and a black collar.

The reports and debates were very disagreeable for whites; few kind words were said about them. It seems important to me to point out, in this connection, that there are whites who are attempting to replace force with justice. But don't they run the risk of being branded traitors to their own race? I didn't hesitate to ask Michael Scott about this. His reply:

"I have my external commission to this conference from the Herero, and other oppressed tribes of the mandate territory of South-West Africa, the former German colony. I have my spiritual commission through my faith in Jesus Christ. I am convinced that what I am doing for the African is for the good of all mankind. I am not interested in races, I am only interested in the oppressed, the humiliated, the wronged. You will always find me on their side, because I am a Christian."

The closing celebration of the Congress was a little slow getting started because the resolutions had not been prepared in time. A Ghanian minister got up, went to the microphone, proposed a song to be sung by the assemblage, and began the first chorus. The amiable naturalness of the minister was winning. But I was more impressed when Scott stepped before the microphone with his Herero delegation. To bridge the waiting period, he and his friends sang some Negro folksongs from South-West Africa. The entire assemblage forgot that this was a white man standing next to black men. We were conscious only of a human being of goodness and humility: one of the few militant Christians of our time with his friends.

Guthrie Michael Scott was born on June 30, 1907 at Lowfield Heath, on the borders of Sussex and Surrey, the son of an Anglican clergyman, Percival Caleb Scott, and Ethel Maud Scott. His grandfather was also an Anglican clergyman; his great-grandfather a naval captain during Nelson's time.

Michael Scott wanted to study medicine or attend Oxford, but was advised against it because of ill-health. One of his father's churchwardens had a brother who was in charge of a leper settlement for natives at St. Raphael's Faure near Capetown. At nineteen, Scott accepted an offer to work there, and after a year went

on to study theology at St. Paul's College, Grahamstown, in the
Eastern Province of the Cape, a theological college of the Anglican Church in South Africa which trained white candidates for
ordination only. He returned to England in 1929 to continue
his studies at Chichester Theological College, and was ordained
by the Bishop of Chichester himself in 1930.

After ordination, he spent two years at a large country parish
in Sussex, then spent less than a year at a fashionable parish in the
West End of London before moving to the slum areas of the East
End. Here, during a period which saw the worst effects of the depression and the rise of Fascism, he was confronted for the first
time with political and social problems.

In February 1935, Scott sailed to the Far East as chaplain to an
Army Transport, and became domestic chaplain to the Bishop of
Bombay. He was later transferred as chaplain to the Anglican
Cathedral in Calcutta, and after spending three months in a hospital after an automobile accident in 1938, he was sent to Kasauli, a
hill station in the foothills of the Himalayas. During his stay in
India, Scott did much soul searching as he witnessed the conflicts
between his Christian ideals and the sufferings and political repression of the Indian masses. He became even more deeply interested in political questions and an admirer of Ghandi and his
passive resistance movement.

Shortly before the beginning of World War II, Scott returned
to England, worked at a parish church in London, and underwent
an operation that revealed ileitis. He served as an air raid warden
during the Blitz, and then volunteered for the R.A.F., as he had
learned to fly small planes in India. After twelve months of R.A.F.
training, he had a recurrence of ileitis, underwent another operation, and was discharged.

After a further operation, he was advised to return to South
Africa, and while awaiting passage acted as chaplain to a convent
in Bournemouth. Early in 1943, he sailed for Capetown, with
the conviction—as he says in his autobiography—that "I must use
the life that had been given back to me by the skill of doctors and

nurses to fight the evils of oppression and injustice which I knew I should find in South Africa."

Scott became chaplain to the Sisters and orphanage at St. Joseph's Home, Sophiatown, on the outskirts of Johannesburg, and assistant priest in St. Alban's Coloured Mission. This mission embraced the slum areas where the coloureds (half-castes) lived; the poor white quarters on the edges of the native townships; and some of the townships themselves. Scott soon became politically active, and was jailed a number of times after coming into conflict with the government; he spent his entire personal savings on his work and in defending himself at his trials.

In 1947, Scott went to Lake Success to deliver a petition representing the views of the Herero tribe of South-West Africa to the United Nations and the British government. He spoke again before the United Nations in 1949, 1950, and 1955, at the request of the chiefs of many of the tribes of South-West Africa, which the League of Nations, after World War I, had placed under the Union of South Africa as a mandated territory. He described the natives of this area as "disinherited" and protested against the constant efforts of the Union to annex its mandated territory. He warned that the lot of the natives in South-West Africa would be far worse than that of the Negroes in the reservations of the Union of South Africa, if the latter were permitted to replace its mandate with outright annexation.

He also warned the United Nations that conditions in South-West Africa could lead to an explosion if all paths leading to improving its status were sealed off. He said that the United Nations must take action to stop the steady alienation of South-West Africa and the rights of its people, who were powerless to do anything for themselves. For the African, the fate of South-West Africa is closely tied up with questions of human rights and justice. The tremendous tasks facing Africa can only be solved by good faith and voluntary partnership between the white and the colored races. Scott represents the view that South-West Africa should be divided, so that the Hereros can have self-government in their own area.

During the United Nations session of 1951, Scott received a written declaration from the South African Government advising him that he was "a prohibited inhabitant of or immigrant to the Union of South Africa." He has tried in vain for years to have this order rescinded.

After being denied re-entry into the Union, Scott and a number of other prominent Englishmen founded the Africa Bureau, which publishes the *Africa Digest* of news and views on African questions. Scott is director of the Africa Bureau, whose purposes are "to try and ensure that people in Britain are aware of the magnitude of their responsibilities and the nature of the problems that have to be faced in Africa" . . . "that Africans who come to Britain should have adequate facilities for stating their case to all sections of opinion in Britain" . . . "to keep people in Africa, especially the leaders of the different communities, informed about happenings in Britain and the British Parliament which concern their country. . . ."

Reverend Michael Scott is the author of several books: *Shadow Over Africa* (1950); *Attitude to Africa* (1951); *African Episode* (1954); *The Orphan's Heritage* (1958); and an autobiography, *A Time to Speak* (1958).

The events in the Union of South Africa cannot be viewed as isolated incidents, but must be seen in the context of what is happening elsewhere on the continent and throughout the whole world. The differences between Boer and Briton are a carry-over from old inter-European rivalries. The Boers' struggle against the British strengthened their racial consciousness and missionary fervor. The German journalist, Marion Donhöff, writing in *Die Zeit* made this comment: "The whites fail to realize that these events are but part of a great social revolution embracing the whole world, of which the color problem is only an aspect—and one may say one which merely aggravates the larger revolution. It is an aspect of a social revolution which has changed Europe since 1789, seized Russia since the turn of our century, and since the Second

World War has dethroned the maharajas in India, the pashas in Egypt, and now the tribal chiefs in the independent African countries. . . . Everywhere we are seeing hierarchal communities transformed into egalitarian societies. This is exactly what the South Africans are determined to prevent in their country."

Reverend Michael Scott is a Christian-Humanist activist, and belongs to those who view the tragedy in South Africa as part of a universal problem. Therefore he has taken stands on questions which have little to do with Africa specifically. He is among those who are against nuclear armaments for Great Britain. In 1958, he demonstrated against the establishment of an American rocket base in England, and was arrested. In January 1960, he led an international "protest demonstration" of about twenty people—mostly Ghanians and Nigerians—towards the Sahara to compel France to stop its nuclear tests there; the group, however, was turned back fifteen miles from the Ghana frontier.

Reverend Scott always returns to his principal concern, fighting racial discrimination in South Africa. In a message to the Manchester Council on African Affairs, he said that there is no need to fear Communism or South African Negro racism, if attempts at democratic progress meet with success. But if these reforms do not succeed, there is a serious danger from both. Scott is repeatedly advising the British government not to turn over the High Commission Territories of Basutoland, Swaziland and Bechuanaland to the Union of South Africa.

Scott recommends the policy of passive resistance, which he learned from Ghandi, to the natives of South Africa and South-West Africa. He thinks that the injustices should be fought without resorting to violence. And he has even come to the conclusion that the former system of slavery was preferable to present conditions; the former slave owners at least treated their property as well as cattle, which one can no longer be sure is the case in the Union.

In his book, *A Time to Speak,* Reverend Michael Scott set down his thoughts about South Africa and its problems:

"The great South African hypocrisy of segregation or *apartheid* has been too long supported by those well-meaning optimists who confuse the issues by defending the alleged intention of the colour bar, 'to preserve the purity of the races,' whilst at the same time deploring its consequences in the reduction of the African people to a state of servitude.

"We are told that to the white man has belonged the initiative, the intelligence, the skill and the capital wealth for the building of civilization in Africa. We are told that he must hold that initiative. He must make secure his political ascendancy and preserve his social and racial integrity, while simultaneously allowing the native peoples to live their own life in their reserves and build on the foundations of their own tribal culture. And very plausible that sounds when accompanied by appeals to racial prejudice and fears of a submergence of white civilization by a rising tide of colour.

"Given opportunity there is no sphere in which the African cannot prove himself the equal of the white man. Despite the great colour barrier which operates through our social, economic and political life, and the initial disadvantage of learning through the medium of a strange language, there are many Africans who have in fact proved their equal competence with white men in spheres of science, medicine and the arts.

"There are vast development projects waiting for all the pent-up human energy and skill of the African. . . .

"The tragedy of South Africa is that her problem is not a colour problem but a white problem. Those who have the political power do not know how to use it; are using it to erect what they think is a barrier to the black man's advance but what in reality is preventing the progress of the country as an economic whole and is in danger of undermining and eventually crushing the human basis on which the whole economic structure rests. . . .

"There is little time to lose. It is time for South Africa to abandon some of those wicked travesties of Christ's gospel and apply its divinely given intelligence to the use of all the resources of that country in knowledge, human skill and labour—and of good will too, so far as it still exists. But there is needed a vision commensurate with the magnitude of the task of building a multiracial civilization in Africa to which all will contribute and from it take their full share."*

In the Spring of 1960, a revolution of inexhaustible force began in the Union of South Africa and its mandated territory of South-West Africa. The *Times* of London commented that these forces could be suppressed for weeks or months or longer, but that they would sooner or later break through if—and this possibility existed—they were not directed into peaceful channels.

* Michael Scott, *A Time to Speak* (Faber & Faber, 1958), p. 104 ff.

14

JOSEPH KASAVUBU AND PATRICE LUMUMBA OF THE CONGO

*Former Belgian Congo the Scene of
Violence and Sharp Sectionalism*

※

What happened in the Belgian Congo between January 1959 and July 1960 is unique in the history of Africa—and the cause of its still being one of the world's great trouble spots today. This colony received its independence more precipitously than any other. Where the other colonial powers had prepared for years and decades, the Belgians reduced their establishment in an astonishingly short time. Within a few days, chaos ensued. World public opinion was shocked. It was said that no one had expected the disaster, but that was untrue: many informed experts had seen what was coming. But the excellent Belgian propaganda machine, just as it had done for seventy-five years, succeeded in covering up the danger signals. What was really happening in the Congo was either little known or frequently deceptively presented. The true conditions were obscured by government censorship or misleading reports.

The Welshman Henry Morton Stanley (1841–1904), who found Livingstone and gained fame for his African travels on assignment from James Gordon Bennett of the New York *Herald Tribune,* was one of the first white men to explore large areas of the Congo. He was the first to see the tremendous potentialities of this huge area, which is as large as India and 77 times the size of

Belgium itself. But where India has 415 million people, the Congo (905,000 square miles) has only 14 million.

Stanley wanted to supervise personally the opening up and the civilizing of the Congo. He found a willing listener in Leopold II, the ambitious and avaricious King of the Belgians, who called into being the International African Association, which later formed a separate enterprise, the *Comité d'Études du Haut Congo*. The latter, financed in large part by Leopold's private fortune, sent Stanley back to the Congo to negotiate trade and diplomatic treaties with native rulers and build a railway line. On April 30, 1885, the Berlin Conference recognized Leopold's sovereignty over the Congo Free State. From Brussels, Leopold ruled the Congo as his own personal domain for twenty-three years, never once setting foot in Africa.

Leopold's agents in the Congo acted with a severity that was extreme even for the times. They were accused of using forced labor and atrocities (such as lopping off the hands of natives who failed to meet their work quotas) that aroused a storm of criticism throughout the world. Roger Casement, British Consul at Boma, uncovered the "red rubber" horrors in 1903. In 1908, Sir Edward Grey, the British foreign secretary, declared that the Congo Free State had "morally forfeited every right to international recognition." Between five and eight million Congolese are said to have died as a result of Leopold's administration. Belgium's parties of the Left attacked the Crown and its agents so vigorously that Belgium was almost ready to give up the Congo.

Finally, in August 1908, the Belgian Parliament took over the Congo from Leopold, as a colony. Soon—according to Belgian criticism itself—two great forces were in power: capitalism and the Catholic Church. Motto: what Father does is always right. And as long as the children were small, they obeyed or pretended to obey. But when they grew up, they rebelled; Father's authority and his very presence melted away.

In the first days of January 1959, there was a revolt of the Negroes in Leopoldville, capital of the Belgian Congo, against the whites and their system of paternalism. There were many wounded and dead; how many dead it is difficult to determine, for many corpses were thrown into the Congo and washed away. Churches, hospitals, and schools were burned—all institutions built by the Europeans for the Africans. Twenty-five thousand children lost their schoolrooms. When I asked if it wasn't absurd to destroy things which could be of great use to the Congolese, I was told: "This will let you judge how we hate the Belgians. We no longer want any of their help." Catholic institutions suffered great damage, while Evangelical, such as those of the Salvation Army, were spared. "We are striking at the Belgian State through the Catholic Church," the insurgents said.

The Belgians were able to head off an even greater calamity at the last minute. The African side made known a plan to burn the whole European quarter to the ground. (They already foresaw Luluabourg as the new capital.) The atmosphere was weird, ghostly. The Europeans left Binza, the beautiful, cultivated suburb of Leopoldville, fearing arson and attacks by night. In their excitement, the insurgents made no distinction between nationalities. Danish and American diplomats, who had nothing to do with Belgian colonial policies, were molested, their autos overturned and destroyed. The rights of foreigners were not respected.

In order to study the causes of the January revolt, which brought in its wake disorders in other cities and villages of the Belgian Congo, I tried to establish contact with Negro political leaders. Political parties had been in existence only since 1958, and many of the leaders met each other for the first time in that year at the Brussels World's Fair. I visited the meetings of the young parties, and often mixed with the crowds who had gathered outside the homes of the families of those who had been arrested. The people brought them gifts and food, cheered them with tumultuous applause, and encouraged them to stand firm and keep their courage up.

What surprised me most as I was making these inquiries was the behavior of the Negroes. I was hardly able to recognize them as Congolese. They had been very submissive only two years before.

They bowed deeply when a white man approached, did not dare to look him in the eye, and said the things he wanted to hear. How can these people be so humble, so self-denying, I often thought at the time. Now all that had changed. They dared to speak up when they were dissatisfied with something. And they were very dissatisfied!

In few countries did the whites have such unsatisfactory and little contact with the Negroes as they did in the Belgian Congo. This was the reason for the sharp criticism of Belgian Father Placide Tempels against his own people in his book *Bantu-Philosphie,* and of foreign journalists. Perhaps this is why the Belgians granted independence to the Congo almost without clashes or lengthy discussions with the Africans. This latter fact is even used to support the belief that when all is said and done, the Belgians were not really greatly interested in their African colony. One often heard in the Congo: "Brussels is leaving us in the lurch, doesn't think about us, those at home are completely indifferent to what happens to us in Africa." This line of thinking was already beginning to run through all the polemics in Leopoldville in January 1959.

After the uprising, I left Leopoldville for the Lower Congo, because the disorders had originated there. I traveled for some distance on the state railway. At the station stops, we few whites were vilified, our car spat upon, and struck with stones, breaking the windows. When we transferred to an automobile and zig-zagged through the jungle, stones flew about our ears and hateful curses were bawled at us. And everywhere the cry constantly rang out: "Independence!" In several places, Belgian officials told me that the people had stopped paying taxes. Their slogan was: "We'll pay taxes again when we're independent." Whoever failed to pay his taxes was tossed in jail for two months and had to perform forced labor; there were also added penalties. That didn't divert the natives, and the jails were soon bursting. Everywhere one saw those who had been sentenced working in prison uniforms under

police guard. The Negroes greeted them like heroes. The officials
—Flemings for the most part—would have preferred to leave the
country immediately. I failed to meet one of them who saw any
future possibilities for himself there. Naturally I was told this in
strictest confidence.

Belgium has done many astonishingly good things in the Congo.
It borders on the miraculous how Leopoldville (pop. 372,000)
became a modern and beautiful city within a few decades. Four
years ago I was in Katanga Province, near the Rhodesian border,
and went down into a mine seven hundred meters below the earth's
surface. The underground electrical installation that I saw there
will always remain in my memory as a shining example of Belgian
technical ingenuity. But who does all this benefit? The Africans?
No! The Belgians, the *Societé Générale de Belgique* and its numerous subsidiaries such as the *Union Minière de Haut-Katanga,*
which owns not only the mines, but the railroad, the air service,
factories and banks. The *Union Minière,* before independence,
paid about 45 per cent of the Congo's annual revenues, and contributes 60 million dollars a year to the state of Katanga. The
money that flowed out of the Congo into the Belgian treasury
represented from 3.3 to 3.5 per cent of Belgium's entire national
budget.

There were Belgians in the Congo who had a clear understanding of the situation, but their number was not very large. Most of
them put their personal interests first. After the uprising of January 1959, Maurice van Hemelrijk, at that time minister of the
Congo and the trust territories of Ruanda and Urundi, arrived
from Brussels. I met him often, listened to his official speeches,
and came to know him quite well at international conferences and
finally at small discussion groups. He had only been minister for
a few weeks and before that he had never been in the Congo.
Was he supposed to save the situation? After the catastrophe of
July 1960, he complained bitterly that 80 per cent of the Belgians
had worked against him, that no one had listened to him. Cer-

tainly van Hemelrijk tried his best to save what was left to be saved at the last minute. But he was hardly an expert. That's why he was distrusted, a distrust that was expressed—among other ways —by his own countrymen in the Congo pelting him with tomatoes.

Above all, the Belgians in their anger did not even listen to the specialists. Now that is one of the sins of the whites in Africa . . . to disavow reason as well as human feelings. They believe principally in the power of money. Slogan: "With money behind you, you can do anything to anybody that you feel like doing." During the state of emergency, it was suggested that servants no longer be summoned with the cry *boy!* What was the reaction? To call one's servants and chauffeurs, with irony, *Monsieur le boy.* The Africans were only further enraged. Few Belgians understood this, and when one warned them, they replied: "As though that meant anything!" But it means a great deal—for the correct psychological approach to the "colonial peoples" is of prime importance. And that was what was so frequently lacking in the Belgian Congo.

The Swiss journalist, E. C. Schwarzenbach, wrote in *The Belgian Congo:* "The colonial administrations have long realized that the small psychological mistakes and tactlessness of the primitive whites that incite racial antagonism will in the end cause more harm, for example, than the regulations concerning the segregated native settlements. The whites who compensate for their personal inadequacies with a racial superiority complex are the dangerous catalysts of Negro racial madness."

A few years ago I wanted to receive the distinguished Negro composer Joseph Kiwele (whose *Missa Katanga* has been recorded) in my hotel in Elizabethville, the capital of Katanga Province. Although King Baudouin had clearly stated during his tour of the Congo that racial barriers had to go, and himself had decorated this highly deserving artist and music scholar, Kiwele was not permitted to enter the hotel.

When I protested, the director said that he would be willing to set a table for me and my Negro guest behind a screen in the dining room. With this, we left the hotel to eat in the "native

city." At the time, this was closed off at seven or eight o'clock
and whites were denied entry. In the *cité* I was naturally not insulted, but on the contrary welcomed and treated like an honored
guest. Back in my hotel, I reflected on how often attempts at
doing good are futile. King Baudouin had just said of the Congolese: "Your thirst for knowledge, your frankness without affection or artificiality, your natural dignity, and your goodness deserve our respect and our admiration." The royal message doesn't
seem to have made much of an impression in the hearts of his
subjects.

So far I've hardly discussed cultural policies in this book. I would
now like to introduce them briefly. It will become clear how not
only the Belgians, but all colonists, have missed the boat here.

The school system in the Belgian Congo was always rather one-
sided, for it was left principally to the Catholic missions, which
were often intolerant. Non-Catholics were allowed to study at the
Roman Catholic Lovanium University, but not to board there.
"That would be an affront to the spirit of Lovanium," a professor
who took me on a tour after its opening told me.

The Belgians only began to give Africans education on the
advanced level in 1958. In contrast to the natives in French and
British colonies, the Congolese had not been permitted to study
in Belgium up till then which is why the country had hardly a
dozen trained university graduates on the day it received its independence. The Congolese tried constantly to obtain higher education, but it was denied them. This was criticized by the Belgian
Parliamentary investigating committee that studied conditions in
Leopoldville after the bloody disorders.

The Belgian colonial historian and politician, Professor A. J. J.
van Bilsen, of the University Institute for Overseas Territories in
Antwerp, wrote a study in 1955 that has become famous: *Un Plan
de trente ans pour l'Emancipation politique de l'Afrique Belge.*
As a Belgian he expressed strong disapproval of the Belgian system: "It is our fault, not theirs, when there are no Negro doctors,

veterinarians, engineers, public officials, or officers." The Belgians
were not pleased by their countryman's critique. He, who wanted
to help, was branded a "traitor." But in July 1960, Belgium was
subjected to much more violent criticism by world public opinion.

In Elizabethville there was a small art school, founded on the
private initiative of a Frenchman. An innovation was classes for
architecture and advertising art and applied art; it was a worth-
while and useful undertaking. But after the disturbances, the Belgian State wanted to save money and withdrew its small support
from these classes which were doing so much good.

In Leopoldville there was a small, but highly instructive *Musée
pour la vie indigène*—an ethnological museum specializing in the
native life of the Congo. Support for its upkeep was also shame-
fully small. Director Adr. vanden Bossche had no European assistants, only five simple African handymen. The director, an expert of international reputation, had his hands full, for he also
had to give courses, hold lectures—all for an inadequate salary.
Here, too, it was decided to economize after the disorders. The
provincial governor of Leopoldville announced that the director
could only work in his museum in the afternoon; in the morning
he would have to work in the Education Office to—as he himself
told me—"supervise the cleanliness and inventory of toilets, wash
rooms, and kindergartens."

The first Congolese to become politically prominent was Jean
Bolikango, who was born in Leopoldville in 1908. For thirty-two
years he was a teacher with the *Pères de Scheut* and eventually
became President of ADAEPS (*Association des Ancièns Élèves
des Pères de Scheut*). In 1958, he represented the Catholic Mission at the Brussels World's Fair.

He remained in the capital and took a position as assistant commissioner general of INFORCONGO (*Office de l'Information
et des Relations publiques pour le Congo et le Ruanda et Urundi*).
Bolinkango was the first Congolese to receive a senior government
post—but this was not until 1959 and as a propagandist for the

Belgian government! This tall, handsome man, a devout Catholic, is one of the founders of the *Mouvement pour le Progrès National Congolais* (MPNC), and president of the Federation of the Bangala Tribe. He once had hopes of being president of the Republic himself, and backed Lumumba in seeking the latter's help to that end. Lumumba later arrested him. He might be described as the "young elder statesman" of the Congo, and is now vice premier in the new administration of Premier Joseph Ileo.

Joseph Kasavubu, who has been president of the Congo since it received its independence, is still probably the most powerful political figure in a land where the wind of change is blowing with gale force and no leader seems secure. Although he was educated by Europeans, he never liked the Belgians—or Europeans in general—very much.

Kasavubu's grandfather was a Chinese who worked as a laborer on Congo railway construction. He is a stocky man with a round face and thick glasses, who has been described as "astute," "lethargic," "brooding," "tough," and as looking like a "benign, enigmatic cherub." He speaks in a rather high-pitched, soft voice that has just a hint of unction. He has spent much of his presidency in seclusion in his comfortable, modern stone-and-glass villa on a hill west of Leopoldville overlooking the Congo River, where, it is said "he watches for the bodies of his enemies floating by."

Kasavubu was born, probably in 1917, in Kuma-Dizi, a village ten miles from Tshela in the Mayombe mountains, in Leopoldville Province. He received his early schooling, like Bolinkango, from the missionary fathers, the *Pères de Scheut*. He proved to be a gifted student and the fathers sent him to the *Grand Séminaire de Kabwé*, in Kasai Province, where he studied philosophy and theology for three years. There he became general secretary of the *Association des Anciens Élèves* (alumni) of the *Pères de Scheut*. He studied for the priesthood, but did not complete his training.

Although Kasavubu freely criticized the Mission when he left, he felt that he had been unjustly treated, and even today seems to suffer from his personal conflict with the Christian Mission. Kasavubu returned to his native province and began some spirited agi-

Future Rulers?
Left, Libyan Crown Prince Hassan Ridah el Senoussi. Right, Ethiopian
Crown Prince Asfa Wosen, with his daughter, Princess Mariam.

Julius Nyerere, Chief
Minister of Tanganyika,
with his wife during fes-
tivities in Dar es Salaam.

Harry Nkumbula, President of the African National Congress of Northern Rhodesia.

Sir Roy Welensky, Prime Minister of the Federation of Rhodesia and Nyasaland.

Reginald Stephen Garfield Todd, missionary and former Prime Minister, a leader in the fight to preserve the Federation and continue separation of the races.

Dr. Hastings Kamutzu Banda, leading native politician in Nyasaland.

Dr. Hendrik Verwoerd, Prime Minister of the Union of South Africa, in London, following his decision to withdraw the Union from the Commonwealth of Nations.

Dead and wounded lie on the ground at Sharpeville, Union of South Africa, after police fired on native demonstrators against the Union's white supremacy policy, March, 1960.

tation against the Catholic Mission. When he took up a position against the Catholic Church, he was also attacking the colonial administration. For a few years he had an assured income as a teacher at a school in Mayombe. But his heart belonged increasingly to anti-colonial politics. In 1942, he became a clerk in the Belgian Financial Administration. "I wanted to study the enemy on his home grounds," is his explanation for this surprising move.

After moving to Leopoldville, Kasavubu married and eventually became the father of nine children. In 1957, he became mayor of Dendale, one of the Negro townships of Leopoldville. On April 20, 1958, he gave a fanatical nationalist speech calling for independence, which earned him a sharp reprimand. Soon after the uprising of January 4, 1959, the Belgians arrested Kasavubu and held him until March 1960. Along with other politicians, he was brought to Belgium for talks and restored to his office of mayor after his return. In December 1959, he was once again in Brussels and took part in the Round-Table Conference of February 1960. His reputation suffered because of his temperamental outbursts and his occasional disappearances (obviously to Paris, to negotiate with the French). His most formidable opponent, Patrice Lumumba, meanwhile pressed to the foreground.

Kasavubu owes his continued strength to the support of his 1,200,000 Bakongo tribesmen of the Lower Congo, and his unchallenged leadership of the ABAKO, a dynamic cultural association of the Bakongo, which is strongest in Mayombe and the Madimbe region. His first famous speech, *Le Droit du Premier Occupant,* was given in 1946. He declared that the Congolese, and especially the inhabitants of Bakongo, were the original inhabitants and therefore the real owners of the Congo. Correspondingly, the Belgians had no claim at all to the Congo and must "promptly disappear." Even his own supporters were at first dismayed by this radical position. As I have noted, the Belgian Professor van Bilsen published his *Thirty Year Plan for the Political Emancipation of the Belgian Congo* in 1955. It enraged the conservative Belgians, but inspired the Negro nationalists even more. The "Plan van Bilsen" declared that Belgian had no other alternative but to grant the Congo independence in thirty years. Thirty years? The Congo received its independence twenty-five years earlier than this young Belgian scholar had foreseen.

Aside from politics, Kasavubu's interests were constantly centered on social questions. He pleaded for equal wages for Negroes and whites, when they did the same work, for equal representation in the administration, and for the dissolution of all racial discrimination. A young white sales employee could earn around 300 dollars a month; he could live on it, and better than he could in Belgium. Married men received higher salaries, had elegant, comfortable houses with plenty of servants, and the newest American automobiles. A white employee of the partially state-controlled railway system earned around one thousand dollars a month; a mechanic in the *Union Minière* around 850 dollars a month; and an engineer around 1300 dollars a month.

But what did a Congolese earn? A young African salesman earned around 25 dollars a month; a station master—married and with several children—also around 25 dollars a month. Even Belgian official statistics admitted that the Negro's average weekly wage was around four dollars, and the whites around 125 dollars. It was shocking to see how miserably Negro artists and intellectuals were paid. My old friend Albert Mongita was an announcer on *Radio Congo-Belge* for fourteen years, and in addition wrote radio scripts, for which he received no extra compensation. His basic salary after fourteen years service was around 150 dollars a month, about half of what a young white salesman received.

But back to Kasavubu. In 1955, he was elected by 42 out of 60 votes at the Congress of Kisantu as president of the ABAKO (*Association des Bakongo pour l'Unification, la Conservation et l'Expansion de la langue Kikongo*). When Joseph Kasavubu created a political movement out of this tribal cultural association, he became the most popular politician in the Lower Congo, the Leopoldville Province.

For a while, Kasavubu considered the idea of a Republic of the

Lower Congo. Tribal loyalties still play a key role in the Congo. Kasavubu felt closer to the people of the Lower Congo on the north bank of the Congo River than to those in other provinces of his own country. There were negotiations between him and *Abbé* Fulbert Youlou, President of the former French Congo. When the Belgians announced their intention of granting independence to the Congo, the French recalled an old secret treaty that Leopold II had concluded with the French Premier Jules Ferry in 1883. This granted France rights to the Congo, in case Belgium "sold the Congo or was not in a position to protect its rights there."

This *droit de Préférence* was renewed in 1908, when Belgium took over the Congo as a colony. It was also rumored that the ABAKO was financed by France. The future of this section of Africa is therefore uncertain. It is not impossible that one day the Belgian Lower Congo will secede from the rest of the Congo and unite with the former French Congo. It was understandable that Belgian public opinion was enraged when France's ambitions became known, and its press wrote of "a new edition of French colonialism." (The Belgians protested again when Sir Roy Welensky, prime minister of the Federation of Rhodesia and Nyasaland, declared at the same time that Salisbury would give careful consideration to any desire on the part of Katanga Province to join the Federation.)

In addition, it is also known that Kasavubu has negotiated with Africans in the Portuguese Lower Congo. The Portuguese, on the other hand, fear for the boundaries of Angola, which borders the former Belgian Congo and which has been the scene of recent bloody disorders, and especially for its small enclave of Cabinda on the Atlantic, squeezed between the former French and Belgian Congos. Is Kasavubu dreaming of a "Kingdom of the Lower Congo," naturally with himself as its king? He speaks often of the old Bakongo Kingdom, which flourished between the fourteenth and sixteenth centuries. He was obviously flattered when I addressed him as *Roi Kasa*—as many of his followers do. In any case, the Lower Congo occupies a key position. Stanley himself said that the whole Congo—without the Lower Congo—"isn't worth a penny."

One also cannot view Kasavubu only as a politician, but must know something of his religious leanings. His ABAKO is in direct contact with the Kimbanguists. This sect was founded in 1919 by the African preacher, Simon Kimbangu, who died in 1956, reportedly as a repentant Catholic; today it is said to have around 100,000 members. For years it was suppressed, but now operates without restrictions. Kimbanguism is a mixture of African mysticism and Christianity. Islamic theories were brought into its liturgy and teachings by formerly exiled members. Diagienda Kimbangu, son of the founder, whose office is in Kamba (the "Jerusalem of the Movement") is in constant contact with Kasavubu, who lets himself be called *Dieu Kasa.*

Since Christianity has been discredited in the Congo because of its association with colonialism, Kasavubu is willing to make use of this religious movement, whose aims coincide with his own ambitions. "Kimbangu wanted to be the Saviour and the Redeemer of the Negro race, as Moses, Jesus, Mohammed, and Buddha were for the other races," G. Guarighia has written. It would seem that the same idea has occurred to Kasavubu.

Patrice Lumumba is dead, his corpse lying in a secret grave in the Katanga Province controlled by one of his archenemies, Moise Tshombe. But the spirit and influence of the first premier of the Congo are far from dead. He was one of the first major problem personalities among the new leaders in Africa, a figure of importance in world affairs, a man who believed in strong central government as against the federalist concepts of his antagonists Lumumba and Tshombe. News of his death caused an uproar in the United Nations and touched off violent demonstrations in many of the Afro-Asian countries. "The fuss over this evil man will soon die down. The people have no memories here," said Moise Tshombe. But the ideas that Lumumba represented have not died down, and will continue to influence events in the Congo for a long time to come. Antoine Gizenga, leading aspirant to Lumumba's role as a national leader, has set up a regime in Stanleyville in the pro-Lumumba Oriental Province. It boycotted the Tananarive "confederation" conference of March 16, 1961, has the backing of the Soviet Union and several of the Afro-Asian nations, and its troops have penetrated more than 30 per cent of the Congo.

Patrice Lumumba entered politics much later than Kasavubu. It is all the more astonishing how quickly he gained influence. Both men were quite different. Kasavubu is more of an African mystic; Lumumba was more a politician in the Western sense. Kasavubu is transparent; he makes hardly any effort to conceal his sympathies and hostilities. Here, Lumumba—at least until he became premier—was a master. He was anti-European when he had to be to win votes, but quickly became pro-European when it could help his party, the *Mouvement National Congolais* (MNC). Another difference between the two: Kasavubu built his plans on tribal politics; Lumumba wanted to dissolve at all costs the authority and solidarity of the tribes in order to create a single, strong Congo State. Lumumba wanted to build a powerful central government that would dominate the various provincial governments.

Lumumba was slightly over six feet tall, lean, wore a small black goatee, and made a very intelligent impression. He knew how to handle himself at international forums. That is astonishing, when one remembers what little training and education he had for his extraordinary career. Patrice Emery Lumumba was born in 1925 in the Sankuru district of Kasai Province. He, too, attended a mission school. But unlike Kasavubu he remained a loyal Catholic until his death. When I asked him, he told me that he had been able to survive his time in jail only because of his deep religious faith.

Lumumba worked for twelve years in Stanleyville as a post office clerk, and was *Président des Cercle des Evolués*. He was arrested and convicted of embezzling 126,000 Belgian colonial francs (about $2,500) from the post office. Lumumba always spoke quite candidly about this painful episode in his life. He told me: "I took the money, not for myself, but for my political activities. I hurt no private individual, only the Belgian State, which at the time was my worst enemy. It had plundered us, now I plundered it." He was sentenced to two years in prison, but appealed and served only about a year. In prison, he found time to compose anti-colonial texts. He was one of the leading political figures in Stanleyville. He also had influence as president of the Circle of *Evolués*—Congolese who had been educated and were regarded as the nucleus of a future native middle class.

In 1958, Lumumba returned to Leopoldville and became the sales manager of a brewery. He was married to a girl who had also been born in the Congo jungle and had been baptized a Catholic; they had three sons and a daughter and lived in a modest but comfortable European-style house in a Leopoldville suburb.

Lumumba's father, also a Catholic, was a simple, illiterate tribesman—a member of the Batetele, a tribe scattered and crushed by the Belgians after an unsuccessful revolt in 1893. In 1958, Lumumba became president of the Federation of the Batetele. In 1958, he became a member of the permanent committee at the All-African Peoples' Conference in Accra, and turned completely to politics. Now that he enjoyed outside support, he was able to become president of the *Mouvement National Congolais,* which already had well-organized political offices throughout the Congo. One of the reasons for Lumumba's rise was his ability to capture the imagination of the Congolese crowds; his personality and silver tongue were unique among native leaders, and when jailed by Kasavubu he almost talked his guards into letting him escape. It has also been asserted that he appointed himself president of the MNC, a key party: he sent a news release to the Belgian press agency and presented his rivals with a *fait accompli.*

In December 1958, Lumumba had given a rebellious speech in Leopoldville that was the beginning of his political activity. During the uprising in January 1959, the Belgians wanted to arrest him, as they had Kasavubu and his associates. But Lumumba had himself ferried across the Congo River in a log-canoe to Brazzaville and fled from there to Nigeria. When the Belgian Parliamentary Commission sought to determine the reasons for the uprising, Lumumba sent it material on the mistakes of the colonial system.

In April and May 1959, Lumumba was in Belgium, where he took part in conferences and gave lectures. He also participated in the meetings of independence movements in Nigeria, Guinea, and Ghana. He became director of the weekly *Indépendance* and with it gained influence in the politics of the transition period. Kasavubu saw Lumumba's star rising with consternation, and began to fight him publicly.

Lumumba realized that only courage would pay off. On July 1, 1959, he opened a political meeting by pathetically asking his audience to remember those who had fallen during the January uprising. The Belgian colonial administration was enraged. Hadn't they done everything to make light of the uprising and if possible strip it of its political character? Lumumba had other ideas. He needed martyrs for the independence struggle and especially for his MNC. Even within his own party, there were those who were dissatisfied with him. The other party leaders were annoyed by his struggle against tribal loyalties. This led in July 1959 to the defection of one wing of the party. Albert Kalonji, a journalist and trade unionist, who is now president of the secessionist "Mining State" of South Kasai, turned to the ABAKO and a number of the smaller parties—of which there are some thirty in the Congo, most of them of no real importance. With them he created a coalition, which was also active during the independence negotiations in Brussels. This didn't bother Lumumba, for the masses remained loyal to him.

There were outbreaks of serious disorders during the Congress of the MNC in the fall of 1959 in Stanleyville, and the government held Lumumba responsible. He was arrested on November 2, 1959 and sentenced to six months in prison. After three months, he was pardoned by the Belgian colonial minister, De Schrijver, and allowed to participate in the Brussels Round-Table Conference on Congo independence.

Lumumba appeared in Brussels with his wrists bandaged. He had scars on both wrists from the handcuffs he wore in prison, and he reported that his body was covered with the bruises he had received through mistreatment.

Once again, Lumumba displayed his gift for practical politics, and quickly became the most important negotiator: he stood out for both his logic and quickness at repartee. He won the Belgian negotiators—and Belgian public opinion—over to the idea that despite his previous declarations, he now wanted the Belgians to stay on after independence; his party would in future welcome more Belgians becoming active in the Congo. In the name of his party, he guaranteed them every freedom. With this, he trumped Kasavubu.

The historic Brussels Congo Conference took place between January 20 and February 20, 1960. Belgian cabinet members and parliamentarians negotiated with 44 Congolese delegates. Sixteen resolutions were passed, among which these were the most important:

The Congo would become a fully independent state on June 30, 1960. The state would consist of the six provinces with the same geographical boundaries currently in effect. The future Constituent Assembly could change the number and geographical boundaries of the provinces after independence. The Congolese legislature would be formed after general elections in April and May 1960, and would consist of a 137-man Lower House, or Chamber of Representatives, and an 84-member Upper House or Senate. The first Congolese government would be formed by June 10, 1960 and would replace the Belgian administration on June 30. Until then, six Congolese would form a college with the Belgian governor-general, Henri Cornelis, and work closely with him in administering the country. A treaty of friendship, assistance, and co-operation between Belgium and the Congo would be signed as soon as possible that would also guarantee the protection of Belgian and foreign investments in the Congo. Further, the treaty would guarantee the rights of the 100,000 Belgian citizens who would remain in the former colony.

Patrice Lumumba declared at the close of the Conference that his party, the MNC, was completely satisfied with what had been achieved—but people shouldn't forget that the Congolese were receiving their independence "while our brothers in Kenya, Nyasaland, Rhodesia, South Africa and Angola are still fighting for their freedom." He encouraged the assembly to forget the mistakes of the past and "look at the wonderful future that smiles at us."

Soon he went to Ghana, to discuss foreign policy matters with Kwame Nkrumah. Lumumba declared that he was for a foreign policy of positive neutrality without alliances to any blocs. The Congo would welcome foreign capital and technical assistance and build democratic institutions. He favored the idea of a United States of Africa, but preferred a federation of independent states that would retain their own sovereignty.

Joseph Kasavubu had this to say about the Brussels Congo Conference: "Congolese of all provinces and races, we are bringing you independence. . . . This independence has been won by a united front of all Congolese delegates." Kasavubu also expressed the intention of aiding all African peoples in their struggle for independence, above all Ruanda and Urundi. At the same time he asked the Congolese to prove themselves worthy of independence through work, unity, and the regular payment of taxes.

There was hardly anyone who was not surprised by the outcome of the Congo Conference. "The sell-out in the Congo has begun," commented Jürgen Tern in the *Frankfurter Allgemeinen Zeitung*. This was preceded and underscored by falling prices, the beginnings of the flight of capital, and above all by a disastrous economic situation in a country which up till then had appeared to be economically healthy.

Until January 4, 1959, the first day of the uprising, the Belgians had acted as though everything was in splendid shape; it was only the British, the French and so forth who would "have to pull back everywhere." Even General de Gaulle was not spared sharp attacks. On August 28, 1958, de Gaulle gave a speech in the Félix Eboué Stadium in Brazzaville, on the other side of the Congo River, in which he asked for support for the French Community and held out the prospect of independence for the colonial countries. At first the Belgians laughed at him contemptuously, then they became angry and finally persecuted their French neighbors with unconcealed hatred once they realized that de Gaulle's speech had made the *Evolués* in Leopoldville rebellious. Certainly developments in other countries hastened the process of granting independence to the Belgian Congo. Because of that further developments were viewed with considerable anxiety.

The Times of London called the Belgian decision to give the Congo independence without suitable preparation more of a gamble than an experiment. In contrast to the other African countries, the Congo, as we have already indicated, has practically no trained native class (elite), although there are fewer illiterates here by far than elsewhere in Africa. Grammar and secondary schools were considered good enough for the natives. In the *Force Publique* there was not a single Congolese officer and hardly a half-dozen sergeants. As the day of independence approached, the country could not produce a single personality who was really qualified to be a cabinet minister or any kind of senior public official, or the manager of a bank or a factory. The Congolese were in fact completely unprepared to rule and administer. Insofar as any of them had reached the level of civilization in the Western sense, this was limited to commercial affairs.

The hope remained that the Belgians would come to some kind of an agreement with the Congolese at the last minute. Patrice Lumumba continued to proclaim that the Belgians could—even should—stay. Kasavubu, on the other hand, believed that the Congolese could manage without the whites. Or was he already negotiating with the Soviet Union? It was striking how Lenin and Khrushchev were frequently cited in speeches by ABAKO leaders as helping the Africans in their struggles for freedom. As far as the financing of Lumumba's party with 85 million Belgian francs goes, he is supposed to have received a quarter of it from Kwame

Nkrumah and Sékou Touré, a quarter from Western banks, and the remaining half from the Eastern bloc. It would appear that Oswald Spengler was right once again when he wrote in his *Year of Decision* that one day the racial struggle would join up with the class struggle.

In April–May 1960 tribal clashes broke out in several districts of the Congo. The Belgian Air Force started an air lift and brought in troop reinforcements, as the growing uneasiness of the Europeans spread and fear of terrorism arose. In the first general elections for the new Congolese Parliament in May, Lumumba, Kasavubu, and Kalonji scored notable victories, and it became clear that they were the men who would determine the fate of an independent Congo after June 30. At the beginning of June, panic set in among the whites and many of them began to leave the country. There was fear of a "night of the long knives."

Lumumba announced that he wanted to be head of state as well as premier of the new nation. Secessionist tendencies could already be observed in Katanga Province and Leopoldville. Moise Tshombe, leader of CONAKAT (*Confédération des Associations des Katangaaises*) threatened a *coup d'état* and the withdrawal of Katanga from the Congo State; he sent an appeal to the Rhodesian government and the United Nations. The ABAKO made similar threats.

After Lumumba failed to gain the necessary majority for a central government, Kasavubu was charged by the Belgians with forming a coalition government that would have as broad a base as possible. Lumumba called this a "Belgian crime against the Congo," said that he was the victim of a plot and would nevertheless form his own government, in which Kasavubu would be foreign minister.

At the last minute, the rivals worked out a compromise. Lumumba became premier and minister of defense; the latter post gave him control of the *Force Publique*. On June 24, 1960, both houses of the Congo Parliament elected Kasavubu the first president—or head of state—of the Congo. He received 158 votes to 43 for the only other candidate, Jean Bolinkango, who had become in the meantime a Lumumba supporter. At the same time, Parliament announced its decision to name the new state "Republic of the Congo."*

The independence of the Belgian Congo was proclaimed on June 30, 1960. King Baudouin took part in the ceremonies. In his speech to both Houses of the Congo Parliament, the young sovereign exhorted his former subjects to unity: "The principal dangers for you are the inexperience of your people in government affairs, tribal fights which have done so much harm and must at all costs be stopped, and the attraction which certain of your regions can have for foreign powers which are ready to profit from the least sign of weakness." He warned of the danger of the secession of Katanga and its merger with the neighboring British territories. He went on to tell the Parliament not to hesitate to turn to Belgium for counsel; Belgium was prepared to train the technicians and public officials that the Congo needed. Africa and Europe complemented each other, and their mutual co-operation would bring forth wonderful results. He concluded: "People of the Congo, my country and myself are moved in recognizing that the Congo accedes to independence and sovereignty in agreement and friendship with Belgium on June 30, 1960."

President Kasavubu, in his reply, praised the Belgian administration of the Congo. He promised future co-operation and added that Belgium had given "an example unprecedented in the history of peaceful decolonization—leading our people directly, without transition, from foreign rule to independence under full national sovereignty."

Premier Lumumba would have none of this kind of talk. "We are no longer your monkeys!" he shouted (*macac*—monkey—was

---

* This brought forth a vigorous—but vain—protest from Abbé Fulbert Youlou, President of the Former French Congo, which had decided to adopt the name "Republic of the Congo" when it achieved self-government in 1958. The same difficulty arose between the former Anglo-Egyptian Sudan and the former French Sudan, both of which became known as the "Republic of the Sudan." The former French Sudan, however, recently took the name "Mali Republic."

an insult often used by the Belgians, and particularly resented by the Congolese). Despite the presence of the king, he called the former Belgian administration "a shameful regime of oppression."

In a speech of extraordinary ferocity, Lumumba went on: ". . . . no Congolese worthy of the name will ever be able to forget that this independence has been won through a struggle . . . in which we did not spare our energy and our blood. . . . We have known ironies, insults and blows which we had to undergo morning, noon, and night because we were Negroes. We have seen our lands spoiled in the name of laws which recognized only the right of the strongest. We have known laws which differed according to whether they dealt with a black man or a white. We have known the atrocious sufferings of those who were imprisoned for their political opinions or religious beliefs, and of those exiled in their own country. Their fate was truly worse than death itself. Who will forget the rifle fire from which so many of our brothers perished, or the jails into which were brutally thrown those who did not wish to submit to a regime of injustice, oppression, and exploitation, which were the means the colonialists employed to dominate us?"

Despite this sharp attack, King Baudouin was accorded an ovation by the parliamentarians and the people. At an official luncheon following the independence ceremony, Lumumba appeared to have changed to a conciliatory mood. In a toast to the king, he said: "At the moment when the Congo reaches independence, the whole Government wishes to pay solemn homage to the king of the Belgians and to the noble people he represents for the work done here over three-quarters of a century. I would not wish my feelings to be wrongly interpreted. . . . Long live King Baudouin, long live Belgium, long live the independent Congo!" Now Patrice Lumumba had shown that he, too, had two faces.

Immediately after the independence ceremonies, the struggle over the Congo went into high gear. For the first time, the interests of foreign powers added fuel to the fires of internal dissensions.

The Western delegations which had appeared at the ceremonies soon left, but the Russians stayed behind. The Soviet Union bought a Leopoldville skyscraper for its embassy, and announced that it wanted to help in the construction of a new Congo River dam. Above all, it gave generous financial backing to the Lumumba government.

Despite its good relations with the Soviet Union, the Congo government asked the United States to send troops as the tribal clashes spread. President Eisenhower replied that "such military assistance would be better for the Congo if it did not come from the United States or any of the Western nations." The United Nations prepared to send officers and technical advisers. Moscow and Peking reacted quickly with declarations in favor of the Lumumba regime.

Six days after independence, the *Force Publique* mutinied. This ill-paid organization, created in 1891 to maintain public order, was up to then composed of about 25,000 African enlisted men, mostly illiterate, commanded by about 1,000 Belgian officers. The purpose of the mutiny was the deposition of its hated Belgian commander-in-chief, Lt. General Emile Janssens, a fanatical colonial soldier and admirer of Leopold II, and especially of its Belgian officers, who had blocked the Africanization of its cadres.

The mutinous troops at first occupied Leopoldville, then the mutiny spread through the whole country. Panic gripped the inhabitants of Leopoldville, above all the whites. Ten thousand of them fled to the French Congo or to Angola. President Kasavubu stepped in as commander-in-chief of the army. The government succeeded in reaching an agreement with the mutinous troops: the Belgian officers would be relieved, and would in future serve only as civilian advisers. The *Force Publique* would become a national army with a Congolese commander and officers.

On July 11, 1960, Moise Tshombe, the prime minister of Katanga, proclaimed the independence of the province and its secession from the central government. Tshombe accused the government in Leopoldville of being dependent on a parliamentary majority of extremists who had achieved power through election frauds. He said that the central government's purpose seemed to be "the disintegration of the whole military and civil machine, and the creation of a reign of terror which is driving out our Belgian collaborators," and to replace them with advisers "which it already seems to have recruited from the Communist countries."

He requested the prime minister of the Federation of Rhodesia and Nyasaland, Sir Roy Welensky, to send troops to restore order. Welensky believed that his hour had come. But Prime Minister Macmillan forbade him to send troops without the permission of the British government in London. Tshombe was informed that Great Britain would not recognize him as head of state. Paris turned down Katanga's attempts to have it recognize its independence on the grounds that France could not establish relations with a provincial government that had no international status.

In the meantime, Belgian troops were flown into Katanga, the world's greatest uranium producer and the richest area of the Congo, but *Libre Belgique* demanded in vain "the immediate recognition of Katanga's independence." Meanwhile, Tshombe declared that the basic law forced on the Congolese by the Belgians was bad and unsuitable for African conditions. He said that he would like to see a "United States of the Congo" founded, based on "the freedom and harmony of the Congolese peoples." He hoped for the support of President Kasavubu, who was known also to be no supporter of a strong central government.

Moise Tshombe, now the president of Katanga, continues as one of the key political actors in the Congo drama, if only because his secessionist province is the economic heart of the country. A few figures will give a rough idea of Katanga's wealth. At independence it had a white population of about 33,500 and a Congolese population of about 1,650,000; it contributes 60 per cent of the Congo revenue but has only 12 per cent of the total population. Katanga produces about 60 per cent of the West's uranium; 80 per cent of the world's industrial diamonds; 73 per cent of its cobalt; 8 per cent of its copper, and its rich mineral resources that also include gold, zinc, and manganese are far from worked out.

Tshombe is a very self-confident man, but at the same time

courteous, amiable, and possessed of a good sense of humor; he speaks fluent French and English. His full first name is Moise-Kapenda (beloved of Moses) and he was born in November 1919 in Musumba. He comes from the royal family of the Lunda tribe, which has provided chiefs for Katanga for a long time. He himself is married to the daughter of the paramount chief and has ten children. His family was quite prosperous: the father owned plantations; a string of retail businesses in Elizabethville in which he sold groundnuts, fruit, grain, and beer; and a hotel for whites. The son attended American Methodist missionary schools, and later took a correspondence course preparatory to entering his father's businesses. But, unlike his father, Moise Tshombe was never a very successful businessman.

His interest in politics awakened in 1957. He was elected to the Provincial Council of Katanga, later to the municipal government of Elizabethville. He also took over other positions of power, such as the directorship of the African Chamber of Commerce in Elizabethville. In 1959, he became president of CONAKAT and developed this party into an instrument of power. At the Brussels Congo Conference he came out for a federation of Congo states and even then wanted Katanga to have its own government. He has always maintained good relations with the Belgians. He was always pro-European, and never anti-white. His opponents accuse him of being "hostile to progress." Lumumba attacked him during the Congo Conference; he especially did not like Tshombe's co-operation with Belgian capital in Katanga. Tshombe was nicknamed "bank drawer." After the Brussels conference, he toured the United States as guest of the State Department.

After proclaiming Katanga's independence on July 11, 1960, Tshombe appointed a Belgian major to command all armed forces and police in the province. The major—now Colonel Guy Weber— is constantly at Tshombe's side. Despite all the recent difficulties, the economy of Katanga—still run by Belgians—is humming. Tshombe barred Lumumba from landing in Elizabethville, and the premier was obliged to return to Leopoldville. Tshombe at first permitted no UN troops to enter Katanga, but later agreed to a compromise through Hammarskjold's efforts. He created Belgian-Katanganese communities, and attempted to have his state recognized everywhere in the world. On July 14, the Provincial Parliament—which was at first hostile to him—approved his independence declaration, after he had won over the Opposition and, above all, the tribal chiefs. The constitution of the Republic of Katanga went into effect on August 4, 1960.

How much the Belgians (and perhaps even the Americans?) had to do with developments in Katanga will be for history to decide. Tshombe went to Brussels at the end of 1960 and was received by King Baudouin. Katanga has built a defense line 80 miles deep against the rest of the Congo area. President Tshombe has declared that he wants to break the Belgian monopoly in Katanga. There is talk of an "internationalisation of the wealth of Katanga," and this proposal doesn't seem to have met with any opposition from the *Union Minière*.

After Lumumba found himself in increasing difficulties in the summer of 1960, he appealed to the UN to enter the picture and restore order. Dag Hammarskjold interrupted a European trip and returned to New York. The Soviet Union accused the United States, Great Britain, France, West Germany, Belgium, and Portugal of "aggression" in the Congo, and said that ". . . . the United States should take immediate steps to put an end to the aggression. . . ." Henry Cabot Lodge immediately intervened to refute "the outrageous and untrue statements" concerning United States' actions, and declared "it is regrettable that the Soviet Government should have interjected itself into the situation with the truly incendiary statement. . . ." The other governments protested with sharp notes. *The New York Times* commented that the military forces sent to the Congo should not come from any of the great powers, like the United States, Great Britain, France, or the Soviet Union, but from the small non-Communist and non-colonial states.

The Lumumba government broke off diplomatic relations with

Belgium. The Security Council decided to send troops under the command of the Swedish General Carl von Horn. Dr. Ralph Bunche flew to Leopoldville to negotiate with the Belgians and Congolese. The Belgian premier, Gaston Eyskens, told the Belgian Parliament that the mutiny of the *Force Publique* had been led from the outset by Communists. And, in fact, Kasavubu and Lumumba had sent a letter to Khrushchev on July 14, in which they said: "Perhaps we may be compelled to ask for the Soviet Union's intervention, unless the Western camp discontinues the aggression against the sovereignty of the Congo Republic."

Premier Khrushchev immediately dispatched a "Message to the Congo Government": "The Soviet Government and the Soviet peoples take into account the tremendous international significance of the heroic struggle of the Congolese people. . . . The Soviet Union has already raised its voice in resolute condemnation of the imperialist intervention. . . . The demand of the Soviet Union is simple—hands off the Republic of the Congo! The Congolese Government may rest assured that the Soviet Government will render the Congo Republic all the assistance which may be necessary for the triumph of your just cause."

Lumumba's career reached its high point when he flew to New York on July 24, 1960. He asked the United Nations to see to it that all Belgian officials and troops left the Congo, and asked for economic and technical assistance. He returned to a hero's welcome in Leopoldville with the support of the United Nations and most of the African states. But the months that followed saw a deepening of the internal political rivalries in the Congo. Lumumba pressed the UN with constant demands for help in putting down rival forces. His relations with Dag Hammarskjold and President Kasavubu began to deteriorate. Lumumba tried to suppress secessionist movements in Kasai, Leopoldville Province, and Equator. In doing this, he was strongly supported by the Soviet government, which sent him transport planes and trucks.

The political situation changed dramatically between September 5 and 9, 1960. President Kasavubu, who up to then had taken few decisive measures, announced in a radio broadcast on September 5 that he had dismissed Lumumba, was replacing him as premier with Joseph Ileo, president of the Senate, and would himself take over command of the armed forces. Lumumba later went on the radio to reply that he was still premier and defense minister, and that Kasavubu was a "traitor" and no longer head of state. Lumumba's downfall was attributed to his inability to find a formula that would have given him the backing of Kasavubu and his supporters. Lumumba was still fighting for a strong central government, while the provincial leaders seemed to prefer a federal system with provincial autonomy.

In the struggle to arrest each other and gain control of the state, Kasavubu won out, thanks to the assistance of Colonel Joseph Mobutu, the Congolese National Army chief-of-staff. The army seized power on September 15, 1960. Mobutu threw his support to Kasavubu, arrested Lumumba, and was later promoted to major general.

General Mobutu was born in 1929 or 1930 in Lisala in Equator Province. After attending a mission school, he became a soldier in the *Force Publique* in 1949. Seven years later he was discharged as a sergeant-major, as no Negro could become an officer before independence. When Lumumba was working in the post office in Stanleyville and founding his political organization, Mobutu was a writer in the Commissariat in Leopoldville. He began to work on newspapers and became editor of *L'Avenir*. When Lumumba's party founded the journal *Actualités Africaines* Mobutu was appointed its editor-in-chief.

Mobutu went to Europe for the first time to attend the Brussels World's Fair, worked for the Belgian information service INFOR-CONGO, and in addition studied at a Catholic Institute for Social Studies in Brussels. During the disorders in Leopoldville in the spring of 1959, he remained in the background. He attended the Brussels Congo Conference of 1960 as a delegate from Lumumba's *Mouvement National Congolais*—and was then still on intimate terms with Lumumba.

After independence, Lumumba named him state secretary for defense in his cabinet. Soon after the outbreak of the mutiny of the *Force Publique* at Camp Hardy in Thysville, Mobutu was called to duty as chief of staff with the rank of colonel—though his previous military experience had been confined to the accounting department. In this capacity, he was originally expected to launch an attack on the secessionist province of Katanga. But to the world's surprise, he became a strong opponent of Lumumba.

After seizing power, Mobutu suspended Parliament and ruled through a youthful caretaker regime, the *collège d'universitaires,* later called the Council of Commissioners-General. But he voluntarily stepped down as a "strong man" when Kasavubu announced the end of the military regime on February 11, 1961, and named a provisional government formed of members of the suspended Parliament.

Intelligent and sophisticated, Mobutu is a thin, nervous man whose personal conflicts have caused him to be called "the Hamlet of the Congo." He seems to be strongly anti-Communist. It was he who ordered the diplomats, technicians, and doctors of the Eastern bloc states to get out of the Congo. He is not anti-European, and saved the lives of many Belgians during the disorders.

Mobutu's Congo National Army is still not a disciplined and reliable organization, but with it he does more or less control Leopoldville and Equator Provinces, and supports Kasavubu as the legal head of state recognized by the United Nations. In many places, the Congo National Army is unpaid and mutinous and split into quarreling factions. Mobutu is said to control about 7,500 men, while Moise Tshombe in Katanga has a well-trained private army of about 5,000 men under the command of about 150 Belgian officers and noncoms. The third major military force reflecting the crazy-quilt of the country's political and tribal divisions is the approximately 7,500 men controlled by the pro-Communist Stanleyville regime of Lumumba's heir, Antoine Gizenga.

The future of the young Republic of the Congo remains more uncertain than that of the other young nations on the African continent. What happened there, shouldn't have happened. The Congolese and especially the Belgians have left themselves open to strong criticism for the events that unfolded in the Congo. History will not spare Belgium the criticism of having left the Africans fully unprepared for independence. This preparation was necessary, and the French and English colonies were thoroughly prepared.

Ernest Kobbert wrote in the *Frankfurter Allgemeinen Zeitung:* "If anyone has to be called guilty, then it is the colonial Belgians themselves. . . . For too long they were content with the barefaced paternalistic administration of the colony and economic penetration; for too long they put aside all thoughts of preparing for evolution to independence. The lashing of natives was only forbidden just before World War II. . . . Only a few years ago was racial segregation done away with in the capital of Leopoldville. . . ."

To the credit of the Congolese, I must note that there was never any pronounced hostility to foreigners in the Congo. I traveled thousands of miles for days on end, most of the time completely alone with Negroes, and they were always good friends and ready to help. All of which makes it so regrettable that the young country so quickly lost the trust and respect of world public opinion.

The crisis in the Belgian Congo seems to have paved the way for a new phase in African history—"for many generations, work and reparation in such measure that it seems to make taking sides in the East-West conflict old-fashioned." (Benno von Reifenberg.) If the Belgians have lost considerably in reputation, it is because the transition to independence in the other African countries went off as planned. Certainly there are basic differences between West and Central Africa. But they are not decisive. In the countries administered by the British, for example, the Africans for years—for generations, were accustomed to the execution of responsible offices and because of this they were prepared when they received power and were careful not to misuse it. The preparation of a colony for independence requires time, a lot of work, and a complicated technique—otherwise there is anarchy.

15

FULBERT YOULOU OF THE REPUBLIC OF THE CONGO

A Priest Becomes President

᛭

Until September 1958, French Equatorial Africa was a huge land (pop. 4,436,000; 969,111 sq. miles), four times the size of Texas, ruled from its capital, Brazzaville (pop. 107,000) by a French governor-general. When the people of its four territories voted *oui* to General de Gaulle's new constitution for the Fifth French Republic, and its offer to join the French Community, the land was divided into four republics on September 28, 1958: Republic of the Congo (capital, Pointe Noire; pop. 760,000; 138,000 sq. miles); Chad (capital, Fort Lamy; pop. 2,750,000; 495,000 sq. miles); Gabon (capital, Libreville; pop. 403,000; 103,000 sq. miles); and the Central African Republic (capital, Bangui; pop. 1,130,000; 241,000 sq. miles).

For a long time, I have had a special affection for *Afrique Équatoriale Française*. I have traveled through it, lived and made many friends there.

European missionaries began to open up A.E.F. in the 18th century. France purchased its first territory there in 1839. Just as an Englishman, Stanley, acquired the Belgian Congo for Belgium, another foreigner, in this case an Italian, founded a colonial empire for France. He was Count Pierre Savorgnan de Brazza (1852–1905). A federal organization of four territories was formed, known as French Equatorial Africa, in 1910. But this land, so far from France, was the stepchild of French colonial policy. The funds to support it were always too small; there was always poverty, suffering, and unemployment. The experts were all the more surprised when France granted A.E.F.—which is five times as large as France itself—internal autonomy so quickly and regrouped it into four states independent of one another. I spoke about this to many leading French officials and asked: "Couldn't you have held off independence for a while?" The reply: "After all that de Gaulle promised, we couldn't do it. We had to grant A.E.F. its right to sovereignty."

The development of the former province of Middle Congo into the Republic of the Congo is closely tied up with the story of one of the most unique personalities in Africa: the former *abbé* and present president Fulbert Youlou—"black Christ" and politician of very independent stamp. He is the most colorful of the four heads of state of French Equatorial Africa.

Fulbert Youlou was born on June 9, 1917 in Moumbouolo (Brazzaville District), the son of a trader of the Ballali tribe. After studying at elementary schools in the French Congo, he entered a Catholic seminary in Akono, French Cameroon. He completed his studies for the priesthood in Brazzaville, was ordained in 1946, and became a parish priest in the Brazzaville and Mindouli dioceses. In 1955 he was defrocked for having broken several of his vows. It is said that he was forbidden ever again to wear priest's garments. Nobody in Brazzaville knows whether this is true or not. The Church itself keeps its silence on the issue, and also expresses no opinion on the widespread rumor that Youlou has been excommunicated. In any case, he still wears his white cassock and uses the title of *abbé*. His hand is adorned with a huge ring, normally worn only by archbishops. He occasionally likes to be addressed as *Monseigneur,* although he holds more than enough other important titles and offices.

Fulbert Youlou is officially unmarried, but he appears to have many wives and numerous children. The most remarkable rumors about him make the rounds in Brazzaville. Even his closest French advisers keep silent when one tries to learn something of his private life and his relationship with the Catholic Church. In general, the Europeans in the Republic of the Congo don't like him. The Catholics regard him as a traitor, while the others say he is immoral.

Like many short men, Fulbert Youlou is suspicious and vain. It is difficult to carry on a rational conversation with him because he is quite nervous and moreover scents envy, treason, and disloyalty everywhere. It is also practically impossible to receive from him a clear answer to a direct question. But he doesn't take offense when visitors ply him with troublesome questions. He even has a sense of humor.

After Youlou was relieved of his priestly functions, he decided to enter politics. In 1956, he founded the Democratic Union for Defense of African interests (UDDIA). In November of the same year he was elected mayor of Brazzaville, an office he still holds, and then a municipal counselor. His party became the local division of the African Democratic Rally (RDA), an important collective movement that sought to group all races and religions in French West Africa into a united front.

In the elections of 1957, Youlou's party won only 22 of the 45 seats, while the Socialists won 23. The clever Youlou, however, was able to win over one of his opponents, so that when the provisional government of the Republic of the Congo was formed in November 1958, the UDDIA had a majority of one. This one vote was enough to make Youlou's party the ruling party and himself prime minister in December 1958. From May 1957 to December 1958, he was minister of agriculture, and also deputy to the provisional Legislative Assembly of the Congo. As prime minister he was charged with justice and foreign affairs. In the voting for the Legislative Assembly in June 1959, his party won 51 of the 61 seats, and on November 21, 1959, he was unanimously elected president of the Republic by the Legislative Assembly.

President, prime minister, foreign minister, mayor of Brazzaville, president of the ruling party—the defrocked priest today holds in his hands considerable power. He has even succeeded in winning the respect of de Gaulle's government. Certainly, without French support he could never have come to power so quickly. Nevertheless, his rise is worthy of admiration. It's true that many have harsh words to say about him. In this connection, he himself has often said that his "life portrait fluctuates with history." But one must say in his defense that he had to build a new state from the ground up with the help of only a small group of trained administrators. He has never lacked for courage, which can also be said for him. Moreover, he always carries a pistol under his cassock—another indication of his individuality.

An adventurous episode took place in the weeks immediately following the founding of the Republic of the Congo. Pointe Noire (pop. 55,000), a port on the Atlantic, was named capital. Youlou had few supporters there, since it wasn't his tribal area. One day, when the burden of tribal contention became too heavy, he had his official papers, family, household effects, and closest co-workers loaded into a railway car of the Pointe Noire–Brazzaville line. He had some heavily armed soldiers stationed on the car, and went racing off through the Mayombe mountains. Upon his arrival, he said: "Pointe Noire may be the capital, but I'm the head of state, and I'm going to rule from Brazzaville." And he still does today. The most important government offices are in Pointe Noire, but the president lives and works in Brazzaville, the old capital of French Equatorial Africa.

The young republic's first years were critical. It was difficult to rule effectively with a one-vote majority. The opposition, lead by Jacques Obangault and his *Mouvement Socialiste Africain* (MSA), had no intention of coming to terms with "the *abbé's* dictatorship." Tribal warfare broke out on February 16, 1959 in the outskirts of Brazzaville. The *abbé's* supporters, the Ballali, live principally in Bacongo (not to be confused with the province of Bakongo in the former Belgian Congo); Obangault's, the M'Bochi and Batékés, in Poto-Poto (pop. 65,000). The Ballali around Brazzaville number about 60,000; the M'Bochi and Batékés, around

30,000. There are also a number of smaller tribes, who support one or another of the main tribes.

As one of the few Europeans living in Poto-Poto, I saw the political situation becoming ominous early in February 1959. Then, one afternoon, the opposition party held a meeting, and some harsh words were said about the government. Many M'Bochi and Batékés took this as a summons to attack the Ballali. The houses of the Ballili in Poto-Poto and Bacongo were set on fire. Men, women, and children—most of them completely unpolitical —were killed or severely wounded. The Ballali were caught by surprise, but quickly struck back. The Ballali from Bacongo, and another two thousand from the jungle, organized. A tribal war— in which mostly old-style weapons were used—broke out, like those that had raged before the arrival of the Europeans.

My house in Poto-Poto was right in the center of the action. The few Europeans in Poto-Poto were ordered to Brazzaville by the police. Thousands of people began to migrate. The Ballali from Poto-Poto headed toward Bacongo; the M'Bochi from Bacongo toward Poto-Poto. Thousands of Africans sought refuge in the European quarters of Brazzaville. Families camped out in every garden. Many had fled out of fear. For days on end, Poto-Poto and Bacongo were ghost towns; only a few dogs roamed their deserted streets. Soon more than two hundred dead and four hundred wounded were reported.

It was fortunate that many Frenchmen still lived in Brazzaville. Trustfully, the Africans went to them and were given assistance. The military, the French, and Africans tried to stop the warring tribes, but it was difficult in this medieval-type warfare. The army behaved extremely well, and did not use its weapons once. We European civilians worked at the Red Cross and tried to help in every way possible. The victims were as horribly mutilated as those of the Mau-Mau. Police investigations determined that the civilized Negroes had not taken part in these outrages, that they were the work of "savages" from the jungle. The latter had been steamed up by irresponsible politicians, sorcerers, and medicine men to murder in the name of their tribes, often for irrational reasons. I never met a single Ballali or M'Bochi who understood the reasons for this gruesome slaughter, or approved of it. It was "murder in ecstasy."

The spark that kindled the blaze was dissatisfaction with Fulbert Youlou, who continued to put off elections that should have taken place long before. He explained that the whole thing was only "a family quarrel." He added, rather laconically: "One can't hold elections while a civil war is going on." (In previous years, bloody tribal battles had taken place in Brazzaville, Dolisie, and Pointe Noire.)

Although one must pity its victims, one should not make too much of this young republic's tribal warfare, or dramatize the tribal clashes that take place everywhere in Africa today. They are symptoms of growing pains, transitory, comparable to the wars that raged among the small European states centuries ago. They will still break out here and there in Africa for years to come, but will become more infrequent as the influence of the pan-African politicians grows. Shortly after the warfare in Poto-Poto and Bacongo, André Blanchet, a man who knows African conditions, wrote in *Marchés Tropicaux:* "As long as political divisions are based on tribal lines, the map of Africa won't be receptive to any changes worth mentioning." This opinion is slowly being shared not only by the politicians in the Congo, but in all the other African nations.

It is important to note that the uprising of the Ballali and the M'Bochi, which took place a few weeks after the uprising in Leopoldville, had nothing in common with it. On the south bank of the Congo, Africans fought with Europeans; on the north bank Africans fought among themselves. In the Belgian Congo, after the fighting, the whites were hated more than ever, and the Belgians were compelled to grant the Congolese quick independence. On the French side of the Congo River, the wise and patient behavior of the whites gained them greater esteem than they had ever before enjoyed.

I have always regarded the former French Congo as a home away from home, and during those critical months, I gained a great deal of insight into the conditions there. When the white man holds firm to his Christian and humanist ideals, he will be treasured by the African as a friend, a counselor, a helper of the first rank. When the Republic of the Congo formed a new cabinet, in which the opposition party took part, the Africans voluntarily agreed to include three Frenchmen as state secretaries. These Frenchmen—and Africans I questioned about this—told me that they co-operated in an atmosphere of complete harmony and that racial questions never came up for discussion. A considerable difference from the Belgian Congo!

Fulbert Youlou, president and prime minister of a country slightly smaller than Montana, has always been a supporter of close association with France. But he, and the other new leaders in French Equatorial Africa, have taken steps which have wrought great changes in the original 1958 concept of the French Community.

On May 16–17, 1960, in Fort Lamy, Youlou and the prime ministers of Chad and the Central African Republic decided to create a Union of Central African Republics which would seek complete independence. The Union would remain a member of the French Community, but would have transferred to it the powers exercised by the Community. Gabon, richest of the four states of former French Equatorial Africa, decided to seek individual independence, but not to join the proposed Union, perhaps fearing the burden that the three poorer states would place upon it. The four states had earlier established a customs union and an economic federation "in which merchandise, capital, and property would circulate freely."

The French Parliament and the Senate of the French Community adopted a law on June 4, 1960, making it possible for member states to become independent without leaving the community. Agreements were signed in Paris on July 12, providing for the independence within the French Community of Chad, the Central African Republic, and the Republic of the Congo; agreements for Gabon were signed on July 15. The first three, however, received their independence as individual states, reversing their earlier decision to seek independence as members of a single Union.

On August 15, 1960, in Brazzaville, Youlou proclaimed the independence of the Republic of the Congo; the new state was admitted to the United Nations on September 20, 1960, under French sponsorship.

President Youlou said that independence had been achieved "in peace, friendship, and complete agreement with France, to whom we express our gratitude and affection." He added that "our thoughts turn towards General de Gaulle, the man of Brazzaville, the glorious creator of our freedom and independence." Through André Malraux, Minister of State, who was present at the independence ceremonies, de Gaulle sent his best wishes.

Youlou, in his independence day speech, had this to say about his future relationship with France: "This, gentlemen, is what the Congo is and what it must be: a harmonious synthesis of two civilizations, one of which is rooted deep in this Africa—eternal, massive, but so varied nonetheless—land of broad savannas, deep forests, immense rivers that cause us to live close to the very sources of our life; the other is French civilization, which has itself sprung from the various origins out of which modern France has grown. . . .

"At the very time that our independence is proclaimed—which means in particular that we are going to have our own army and our own diplomacy—we have been anxious to reaffirm our attachment to the renovated Community in order that France may continue to give us her technical and material assistance and that we may harmonize the broad lines of our policies within a great ensemble, with a common language, culture and sentiments."

Although the Union of Central African Republics fell through, at least for the present, Fulbert Youlou's political dream seems to be to make Brazzaville the seat of a federal parliament. Perhaps he was already dreaming of this as he raced in a diesel train with his official documents, family, and parliamentarians through the three hundred miles of mountainous jungle from Pointe Noire to Brazzaville.

16

AHMADOU AHIDJO

Cameroon on the Brink of Anarchy

⁂

Germany's West African colony of Kamerun was split up after World War I, and its administration turned over to France and Great Britain by the League of Nations Mandate Commission, a system continued by the Trusteeship Council of the United Nations. The British Cameroons (34,081 sq. miles; pop. about 1,620,000) were administered from adjoining Nigeria. The French Cameroons, by far the bigger slice, slightly larger than California (166,800 sq. miles; pop. around 3,400,000) achieved independence as the Cameroon Republic, or *État du Cameroun,* on January 1, 1960.

The French Cameroons had strong ties with France during World War II. After French Equatorial Africa, it was the second French African territory to join General de Gaulle. It received its internal autonomy through the *loi-cadre* (skeleton law, or enabling act) of 1956, and its first native government in 1957.

The African Democratic Rally (RDA), which has been mentioned in the previous chapter, became Cameroon's leading party, and out of it developed the *Union des Populations Camerounaises* (UPC). The RDA, founded by Dr. Félix Houphouet-Boigny of the Ivory Coast, originally had strong Communist tendencies. The Great Soviet Encyclopedia reported that the RDA was founded with "the active support of the French Communist Party." The RDA soon broke with the Communists, but the UPC continued its leftist course and was banned in 1955 as a "Communist cover organization."

The UPC was responsible for several bloody insurrections in 1955 and 1958. It was not until the winter of 1958/59 that its last military units (around two thousand men) were wiped out in the Sanaga-Maritime Province. Its president, Ruben Um Nyobé, was killed by a patrol on September 13, 1958. Though the UPC had been declared illegal, Nyobé chose to remain in Cameroon at all costs, even as a guerrilla. He represented a strong nationalism with a socialist base, and believed that his presence alone could ensure its success throughout the country. The pro-Communist leaders of the UPC fled to the British Cameroons, and, after being expelled, to Cairo. Financed by Cairo or Moscow—or both—Dr. Félix-Roland Moumie, Ernest Ouandié, Abel Kingue, and Ahama Ossende began a violent propaganda campaign against the British and French administration of their trust territories.

United Nations commissions visited Cameroon and investigated the complaints of the UPC politicians. The delegates found that the UPC pamphlets and its petition to the UN contained misrepresentations and falsehoods. Nevertheless, the widely-distributed UPC propaganda shook confidence in the government and the French trust administration.

One of these brochures was called *L'UPC Dénonce L'Erection des Tortures en Système au Kamerun*. The accusation was grave. Like many others in Cameroon, I tried to find out the truth of the matter. I hesitate to give extracts from this brochure, but it must be quoted from if we are to understand why there is a permanent state of unrest in Cameroon.

Tortures and other atrocities are given detailed description. Some examples: tortures practiced by the police, the *gendarmerie,* and in "concentration camps" are described in a letter from Dzukam Chrétien to the attorney general. The most gruesome methods of repression are also described, such as soldiers—ostensibly from the "Franco-African Community"—burning 250 people to death in the small village of Ekite in Sanaga-Maritime. "For three days the soldiers stood guard and shot down everyone who attempted to flee." Women and children were allegedly tortured in the most horrible fashion. Around 130 children under fifteen, some under five, were jailed in Douala New-Bell and Douala Akwa. "Police headquarters in Douala Bonandjo was not to be outdone in showing how cruel it could be to prisoners. M. Cau, the examining magistrate, declared that it was normal for a prisoner to be given a hundred lashes in a single day. Other prisoners were forced to kneel on files and nails for from five to eight hours daily. . . . In Loum, Father Bernard shot a pregnant woman and a schoolboy who had obeyed his priestly summons; neither the French administration nor the Church has been able to deny that this happened. They also have made no protest about it."

On July 4, 1958, the UPC in Cairo petitioned the International Red Cross to investigate the political situation in Cameroon. It is a lasting pity that the IRC has not had the time to examine all of the events that have unfolded in Cameroon since May 1955. On April 10, 1948, the people had founded a powerful nationalist movement—the UPC. Despite the fact that the status of Cameroon was guaranteed by the United Nations, the French trust administration did not hesitate to use force when it felt its authority weakening. And so it came to the bloody massacres which have claimed at least five thousand victims since May 1955. The protests of the nationalists being ignored, open warfare broke out after the "show elections" of December 1956.

A protest to the General Assembly of the United Nations was followed by newspaper reports from Cameroon, France, and the United States in which one could perceive the bloody course of events. It was no longer a question of maintaining public order, but of warfare by France against a people entrusted to it by the UN. A proposal by the Indian UN delegate, Krishna Menon, to investigate the situation was not followed up, although the UPC expressed confidence that the UN would eventually uncover the crimes that were being committed in Cameroon. The International Red Cross was asked to send an investigating committee, since the country did not come under the jurisdiction of Article II of the UN Charter.

Reverend Michael Scott, fearless spokesman for the rights of Africans, appeared before the United Nations to speak for the Herero tribe of Southwest Africa.

Chief Albert Luthuli, President of the African National Congress of the Union of South Africa.

Joseph Kasavubu (right) first President of the former Belgian Congo Republic, listens to Senator Jonas Fele, of Stanleyville.

Moise Tshombe, Prime Minister of Katanga Province, Congo Republic.

President Fulbert Youlou of the (former French) Republic of the Congo, in white cassock, with France's President de Gaulle, Jacques Soustelle (smoking) and Prime Minister Houphouet-Boigny of the Republic of the Ivory Coast. Behind the latter is Premier Debré of France.

President Ahmadou Ahidjo, of the Cameroon Republic votes in election. His wife looks on.

Nigeria's Prime Minister Abubakar Tafawa Balewa, left,
meets Soviet Premier Khrushchev in New York during
United Nations General Assembly meeting, October,
1960.

Women are becoming a decisive factor in the Africans' struggle
for freedom. They have the right to vote in all independent
nations. Below, election in Republic of the Congo (Brazzaville).

The IRC investigating committee was freely permitted by the UPC to visit six French prisoners, and finally arrived at the conclusion that in Cameroon it was a matter of a "liberation army," and not of "terrorists" or "rebels." "For eight years, the Vietnamese were officially described as rebels. They lost this derogatory name for the first time when they administered a bitter defeat to the French Forces at Dien Bien Phu."

The first premier of Cameroon when it received internal autonomy was André-Marie M'Bida, founder of the *Parti Démocrate Chrétien* (PDC), who resigned after clashing with the French high commissioner. His successor was Ahmadou Ahidjo, who was premier when the country became independent on January 1, 1960, and who was elected president of the republic on May 5, 1960. Like the late Patrice Lumumba, Ahidjo was a post office employee. He was born in 1924 in Garoua, in the Benoué Region. After primary and secondary school, he attended the *École Supérieure d'Administration* in Yaoundé, the capital (pop. about 40,000). He worked in a telegraph office and distinguished himself during the Second World War as a radio operator.

The industrious young man became interested in politics and was elected to the *Assemblée Répresentative du Caméroun* in 1947 as deputy from the Benoué Region. He became general secretary and then president of the administrative division and finally vice-president of the whole Assembly. In October 1955, he became *Conseiller de l'Assemblée* of the French Union, and after the elections of December 23, 1956, president by acclamation of the Territorial Assembly of Cameroon. He now began to exert a decisive influence in the debates over a new statute for Cameroon.

On May 16, 1957, Ahidjo became deputy premier and minister for internal affairs in the first administration. After M'Bida's resignation, he was asked to form a second administration, and then was elected its premier. He is also president of the *Mouvement d'Union Camerounaise*. This party, like President Youlou's in the Republic of the Congo, has close connections with the African

Democratic Rally. The latter is the largest West African collective people's movement, and is one of the cornerstones of General de Gaulle's African policies.

The thirty-seven year old Ahmadou Ahidjo appears to be younger than he is. He looks more like a young teacher than a president. He is a Moslem, and usually wears a colorful cap and a white or colored robe, the preferred costume of many Cameroonian natives. His pleasant laugh is disarming. His speech is unhurried and almost without passion. He still retains numerous French advisers, who, as they told me, had "trained crown princes" in other places. Ahidjo's most striking qualities are his common sense and his industry.

In order to understand Cameroon's problems and objectives, let us read a few sections from speeches given by its head of state. Speaking before Cameroon's Legislative Assembly on February 18, 1958, Ahmadou Ahidjo said:

"As I have repeatedly declared, we must realize the indispensable connection between tradition and progress in such a way that neither feels unjustly held back, or that the first fears that it will be irrevocably dissolved by the second. . . . If development is the country's major concern, tradition represents reason and experience—it is our history; to ignore the past would mean that we would remain children eternally. There can never be any question of reforming the traditional framework by force. . . . The structure of every country's institutions must always accord with its economic and social environment. . . .

"Our duty is to preserve what is viable and healthy in our traditional institutions. It would be regrettable for the whole country if the cadres, who are daily giving evidence of their vigour—and I am especially thinking of those in North Cameroon, which I know well—should be seized by a wave of reforms which find their justification only in the superfluous desire to create something new."

In this same speech, Ahamadou Ahidjo defined his conception

of democracy: "If certain people contrast us with a starry-eyed picture of democracy, we will not hesitate to reply to them that a literal imitation of the systems of the European countries is not always suitable for Africa. African democracy, too, is not without magnanimity, and the work of numerous sociologists has helped us to find again in our customs those methods which the West often discovered after us. In our time, our conception of democracy lies much more in the recognition of the worth of the individual and in offering to everyone the possibility of satisfying his essential needs than in more or less skillfully worked out legal formulas that will collapse in the first breeze."

Ahmadou Ahidjo spoke before the General Assembly of the United Nations about the general situation in Cameroon, the Opposition, and the civil war unleashed by the UPC. The UPC was charged with the same acts of violence of which it had accused the French and the national administration.

"The General Assembly of the United Nations knows our difficulties well. It has been told of the events of May 1955, when certain political groups tried to stir up bloody disorders. After these outbreaks, those who had incited them fled over the borders or into the forests of Sanaga-Maritime. When the responsible authorities determined that these groups had ceased to operate within the law, they were outlawed by the decree of July 13, 1955. These groups continued their activities from hiding or from abroad. When it was decided in December 1956 to hold elections for a renovation of the Territorial Assembly, the supporters of the UPC increased their agitation, in which they attempted to paralyze every peaceful political development by force. . . . In the eyes of public opinion, their supporters were only a tiny group, and their disappointment was especially great when all the nationalist movements decided to take part in the elections.

"It appeared that these party leaders had nothing in mind but an armed revolt. They decided to form a para-military organization to fight by force of arms those of their countrymen who resisted their actions or denied them aid. They carried out sabotage, burned houses, plundered villages, and wounded, or murdered in a terrible fashion, Cameroonians. Among the victims were two candidates for election: a doctor and a lumber contractor. A third, who is now a representative in the Legislative Assembly, escaped with his life only by a lucky coincidence.

"Military intervention was necessary to restore order. The attacks ceased. Prisoners were brought to justice and sentenced. In September 1957, the extreme agitators took advantage of the withdrawal of the police troops to re-organize and, despite the appeals of the government of Cameroon, a new series of attacks took place in Sanaga-Maritime. . . . At the same time, armed bands, who seemed to have been trained along the borders of neighboring countries, began to commit crimes. Among their victims was Samuel Wanko, a member of the Legislative Assembly, a young engineer with a promising future. Security measures had to be taken to protect the civil population; villages especially had to be re-grouped in order to assure their safety.

"There was a lot said about reprisals, a state of war in Cameroon, concentration camps, bombings, tanks, and thousands of soldiers employed in the counter-action. We have a very high opinion of your organization. We are too well aware of the earnestness and the moral stand of the United Nations to let ourselves be talked into a discussion of these accusations, which are so obviously laughable to any impartial observer who knows— or has known—the situation in Cameroon. When the United Nations sends its delegates into those countries which stand under its protection to get a detailed picture of their political situation, I think that the UN does this in order to judge their findings, so that it won't have to rely on political pamphlets.

"We directed appeals to the rebels to end the civil war and return to their villages. We promised immunity to those who had been led astray, and impartial, un-political justice before the law to those who had committed crimes. The results of this patient and constructive action of the Cameroon government were remarkable. I am happy to be able to say that hundreds from the

Sanaga-Maritime responded to our appeal to cease fighting; their number is increasing daily. I am especially happy that among them are many leaders and supporters of the illegal action, who became convinced through the work of the Cameroon authorities that they had previously been living in error. . . .

"Let us hope that those others who have been led astray will come to us! After these disorders and futile acts of violence, after the loss of so many youths who comprised our elite and on whom the land thought it could count, our people now desire work and peace. If many ask for amnesty for the guilty ones, it is principally because they want to see an end to terrorism, sentences of death, the lies and the hate campaigns. . . . We extend a brotherly hand to those who voluntarily chose to place themselves outside the Cameroonian community. We want all families of Cameroon to take part in the building up of Cameroon in peace, unity, and work."

During his first official visit to the port city and important commercial center of Douala, Ahmadou Ahidjo emphasized his determination to work for re-unification of the French and British Cameroons.

"The unity of the Cameroons is the first ideal goal that we set for ourselves. Because of this, I ask all inhabitants of the Cameroons to unite in a spirit of harmony and mutual understanding. I am certain that the moment seems to have come, and not only for the most reasonable among us, to free ourselves from these terrible tribal battles, from these pernicious separatist ideas, from this exaggerated regionalism. Although thinking about this 'Balkanization' of our homeland arouses our indignation, at the same time we feel a desire to pardon this aberration and go on to pursue the task of re-uniting all the inhabitants of the Cameroons. . . . In this connection, I am of the opinion that every native of Cameroon should feel like a brother toward each of his fellow citizens.

"These efforts to re-unite the Cameroons, which my govern-

ment intends to bring to reality, are not limited to the present
boundaries of the trusteeship territory of the State of Cameroon.
For this reason, I took up, during my inauguration, a positive
position for the re-unification of both sections of the Cameroons.
I also discussed this problem with the responsible leaders of
France, when I was in Paris . . . for another of our ideal goals
is co-operation between France and Cameroon. The alliance with
France is indispensable for the realization of our goals. . . . We
can only proclaim or experience one hundred per cent the actual
solidarity that is being created between our two countries if we
join together in a French-inter-African union, in which genuine
friendship will be fulfilled just as much as freedom. Although
our efforts should concentrate on the attempt to materialize the
three ideals, 'The Cameroon Nation,' 'Cameroon Unity,' and
'French-Cameroon Co-Operation,' we should not forget our other
problems and the necessity for solving them. . . ."

On March 13, 1959, a special Cameroonian session of the UN
General Assembly, after hearing the report of a UN mission that
had visited Cameroon in the fall of 1958, approved the ending
of the French trusteeship and Cameroon's accession to independence. This was officially proclaimed in Yaoundé on January 1,
1960. The Cameroon Republic became the eleventh independent
African state and the first UN trust territory to receive its independence. Because of this, Dag Hammarskjöld appeared at the
ceremonies. Others in attendance were Henry Cabot Lodge, representing President Eisenhower, and Mr. Firubin, the Soviet deputy
foreign minister.

Hammarskjöld thanked France for its important contributions
to the social and political development of the territory. M. Louis
Jacquinot, minister of state in the Debré government, recalled
the friendly cooperation that had existed between France and
Cameroon, without attempting to deny the political problems that
had arisen. Ahidjo took up these problems. Only a few days before he had had to declare a state of emergency in eleven of the

twenty-one departments of the country. Part of the Bamiliké tribal area was in complete chaos. With great earnestness—no one saw him smile once during the independence celebrations—Ahidjo once again asked his opponents to end the civil war and co-operate with the government.

His provisional government could soon point to a string of successes. On January 26, 1960, Cameroon was admitted to the UN. A referendum was held in late February, in which the electorate was asked to vote on a new constitution. Despite appeals by the UPC to boycott the referendum, 77 per cent of the registered voters went to the polls and approved the constitution by a majority of 65 per cent.

On February 26, the government abrogated the French decree of July 1955 banning the UPC and its affiliated organizations. This move was a foreign policy success for Ahidjo. Ghana, Guinea, and Liberia recognized the Cameroon Republic, which they had not done before because of the influence of the UPC abroad.

On April 10, the first general elections for the National Assembly were held. Ahidjo's *Union Camerounaise* won 60 seats; the UPC, 22; the Democratic Party, 11; Moderates, 2; and eleven seats went to other opposition parties. On May 5, 1960, Ahidjo was elected president of the republic by the National Assembly, with powers comparable to those of the president of France.

Cameroon achieved its independence in a bloodbath. In December 1959, the English journalist Colin Legum (author of *Must We Lose Africa?*) wrote that the Cameroonian civil war had taken on a Mau-Mau character. Legum travelled throughout the country under French military protection, and came to the conclusion that between three and five thousand Cameroonians had been killed in the past five years (his figures confirmed the allegations of the UPC). At the end of 1959, many Europeans were killed.

During the independence day celebrations in the capital, Yaoundé, and in the port city of Douala, there were bloody outbreaks as the rebels went about swinging clubs and razor-sharp *pangas.* Shortly before Ahidjo flew into Douala with his honored guests, the rebels attacked the airport. The urgent appeal of Ahidjo that it was senseless for the nation to be "born in blood" went unheeded, as did his hint that this was no way to win confidence in the country, that foreign capital would vanish unless order was restored. (The EDEA Aluminum Works is France's most important industrial enterprise. It is capable of producing 45,000 tons of aluminum a year, and puts Cameroon in eighth place among the world's aluminum producers.)

The Opposition, represented mostly by the largest tribe, the Bamiliké, had no thought of abandoning its intimidation. The Opposition accused Ahidjo more violently than before of handing over the country to France. Old grudges played a part in this. The UPC was the first party to demand independence and reunification of the French and British Cameroons. Now the country had become independent, but the UPC leaders were in exile or hiding. Ahidjo put his hopes on the small contingent of French troops stationed in Cameroon. It soon became clear, however, that the rebels had received Czech arms, were better equipped than before, and that the government was powerless to suppress them. Terrorism increased; each day brought new attacks, wounded and dead. On February 22, 1960, eighty people, including 24 women and 37 children, were burned and hacked to death by young Bamiliké tribesmen in Dschang. The Opposition even succeeded in winning over other countries—at least for its propaganda purposes.

Dr. Félix-Roland Moumie, president of the UPC, and leader of its Marxist wing, broadcast from exile over Radio Ghana that his party planned to form a "provisional government of the revolutionary forces" on the model of the provisional government of the Algerian Republic, whose ministers would reside in Cameroon or abroad. He demanded the immediate withdrawal of all French troops, unconditional amnesty for the UPC, release of all political

internees, and postponement of the general elections from April
to July 1960.

In further speeches and announcements, Moumie admitted that
his followers were responsible for the terrorism in Cameroon. He
claimed a following of fifty thousand "active fighters" and many
hundreds of thousands of "silent fighters" in Cameroon. Tri-
umphantly, he announced that his former opponent, ex-premier
M'Bida, although a Catholic and anti-Communist, had joined forces
with him, because the latter had come to believe that only the extreme wing of the UPC could save the country.

Moumie further declared that he himself was a Marxist-Lenin-
ist, that Mao Tse-Tung and Ho Chi Minh were his models, and
that he would carry on the fight in their spirits. (Moumie had
visited Moscow and Peking repeatedly.) He called for a "total
economic boycott"; the businesses of those who did not contribute
to the UPC were to be paralyzed, another parallel to the Algerian
rebels. Another Moumie slogan: "Take money wherever you can
find it!" Banks and cash registers were to be plundered regularly, and no taxes paid in order to cripple the government.
Finally, Moumie attacked those more moderate UPC leaders who
presented themselves as candidates in the first general elections,
after the ban on the party had been lifted, and claimed to be the
legitimate heirs to the party as it had existed before it had been
outlawed. Moumie threatened that "revolutionary justice will deal
with them."

These were not empty threats. Ahidjo was hardly in a position
to be able to combat them effectively. The means at the disposal
of this "darling of the French," as he is called, were—and are—
limited. Cameroon needs a prudent, experienced elder statesman,
and not a representative of the small bureaucracy, of the African
small middle class, who—because of his religion—can rely only
on a group of Moslem feudal chiefs in the north. French arms were
a decisive support for him after independence. But what will happen when the French forces leave? A police force of 2,000 proved
incapable of coping with the situation before. President Ahidjo

would willingly bring additional French military forces into the country, but even his most loyal followers are against this.

And the programs of the many different political parties? They are hazy, fanatical, without rational motives. And the intelligentsia? They are few and far between in Cameroon and also have no clear program. Let us keep in mind that many promising youths were killed in the five-year civil war. The greatest human loss was the leader of the nationalist wing of the UPC, Ruben Um Nyobé, which even opponents of the UPC admit. A certain hope lies in the moderates within the UPC, who now form the "legal Opposition" in the National Assembly. Their leader is Théodore Mayi Matip, Nyobé's last trusted lieutenant in the active rebellion that raged in the Sanaga-Maritime chiefly from September 1957 to September 1958. Matip is for a "constructive opposition," and a *"force de réconciliation."* He is also for a nationalism without pronounced leftist tendencies. Perhaps he may be able to work out a compromise with Ahidjo's government that will avert another catastrophe at the last minute.

The tasks of the moderates would seem to have been made easier by the removal from the political scene of the pro-Communist, anti-French Félix-Roland Moumie. He was admitted to a Geneva hospital following a small dinner party on October 16, 1960. He died there, at the age of 34, on November 3. Tests at the Medico-Legal Institute in Zürich showed that he had been poisoned by thallium, a substance used in rat poison. The circumstances of his death remain a mystery, although it has been alleged that he was poisoned by the "Red Hand," a French organization engaged in counter-terrorist activities against the Algerian rebels.

It is necessary here to mention the British Cameroons. What will eventually become of this area is, for the moment, unclear. The Cameroon National Congress wants the trust territory to remain a part of Nigeria. The Cameroon National Democratic Party, which evolved out of the Congress Party, wants complete self-government, separated from Nigeria, and even a union with French Cameroon. But as the last British governor-general of Nigeria, Sir James Robertson, assured me, these plans change constantly.

Soon after the proclamation of independence of French Cameroon, John Ngu Foncha (b. 1916), leader of the government in the British Cameroons, asked Ahidjo's government to co-operate with him in bringing about the unification of the Cameroons. He proposed that both areas consult each other in international questions. In the meantime, the United Nations decided to hold a plebiscite sometime between September 1960 and March 1961, in which the people of the British Cameroons could vote on remaining a part of Nigeria or joining French Cameroon.

The desire of the Cameroonians for re-unification is understandable. They once lived in unity, even though the boundaries were of cultural construction. Other nations of the world, for example in Europe—say the Cameroonians—are an expression of cultural boundaries, and they have no thought now of dissolving themselves into small nations, duchies and principalities. However, many difficulties stand in the way of making re-unification a reality. In the first place, the Cameroonians still do not have any feeling of belonging to a single nation or community, as do the Nigerians. They think of themselves principally as members of a tribe, of which there are many—Bantu, Fulbe, Hausa, etc. They are further divided into Moslems, pagan animists, and Christians. And each ethnical or religious group seeks advantages for itself first of all.

Since the World War I division of the Cameroons, each area has developed differently, on the French or British political pattern. Foncha is a devout Catholic; Ahidjo a devout Moslem. In one area the youth grows up speaking French, in the other English. Problems arise from this one fact alone. What should be the official language of a re-united Cameroon? And what should be the official currency, the colonial franc or the West African pound? The same problems stand in the way of the re-unification of Togoland, another German colony that was partitioned by the League

of Nations. When I mentioned this problem to African politicians, they told me: "That is exactly why we are for Pan-Africa, so
that these language, boundary and other problems of secondary
importance will no longer carry great weight." Pan-Africa, however, is still a long way off, but chances do exist for a re-unification
of the Cameroons. As in Togoland, tribes and families are not only
separated, but literally individual families and their landed property. And it is in these areas that there is a permanent "land
hunger," which is why the situation of the Bamiliké has been compared to that of the Kikuyu in Kenya. Perhaps re-unification will
be accomplished under the pressure of these conditions.

In the meantime, independent Cameroon is living on the brink
of anarchy, under the permanent threat of total civil war. The
Communists are standing by, watching and waiting. In 1959, the
London *Economist* predicted that Cameroon could perhaps become
the first Communist African state, that it was in any case a fertile
hunting ground for the Communists. The Soviet Union and the
satellite countries have up to now appointed no diplomatic representatives to Cameroon. This can be taken as a sign that the Eastern bloc doesn't take the present government seriously, that it
regards it as a "puppet regime," and is waiting for the UPC to
triumph before becoming active.

Moumie made no secret of the fact that he wanted to make
Cameroon the first socialist country on the African continent. His
contacts with representatives of the Eastern bloc during his exile
in Conakry were as close as they were public. His deputy, and
probable successor, Ouandié, frequently visits the Eastern countries. An increasing number of UPC members are taking special
courses there. Moumie's followers have not only tied themselves
economically to the Eastern bloc, as has Guinea, but are quite prepared to serve as a bridgehead for Communism to enter Cameroon.

Cameroon is a small country on a huge continent. Ahmadou
Ahidjo is perhaps not a great statesman, but destiny has forced
him into a highly responsible position. The consolidation of

Ahidjo's regime, and the stabilization of the whole political situation, is a necessity not only for Cameroon, but for the whole Western world. If Cameroon is lost to the West, the East will fall heir to a base that should not be underestimated. Cameroon's Western neighbor, Nigeria, is in no danger of going Communist, but its neighbors to the North and West, the four states of former French Equatorial Africa, and even the former Belgian Congo, may well one day become Communist states. The Cameroon Republic today is called "a little Algeria." Can Ahmadou Ahidjo succeed, at the last minute, in finding a solution for its many problems?

17

FROM ABUBAKAR TO AHMADU

Five Statesmen of the Federation of Nigeria

⁕

On October 1, 1960, Africa's most populous country became a sovereign and independent state within the British Commonwealth. The Federation of Nigeria, with approximately 38 million people, dwarfs its West African neighbors like Ghana, Guinea, and the Ivory Coast. Its 374,000 square miles make it the size of Texas and Oklahoma combined, and larger in area than any European country except the Soviet Union.

In contrast to the bloodshed that accompanied the birthpangs of the Congo and Cameroon, and Guinea's abrupt defection from the French Community and drift toward Marxism, Nigeria's path to independence had been carefully prepared and the transfer of power was achieved in an atmosphere of order and stability. Nigeria seems to be an encouraging sign that democracy can work in Negro Africa.

Nigeria is a complex land made up of three separate regions and over two hundred different tribes. Northern Nigeria is by far the largest region (281,782 square miles, including the Northern Cameroons; pop. nearly 20 million; capital, Kaduna, pop. 50,000). Then come Western Nigeria (45,376 sq. miles; pop. around 8 million; capital, Ibadan, pop. 500,000); and Eastern Nigeria (29,484 sq. miles; pop. around 9 million; capital, Enegu, pop. 70,000). The Federal capital of Lagos, on the Atlantic, has a population of around 350,000. Non-Africans number only around 17,000 of the total population, and Nigeria, perhaps because of its climate (it was once known as "the white man's grave") has not had to contend with a white settler problem like British East Africa.

Nigeria has many active and varied political parties. The most important are represented by the prime minister and the three premiers of the Regions which comprise the Federation. These four personalities, and the leader of the Opposition, overshadow the other politicians and statesmen in Nigeria—although there are a number of capable men just behind them.

ALHAJI SIR ABUBAKAR TAFAWA BALEWA

The prime minister of Nigeria, Alhaji Sir Abubakar Tafawa Balewa, O.B.E., K.B.E., C.B.E., LL.D., is usually called simply Sir Abubakar. Tafawa Balewa is the name of the northern village where he was born—according to local custom and out of love for his homeland he later added it to his name. *Alhaji* is the prized title given to one who has been to Mecca; Sir Abubakar made his pilgrimage in 1957. He became prime minister of the Federation on August 30, 1957. He is also deputy president general of the country's largest political party, the Northern Peoples' Congress (NPC), and its leader in the Federal House of Representatives.

As prime minister, Sir Abubakar is head of a national government which embraces the other large political parties in the country. The NPC is conservative and represents the Moslem north, which contains more than half the country's population. The second important party is the Action Group, headed by Obafemi Awolowo, leader of the Opposition. It draws its chief support from the Yorubas of the Western Region, the most advanced of the many Nigerian tribes. The third important political party is the National Council of Nigeria and the Cameroons (NCNC), led by the president of the Federal Senate, Dr. Nnamdi Azikiwe. Its main support comes from the Ibos of the Eastern Region, an industrious tribe half Christian, half pagan. The NPC is organized on a regional basis, but the NCNC and the Action Group present candidates throughout the country.

Abubakar was born in 1912 as a member of the Geri tribe. His father, Alhaji Yakubu, was district leader of Lere in the Emirate of Bauchi. It is said that Abubakar's simple origins aided his rise. Had he been a member of the Northern aristocracy, the Eastern and Western Regions would have opposed him; as a *Talakwa,* the son of a poor commoner, he was accepted. From 1922 to 1925, young Abubakar attended a village school; then the Bauchi provincial school until 1928; and the Katsina Teacher's Training College from 1928 to 1933.

His first assignment was to the secondary school in Bauchi, of which he later became director. He educated himself further privately, received the Senior Teacher's Certificate, and specialized in history, which remains his chief scholarly interest. In 1945, he received a scholarship to London University's Institute of Education, won the Ministry of Education's Teacher's Proficiency Certificate, and after his return to Nigeria in 1949 was appointed to many leading posts in the education field.

After World War II, Abubakar turned to contemporary history and politics. In 1946, he became a member of the emir's council in Bauchi. When the new constitution went into force in 1947, he became member for Bauchi in the Northern House of Assembly, and then was elected to the Central Legislative Council. In 1948, he was for the first time a member of the Nigerian delegation sent to London to discuss constitutional changes. In 1951, he was one of the representatives of the Legislative Council at the opening of the Festival of Britain. He was invited to Buckingham Palace and presented to King George VI and other members of the royal family—an experience he still likes to talk about today.

When a new and improved constitution was inaugurated in 1951, Abubakar was returned again as first member for Bauchi in the Northern House of Assembly and re-elected to the Central House of Representatives. Together with his supporters, he founded a Joint Select Committee in the Regional government in 1951 that sought new legislation for Northern Nigeria. In 1952, he received his first ministry: minister of works. After the general elections of 1954, he became minister of transport and was faced with extensive problems. He traveled to the United States and Holland to study water transport and river conditions. During his journey to America, he was made an honorary citizen of New Orleans. Among his British titles, he was named O.B.E. (The Most Excellent Order of the British Empire) in 1952; and, in 1955, C.B.E. (Commander of the Order of the British Empire). In 1955, he also became a member of the governor-general's Privy Council. During his stay in America, he learned that many different nationalities could live among one another in peace. "Until now I never really believed Nigeria could be one united country. But if the Americans could do it, so can we."

His superb speaking voice and command of English have won him the nickname, "The Golden Voice of the North." He loves the North above all, but is careful to think Nigerian and not to give any special privileges to his native region. He is married and has nine children. Although he is Moslem, he does not avail himself of the privilege of having many wives. His chief private interest remains history. He has published a short biography, *Shaihu Umar*. In his youth, he was a zealous track athlete and cricket player.

There is no doubt that the British were wise to name this admirable man from the North as the first prime minister of the Federation of Nigeria in 1957. He is no demagogue, which Nigeria has no need of, but more the modest professor type. It is said that because the prime minister is a man of the North, this region with its many different peoples was won over to the federation idea; otherwise Northern Nigeria might have made itself independent.

Sir Abubakar, like the premiers of the three regions that make up the Federation, always wears flowing native robes and an embroidered cap. He received me in his study in the federal government building on the *Marina,* the waterfront street of Lagos. His working quarters are simple, but admirably decorated. Dressed in a blue and white *Agbada* (cape), he sat behind a huge, heavy mahogany writing desk that was in a remarkable state of order, considering the presence of many official documents on which he was obviously working. His voice is slow and resonant. He struck me as a man from another era. There is something old-fashioned, patriarchal, about him, and one gets the impression that he combines in his person the best of the old and the new. People are right in comparing him to "the lofty and noble figures of the old Sudan."

There is still a great deal of contention between the different regions of Nigeria. One doesn't want to be told what to do by the other. I mentioned this to the prime minister. He replied: "You're right, there are still difficulties among our three lands. But I'm convinced that we will remain a federation. Think back on European history! Even today, your peoples are still at odds with each other. Think of the English and the Scotch, the English and the Irish! But they still manage to get along with each other. Think of the differences between the Flemings and the Walloons—yet the Belgian nation survives. I am always telling the Nigerians to respect each other's customs and traditions. Nigerian unity can only survive through peaceful co-existence—the world, too, for that matter."

African nationalists keep bringing up the subject of a "United States of Africa" in one form or another. But in Nigeria, this idea doesn't seem to come up for much discussion. What did Sir Abubakar think about this? His reply: "I think we're not yet ready for it—just as we're not ready for a World Parliament. I mention this because I was once the member of a committee that wanted to found a World Parliament. In any case, we in Nigeria have so many other pressing problems to solve that we hardly have time to think of foreign policy. First we have to put our own house in order and create prosperity in our own country. We are in fact still an underdeveloped people [he used the word 'underdeveloped,' which is considered taboo by other nationalists]. The recently widely-discussed plan for a United States of Africa will only create new problems. Nigeria still needs many decades to attain the level of other countries. Our most pressing problems are here, and only here."

And the Arabic world? Islam? Communism? It seemed important to me to raise these questions with this devout orthodox Moslem. Sir Abubakar: "We Nigerians who aren't Christians are conservative Moslems. We hardly regard the Egyptians as Moslems at all. We have another way of living up to the word of the Prophet. And we don't like this flirtation, this making pacts with the East. That's easy to do, and shouldn't be expected of us in future. We've decided for the West, and also for the Commonwealth. That will bring us further along."

"Your excellency, then, is not a supporter of neutralism, like so many other politicians in Africa today?"

"I'm against it. Today one must be able to make a choice. The study of history taught me the importance of continuity. One can't shift sides at whim, one minute supporting the East, another the West. This can only lead to conflict, to catastrophe. We young African nations can make a contribution to the stability of world politics. That's why I believe in clear, sober decisions."

Sir Abubakar went on to speak of his trips abroad, of his study of the water transport on the Ohio and the Mississippi Rivers, of the inland waterways and land reclamation projects of Holland. He knew that my family lives in Holland, and said: "The centuries-old struggle of the Dutch with the sea has become a symbol for me of what human will-power can accomplish. Whenever I'm faced with difficulties that seem insurmountable, I think of the Dutch and their struggle with the sea. It always gives me confidence to find new ways of solving Nigeria's problems."

This history teacher, who is making history himself, made an extraordinary impression on me. I felt so much at ease with him that I permitted myself a personal question: "As a youth, did you ever think that you would one day serve your country as its leader?"

"Yes," he said, with a laugh. "Even as a boy, I knew something like this would happen. My father and mother knew it, too. I was raised with the idea that I would one day become what I am: a teacher in the broadest sense of the word."

An extraordinary life! A teacher from the backward North of Nigeria who now rules the most populous land in Africa—a man who deals with kings and queens as though he had been destined for it from the cradle. When I mentioned this, he said:

"When I was a boy in my parents' home, I heard them speak of the English king and the English queen, of princes and princesses. Once I had a dream in which I saw myself walking in London with a beautiful queen. When I went to London for the first time, and then met the royal family, nothing was really strange to me. I knew London and the royal family from my dreams. Don't laugh," he added hastily. "My studies in history helped me, too."

I left the prime minister unwillingly, this man who knows how to combine deep learning with charm and dignity.

"When you travel about Nigeria," he said, as we stood at the door, "beware of the politicians most of all. They try to make capital of everything. It's best to study the people!"

Here are a few paragraphs from a speech by Alhaji Sir Abubakar Tafawa Balewa, which are an indication of his political philosophy, and also a witness to his sagacity as a statesman.

"What has impressed me very much during the past year is the goodwill and encouragement which we are receiving from our friends all over the world. An example of this was the loan which the World Bank made to us last April. That Bank has sixty-seven members, all of them independent nations, and they lent us ten million pounds to help develop our country by extending the railways through the northeastern part of Nigeria right up to within a few miles of the border. It is good to have so many friends ready to help us and we should welcome these demonstrations of goodwill. At the same time we must also learn of Nigeria, so we ourselves have increased responsibilities. Those other people are ready to think well of us and our first duty is to foster their goodwill and to retain their respect by showing that we do indeed deserve it.

This we can do if we really set our minds to it, but much will depend on how we conduct ourselves inside the boundaries of our own country. . . . I suggest to you that we in Nigeria are at present like a community which co-operates to turn a piece of useless bush into fruitful farmland. First we must clear away all the undergrowth of prejudice and sectional quarrels and burn up the weeds of internal dissension, so that when we plant the seeds of independence they will all germinate and grow into strong and healthy giants. . . .

"Differences of opinion there are bound to be in any country, and in a free country they will be expressed openly and, I hope, fearlessly, but let them also be expressed honestly and unselfishly. The fear of God, honesty and tolerance are the foundations on which a nation can build peace and prosperity. . . . And not only among the leaders but especially between the members of different religious and political parties let there be tolerance. Many difficulties lie ahead of us, some of them not even in sight at present, but however great they may be I am confident that we shall overcome them."

NNAMDI AZIKIWE

Of a completely different type is a man who for years has longed to be prime minister himself. And perhaps he will be, for it is his most cherished ambition. The Ministry of Foreign Affairs also attracts him. His name: Dr. Nnamdi Azikiwe, Nigeria's leading political firebrand, commonly known as "Zik."

Dr. Azikiwe can be friendly and obliging when talking to whites, but he is suspected of "black supremacy racial madness," as it is called in Africa. Among his more famous expressions: "Before we reach the year 2,000, the United States will be almost destroyed, and Europe completely destroyed. By whom? Naturally by black Africa."

Dr. Nnamdi Azikiwe is governor-general of the Federation and commander-in-chief of the armed forces. He has been a rabid nationalist for twenty-five years, leader of the National Council for Nigeria and the Cameroons (NCNC), is a fanatical Easterner and, before he became president of the Senate, he was premier of the Eastern Region. When he held this office, one heard now and again of plots to assassinate Zik. "That always happens," Nigerians said mockingly, "when the premier can't think of anything better." Nevertheless, he, too, has done a lot for his country.

Nnamdi Azikiwe was born on November 16, 1904 in the Eastern Region, and is a member of the large Ibo tribe. His father was a minor government employee. Young Zik attended the C.M.S. Central School in Onitsha, his home town; the Hope Waddel Training Institute in Calabar; and finally the Methodist Boys' High School in Lagos. He was a gifted student, always at the head of his class, and early displayed the desire to study abroad. When his father retired as a first class clerk, he turned over his savings of three hundred pounds to young Zik and said: "Now you can go to America. This is all the money I can give you. From now on, it's up to you."

Zik spent nine years in the United States. He studied at Howard and Lincoln Universities, and did some graduate work at the University of Pennsylvania and Columbia. He won a Master of Arts degree in philosophy, and a Master of Science in anthropology. During his last four years in the United States he taught political science at Lincoln; later he received honorary doctorates from both Lincoln and Howard. Like his friend Nkrumah of Ghana, or Banda of Nyasaland, he worked at a lot of odd jobs to finance his studies, especially during vacations. He was a coal miner in western Pennsylvania, a laborer, handyman, porter, dishwasher, cleaned vegetables in a Pittsburgh restaurant, milked cows on a farm, and was even a professional boxer for a short time.

In 1934, Zik returned to Africa. He worked for three years as a journalist and propagandist for African nationalism on the Gold Coast, and gave lectures in Accra. Zik exerted a great deal of influence on one of his students: Dr. Kwame Nkrumah, now the President of Ghana. In 1937, Zik returned to Nigeria and quickly became one of the leading personalities in the nationalist movement because of the experience he had gained abroad. He founded a chain of newspapers, the most important of which is the *West*

African Pilot. He endeavored to spread the nationalist gospel among all classes: teachers and trade unionists, peasant farmers and laborers, clerks and market women.

During the Second World War, the radical elements among the nationalists tightened their organization and founded the NCNC in 1944. Azikiwe was first the general secretary of the NCNC, which draws its support from the Ibos, and then became its president for life two years later upon the death of its first president, Herbert Maccauley. He became a member of the Legislative Council in Lagos, held important posts in the Eastern and Western Houses of Assembly, and was named premier of Eastern Nigeria for the first time in 1954; he was re-elected in 1957.

On December 11, 1959, elections were held for a new and greatly enlarged Federal Legislature. The Northern People's Congress won 142 seats, and the NCNC 89. Azikiwe was offered a post in the federal cabinet, but declined to become president of the Senate. He was replaced as premier of the Eastern Region by Dr. M. I. Okpara, deputy leader of the NCNC. On August 10, 1960, he resigned as national president of the NCNC, and on November 16, 1960 he was sworn in as governor-general, largely a ceremonial office, in succession to the Sir James Robertson, who retired. At the same time, Dr. Azikiwe was appointed a privy councillor by Queen Elizabeth.

In addition to his political ambitions, Zik has always displayed an ardent interest in business. He founded banks, one of which failed and brought him into financial difficulties; his chain of newspapers have also caused him repeated financial difficulties. As premier of Eastern Nigeria, he took a leading role in developing the cement industry, the refining of palm oil, the chemical industry, paper and textile factories, and a steel works. His administration displayed an extensive interest in education, built schools, trained many teachers, and saw to it that greater attention was given to technical subjects in the advanced schools.

Ever since the NCNC came into power in Eastern Nigeria, all adults have had the right to vote in local, regional, and national elections. Azikiwe succeeded in interesting women in politics.

They now have the right to vote, and are to have more opportunity for education. Zik put two young cousins and two young nieces through college. When the girls graduated, he took them with him to America, where they went on to earn their doctorates. He often presents them in public with the comment that they are an example "of what Nigerian women can accomplish."

Nnamdi Azikiwe originally had the Christian first name of Benjamin. He abandoned it after having been insulted at an Empire Sports Festival in London by white South Africans. He still plays excellent tennis, and is president of the Lagos Football Association, the Nigerian Amateur Athletic Association, a table tennis club, and is a member of the Nigerian Olympic Committee. He likes to referee boxing matches, and tries to stimulate interest in the sport in Nigeria. He is married and has three sons and a daughter, all of whom are attending advanced schools. Zik has written several books on West African problems, among them: *Liberia in World Politics* (1934); *Renascent Africa* (1937); *Political Blueprint of Nigeria* (1943); *Economic Reconstruction of Nigeria* (1943).

Dr. Nnamdi Azikiwe bases his political philosophy on five unshakeable, unchanging points:

(1) Political Freedom
(2) Economic Planning
(3) A New Social Order
(4) Intellectual Emancipation
(5) Religious Tolerance

In his book *Renascent Africa*, Azikiwe wrote that history was filled with movements seeking to create a new social order: the Renaissance, the Reformation, the Counter-Reformation, the American and French Revolutions, as well as the Bolshevik Revolution. But the flowering of Ethiopia in antiquity, of Songah in the Middle Ages, had come to stagnation. The slave trade and the "devil of imperialism" had contributed to holding the African to the status quo. Now a radical change had to take place, characterized by his five points.

Although Azikiwe is a hothead, and frequently goes too far, he is extremely intelligent and perhaps even a genius. He is often compared to Kwame Nkrumah and Sékou Touré. He is an intellectual revolutionary, but has warmth and heart and doesn't mind showing it. In his spell-binding oratory he continually told his followers—and his enemies:

"Let bygones be bygones. I mean it with all my heart. Let us go forward together towards the great day of our independence with no bitterness and no looking back to the wounds of the past. I have fought as a nationalist for nearly twenty-five years, and I tell you honestly that if we spoil this magnificent opportunity that lies ahead of us by quarrels amongst ourselves, by intrigues and slanders and dirty politics, it will be the biggest disappointment of my life.

"Much more than this, millions hang on us in all parts of this continent of Africa. We must not disappoint them. Nigeria, when it is self-governing, will be by far the biggest independent African state. Here is a target before you in 1959; not just self-government, but good government and a people united—a federation which is a model of democratic and honest government to give hope to all Africa and a challenge to the rest of the world. Selfish men cannot build lasting unity to make a great new federation work. Morally defeated men, motivated by self-aggrandisement, cannot rise above self-interest to build the independent new Nigeria we all long for. . . . I ask you to work harder than ever before, in a spirit of selfless patriotism. . . . Now with the help of God, let us set ourselves, in the words of Abraham Lincoln, 'to bind up the nation's wounds and set the people free.' "

OBAFEMI AWOLOWO

There are those who have accused Azikiwe of acting like a dictator within his own party, and of permitting negligence and corruption of all kinds in Eastern Nigeria when he was its premier. The former premier of Western Nigeria, Chief Obafemi Awolowo, who, since the elections of 1959, has been the powerful leader of the Opposition in the Federal House of Representatives, told me during an interview: "Above all, let's have no black dictators!" Nothing that he said rang out as sharply and clearly as that. And he quickly added: "If we're going to allow dictators in Africa, we might as well keep colonialism and imperialism at the same time."

Awolowo belongs to the more moderate nationalists in Nigeria, and has therefore often found fault with Azikiwe. He also does not approve of Kwame Nkrumah of Ghana, and has publicly attacked President Tubman of Liberia; Awolowo thinks it intolerable that the small Americo-Liberian elite in Monrovia should tyrannize the native masses in the hinterland. One meets impetuous hotheads so often in Africa that it is a relief to meet a man of compromise like Awolowo, who resembles the prime minister in this respect. The colonial edition of the *Times* has never been stinting in its praise of Awolowo, and once said that parliamentary democracy on the British model would have its greatest chance for success in West Africa if the Opposition were led by a man like Awolowo.

Obafemi Awolowo was at first minister of local government in Western Nigeria, then founded the Action Group and has been its leader since 1951. He gave up his post as premier of Western Nigeria in December 1959 in order to leave himself free for a ministry in the federal cabinet, and was replaced by Chief Samuel Akintola, also a member of the Action Group. He led the Action Group's campaign in the federal elections of 1959 and made use of the most modern methods: for example, he flew to the remotest parts of the country in a helicopter. This made a deep impression on the Nigerians, and angered Zik, who saw his antagonist stealing some of his propagandist thunder. In contrast to Azikiwe and Sir Abubakar, Awolowo has been deep in politics since his teens. He was a member of the nationalist Nigerian Youth Movement, and as a law student in London in his thirties, he wrote a book that was well received and made him well-known, *Path to Nigerian Freedom*.

Obafemi Awolowo was born in March 1909 in the small village of Ikenne in Western Nigeria. His father was a poor peasant farmer. Awolowo attended primary school in his native village, and then Wesleyan secondary schools. His father died when he was still a youth, and as the oldest son he had to quit school and support his family. He worked for several years as a wood cutter, and it was not until he was sixteen that he was able to return to school. He attended the Methodist School in Abeokuta, and later taught a village school.

Studying never bothered Awolowo. He learned shorthand and typing, worked for several business firms and was a newspaper reporter. He studied at night, and in 1944 received the B.Com. (Bachelor of Commerce), a correspondence course degree conferred by London University. He lived a Spartan existence, and his health left much to be desired. He worked and saved, hoping one day to go to London to study. When he finally achieved his goal, he was already married, and left his wife and two children behind in Nigeria.

He won his Bachelor of Laws degree at the London University, but saw little of the city, as he spent most of his time in libraries. He cooked his own meals in his primitive student's quarters, and studied long into the night before falling into bed exhausted. One of his fellow students told me that he had "to drag Awolowo forcibly into restaurants or theatres or cinemas."

He permitted himself only one relaxation from his legal studies: the study of politics, principally British colonial politics. He visited the Fabian Bureau, the Royal African Society, and became a member of the Royal Empire Society. He visited the House of Commons, became friendly with Sir Stafford Cripps (whose daughter Peggy married the present leader of the Opposition in Ghana, J. Appiah), and gave speeches in Sir Stafford's behalf during the elections of 1945.

With the help of Nigerian friends in London, Awolowo founded the Egbe Omo Odudua, a group with cultural and political aims that sought to give voice to the Yoruba's tribal and nationalist aspirations.

In 1946, Awolowo returned to Nigeria, and became a lawyer in the university city of Ibadan. He quickly became popular, and the Egbe Omo Odudua gained great influence in Western Nigeria and also won supporters in the Eastern and Western Regions. The Action Group, founded in 1951, became the political arm of the Egbe Omo Odudua. Awolowo founded a newspaper, *The Tribune,* and with it he attacked Azikiwe's NCNC and became premier of Western Nigeria.

He visited Pandit Nehru, his great hero; even as a student he had been deeply impressed by Nehru's autobiography which he published in *The Tribune.* He discussed with Nehru the problems of native government, independence, and other Afro-Asian problems. With his minister of agriculture, he visited Pakistan, Ceylon, and Egypt.

One day Awolowo invited me to the house he had built in his native village of Ikenne; it lies far off the main roads of Nigeria and I had to drive through miles of jungle to find it. I asked him why he had chosen such a remote spot.

"My native village gives me a lot of energy," he said. "My roots are here, the sources of my strength. . . . Modern civilization is hard on us Africans, and often hard to master. That's why we need complete relaxation. When I walk through the village streets in which I once played as a naked child, I feel happy and gain the strength to take on new tasks."

Obafemi Awolowo ranks as one of the most learned of the Nigerian politicians. He is a devout Methodist and attends church regularly. He told me: "Christianity has done a lot of good in Nigeria. That's why we Western Nigerians are not receptive to Islam, or Communism. In addition, I am seeking to keep my countrymen away from racism through Christianity. Nigeria can no longer afford the racial battles between tribes that were once the usual thing here. That's why, during the independence talks in London, I pressed for the inclusion in the new constitution of paragraphs guaranteeing the protection of human rights."

Awolowo is also a chief. As a democratic politician he makes use of the chiefs and obas (kings), the old feudal rulers of tribes, clans, and villages, because in his opinion they offer the greatest guarantee for confidence and peace in the country.

Awolowo continually devotes himself to questions of education. His school program stirred up lively debate in Nigeria. He is for compulsory education in the entire country, but up to now has not succeeded in putting this through. His political opponents think that the people are not yet ready for compulsory education, and that there is a danger of the youth being educated "only in the spirit of Awolowo."

He had to yield to this political pressure with a heavy heart. "As a youth," he told me, "I had such a difficult time getting an education that the memory of it is still like a nightmare to me. I would like poor peasant boys, such as I once was, to have an easier time of it in future. I had to deny myself many pleasures." The words pleasure and happiness occur frequently in his conversation, and seemed to me to be characteristic of him. This Negro statesman and politician lives a middle-class life. Like his colleagues he always wears the national costume—a flowing, toga-like robe. He has five children, and one of his sons is at Cambridge. He relaxes with his books, or by attending the theatre and concerts in Lagos.

SAMUEL AKINTOLA

Chief Samuel Ladoke Akintola succeeded Awolowo as premier of Western Nigeria when the latter became leader of the Opposition in the Federal Legislature. There is probably no other African nation where the Opposition plays such an important role. If there had been no provision for a parliamentary opposition, the Nigerians themselves undoubtedly would have established one. One also observes that the level of the press in the lands once ruled by the British is relatively high. Most of the newspapers in Nigeria and Ghana belong to well-known English press concerns. When Chief Akintola succeeded Awolowo he was far from an unknown; he had been Awolowo's deputy in the Action Group for years.

Samuel Ladoke Akintola was born on July 6, 1910 in Ogbomosho, the son of Solomon Akintola, a trader of the Yoruba tribe. At four, his father took him to Northern Nigeria, where he learned the Hausa language. He was sent to the Sudan Interior Mission School in Mina. At twelve, he returned to Ogbomosho, went to a Baptist day school and then to a Baptist college, where he was trained to be a village teacher.

From the age of twenty to twenty-one, he taught in a Baptist academy in Lagos. He became secretary of the Baptist Workers' Union and editor of the newspaper, *Nigerian Baptist*. He gave up the latter post when the Mission Executive Committee refused to hear the defense of two discharged teachers, in whose behalf Akintola had intervened as union secretary. He did, however, remain a lay preacher at the mission. He is still deeply interested in education. He was responsible for managing "Education Day," sponsored by the Baptist Mission, and for collecting funds that enabled teachers and ministers to be sent abroad for training every year.

For a time, Akintola was a railway official in Ebute Metta, but politics began to claim more of his interest. In 1943, he was offered the job of editor of the *Daily Service,* a publication of the Nigerian youth movement, which was beginning to play an active role in politics. In his native village, he founded a political movement: The Ogbomosho Progressive Union. The British Council gave him a grant for study at Barnet House in Oxford and at Lincoln's Inn. He was able to study public administration, and, like Awolowo, he gained practical experience by working as a junior barrister in London.

In 1950, Akintola returned to Lagos, worked as a lawyer, and was legal counsel to Awolowo's Action Group and the Ogbomosho Native Authority. In the 1951 elections, Akintola was sent to the Western Region House of Representatives and the Central House. When the first federal cabinet was formed, he was named the first central minister of labor. Awolowo sent him to London in 1951 to represent the Action Group in talks with the Colonial Office, and he became deputy leader of the Action Group.

In 1953, Akintola became central minister of health and took an active interest in the Lagos public health service. He stimulated the immediate establishment of health stations, children's clinics, and hospitals. After the federal elections of 1954, he was the first official leader of the Opposition in the Federal House of Representatives. He held this position until 1957, when Sir Abubakar, as prime minister, formed a broadly-based cabinet and offered membership in it to two members of the Action Group. One of these was Akintola, who was named minister of communications and aviation. In this capacity he travelled to the United States and Great Britain to study their telephone and post office systems, but concerned himself principally with aviation upon his return to Nigeria. He was summoned from his ministry in December 1959 to succeed Awolowo as premier of Western Nigeria, and shortly thereafter also became a member of the Western House of Assembly.

In the spring of 1960, Akintola gave an interpretation of Nigerian politics to a United Press International correspondent that has seldom been matched for frankness and farsightedness. Since Akintola is Awolowo's deputy leader in the Action Group, and the latter has a decisive voice in the Federal Legislature, Akintola's views can be taken as representative of the widest political circles in Nigeria.

The premier first spoke against the idea of a "United States of Africa," and recommended instead an organization of African states on the model of the British Commonwealth. He explained that, without wanting to criticize the leaders of other nations, he had to regard the abdication of individual sovereignty as unrealistic. In an association modeled on the Commonwealth, each state could remain completely independent, and yet at the same time a central organization could be formed. Akintola said that the concept of a "United States of Africa" had not been thought through. One couldn't follow the American model, unless each individual state was prepared to renounce its sovereignty. He pointed out that there was as much difference between some of the widely-separated races of the huge African continent as there was between the Irish and the Japanese. He warned of the danger of being too pretentious. Africa was young, and all of its peoples were united against imperialism. But when imperialism had completely vanished, it might be difficult to find another common, positive cause. The thing to do was to gradually build up economic co-operation, principally on a regional basis.

Akintola stressed that the map of Africa would change drastically in the next few years. In many places boundaries might be changed by armed conflict; he hoped that this would not happen, but the danger did exist. He thought that it would be a good idea to establish an organization of African states that could impartially referee such problems, so that only the most important questions would have to be submitted to the General Assembly of the United Nations.

Akintola went on to say that the fight against imperialism would quickly lose all meaning in the coming years. The fight against racial discrimination would then be the only common goal of the young African nations. He warned that the racial discrimination of the Union of South Africa could touch off a conflict. Not a military conflict, which, for the time being, was not to be taken seriously, but psychological and economic warfare. A solution to this problem had to be found, but one had to proceed cautiously. He himself recommended sending a Nigerian ambassador to South Africa, in order to learn the facts of what was going on there so that Nigeria could be objective towards the Union.

Concerning the prospects for genuine democracy in Africa, Akintola said that this was a problem confronting the young African states. He did not believe that democracy should be diluted, nor that the idea should take root that the average man didn't know what was good for him. He was disturbed when he heard this idea expressed at the All-African People's Conference in Accra. It had been tried and found wanting numerous times in history. Sooner or later, the people came to realize that a one-party dictatorship was not a good form of government. In Nigeria, the leaders had to reckon with a strong Opposition. The Nigerians

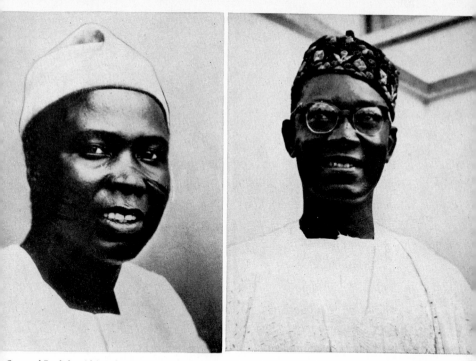

Samuel Ladoke Akintola, Premier of Western Nigeria. Note tribal scars on his face.

Dr. N. Azikiwe, governor general of the Federation of Nigeria.

Alhaji Sir Ahmadu Bello, Sardauno of Sokoto, Premier of Northern Nigeria.

Nana Sir Osei Agyeman Prempeh II, King of the Ashanti (Ghana), and his retinue.

Félix Houphouet-Boigny, Prime Minister of the Republic of the Ivory Coast.

Sylvanus Olympio, Prime Minister of the Republic of Togo.

Kwame Nkrumah, President of Ghana, at the All African Peoples' Conference.

William V. S. Tubman, President of the Republic of Liberia, signing the Golden Book at the Arch of Triumph, Paris.

President Sékou Touré of Guinea greeted by U.N. Secretary General Dag Hammarskjold as the African leader visited the United States in 1959

Léopold Sédar Senghor, President of the Republic of Senegal

believed that this system would bring lasting good results, because there was less danger that one group would come to dominate another. In a dictatorship, Akintola believed, a war machine could be built up without the people even being asked about it.

ALHAJI AHMADU

The third premier of the Nigerian Regions is quite a different personality from Azikiwe, Awolowo, or Akintola. But then Northern Nigeria differs from Western and Eastern Nigeria in many ways, and is larger and more populous than the other two regions combined. As far as modern civilization goes, it is much more backward than the other two. But it is a stronghold of an imposing Islamic tradition and culture, personified by its leading statesman. He is an aristocrat and an autocrat. His party, the Northern People's Congress, is rather autocratic and represents the interests and viewpoints of feudalism. Without question, Alhaji Sir Ahmadu Bello, K.B.E., the sardauna of Sokoto, is Northern Nigeria's most prominent personality. He is usually referred to as the sardauna, and less as premier. In the feudal period, the sardauna was commander-in-chief of the noble warrior class or the royal army.

Ahmadu was born in 1910 in Rabah in the Sokoto district of Northern Nigeria. He belongs to the royal family of Sokoto. He and the sultan are both great-grandchildren of Othman dan Fodio, who founded the Fulani Emirate 156 years ago, and the present sardauna is recognized as their leader by the Northern princes. Thanks to his ability and spotless character he became president of the Northern Peoples' Congress (NPC). The prime minister belongs to this party, the largest in the country (of the 312 representatives in the Federal Legislature, 144 belong to the NPC).

Ahmadu was raised in the historic city of Sokoto. Until he was sixteen, he attended a regional school there, and then (like Sir Abubakar) the Katsina Teachers' Training College, where he later became a teacher. He was an excellent student, and played a leading role in the academic and social life of the college. He became a prefect and distinguished himself at cricket.

Ahmadu taught for three years in Sokoto before becoming a government official. He was district leader in his birthplace, Rabah, and in 1938 became sardauna, the chief adviser to the sultan. The Sokoto area was divided into forty-seven districts. Ahmadu was made responsible for the eastern area, which comprised fourteen districts. In 1944, he returned to Sokoto as general secretary of the native administration. He distinguished himself as a tireless worker. When he left his post in 1948, the work that he had done had to be divided among three men.

In order to broaden his knowledge, he traveled to England in 1948, where he studied forestry and agriculture and above all the British form of government. In 1949, Ahmadu became a member of the Northern Region's House of Assembly. With his colleagues he worked on constitutional changes, and was appointed to increasingly important government posts. He was appointed to the Northern Regional Development and Production Board, and Northern Regional Loans Board, the Nigerian Forests Inspection Board, and the Nigerian Coal Board.

When the new constitution went into effect in 1951, the sardauna served as minister of works and surveys for a year. He became premier of Northern Nigeria in 1953. As premier, he travelled frequently to London to prepare legislation for Nigerian independence. His administration has many plans for developing the region. Local industries, like weaving and milk production, are to be especially encouraged. Northern Nigeria is well known for its groundnuts, hides and furs. In Sokoto itself, the premier has developed plans for the cultivation of rice, and the improvement of cattle breeding by importing cattle from overseas. He is also interested in improving education. He has worked out a plan with the emirs of Kano and Katsina to send Nigerian youths to British schools and universities.

The sardauna, like Awolowo, is an extraordinarily tireless worker. He, too, lacks enough qualified assistants who can relieve him of some of his burdens. When I visited Kaduna, the capital of Northern Nigeria, the premier was sick for the first time in seven years. He was overworked, and had to leave a meeting of the cabinet council out of sheer exhaustion. There seemed little chance that I could see him, but friends of his heard of my misfortune, and, against the advice of his doctors, the sardauna got out of his sickbed and received me in his home, a country estate furnished in the English fashion.

He was pro-Western, and quite well-disposed towards Great Britain—Queen Elizabeth, in fact, had just made him a Knight of the British Empire. He told me of his inspection of the Zuidersee Works in Holland, of his political talks in Bonn, and of his pleasant vacation in the Black Forest. The sardauna is a mighty figure, of truly royal appearance. For the most part, he wears imposing traditional costumes, speaks flawless English, and is a superb orator. He makes every word count, and many English parliamentarians told me that an English minister might well envy his ability to handle questions from the floor. As a Moslem, he has three wives and numerous children. He loves to hunt, and in his house I saw all kinds of hunting trophies, leopard skins and antelope antlers.

More than anyone else, the sardauna has tried to modernize Northern Nigeria. He knows that his region still lags behind the other two. The three regions received their internal autonomy in June 1957, but the sardauna put off self-government until March 15, 1959, in order to prepare for an orderly transition. He told me: "Many people could not understand why I did not press for immediate independence and self-government like other statesmen. Why did I hesitate? I wanted to avoid every risk! We needed time to train qualified personnel. We still don't have enough technicians, although we can now fill many posts with our own people. The founding of a state must be carefully thought out, it must have a foundation. Words alone serve no useful purpose in the long run."

In Northern Nigeria there is a law that calls for preferential treatment for its inhabitants. When a job can't be filled by a Northern Nigerian, a European is given preference, not a Western or Eastern Nigerian. This is an astonishing law—unique in Africa—and I asked the Premier to explain it.

"Formerly Nigerians from the other regions were given preference for all posts, even when Northern Nigerians applied. The result was that Nigerians from the other regions flooded into our land and acquired a great deal of power. The Northerners were pushed aside. These foreign elements presented a great potential danger. One day they could oppress us. It was my duty to prevent this. The law has nothing to do with tribal pride or racial discrimination, it is simply a law for self-preservation."

Religion, however, must have had something to do with it. The Northern Nigerians are orthodox Moslems and against any violation of tradition. The sultan, the emirs, obas, and chiefs, are to retain their authority, even when the government is made democratic in the Western sense. The sardauna said: "Too many foreign influences would violate tradition. That does not conform to the will of God."

Alhaji Sir Ahmadu spoke frequently of the will of God during our interview—simply, modestly, without pathos. It was a pleasurable experience to perceive that men still lived here who held to an undestroyed, traditional philosophy of life. This is probably the reason for Sir Ahmadu's objections to Nasser and other radical leaders of the pan-African movement, and his sympathy for Saudi Arabia. And yet the sardauna is for modernization. He sees to it that the emirs and chiefs attend regular courses of instruction in all areas of modern knowledge and techniques.

Twentieth century development is certainly following a slower pace here than in Eastern and Western Nigeria, but perhaps just for that reason it may be more intensive and longer-lasting than in those African lands which are making a quick leap from the Stone Age into the atomic era. The Nigerians may well be grateful for the statesmanlike sagacity of the sardauna, and his friend, Prime Minister Alhaji Sir Abubakar Tafawa Balewa.

Northern Nigeria is a decisive factor in Nigeria as a whole. The prime minister and the sardauna can be thanked for the pro-Western, and, in national affairs, moderate policies of this area. If there are any two men who hold the keys to power in Nigeria, it is these two.

The most significant event in a year that brought sweeping changes to Africa was Nigeria's attainment of independence in October 1960. All African nations will be watching Nigeria closely in the coming years to see what happens there. During a trip to Lagos, Prime Minister Macmillan referred to the developments in Nigeria as a "triumph of partnership," and added that he was convinced that this partnership between equals would be continued in future.

Nevertheless, the Nigerian political parties engaged in some fairly dubious manoeuvres during the federal election campaign of December 1959. When Dr. Azikiwe was about to give an election speech in a West Nigerian town, shortly before his arrival a costly bridge was dismantled so that he could not drive over the river. All boats were hauled up on land so that he could not be ferried across, and his supporters were obliged to put together a makeshift raft.

Zik's supporters revenged themselves by turning loose some enraged oxen at one of Awolowo's rallies; they dispersed the crowd and injured many. Awolowo employed not only a helicopter, but two television stations and hundreds of small television sets in his election campaign. This was an unheard-of stroke, for up to then there had been no television in Nigeria. The candidates insulted each other in unbridled, racy language; "oppressor of the people" was a favorite epithet hurled by all.

It is apparent that the different leaders differ in their political concepts. Azikiwe may be described as a socialist neutralist, Awolowo as a liberal democrat, and the sardauna as a feudalist. Nevertheless, they are all Nigerian nationalists without qualification. The *Times British Colonies Review* remarked that what Solomon in his wisdom had only dreamed of, had in fact taken place in Nigeria. Despite all cultural, tribal and imperialist boundaries, a country-wide spirit of nationalism had developed. A nation had been forged out of many dissimilar elements.

Because of this, Nigeria has become an example on this restless continent, and should have a strong influence on further developments in Africa. The transition to political independence took place in a peaceful, orderly fashion. The personal ambitions of its statesmen and politicians were subordinated to the concept of unity. From the economic point of view, Nigeria is one of the few African nations that offer fertile ground for investment. The Commonwealth Development Finance Company has announced the formation of a special company for investing in Nigeria.

This is all very disagreeable to the Eastern bloc. The Soviet government, the Soviet propaganda machine, and the Soviet press are all taking an increasing interest in Nigeria. L. Pribytkovski wrote in the Moscow periodical, *Sovremenni Vostok,* of "progressive forces" in Nigeria which are displaying an increasing desire for an independent and neutralist foreign policy "in cooperation with the peace-loving nations of Africa and Asia in their struggle against Imperialism, colonialism, and war." But it is difficult to find any trace of these "progressive forces"—or Communists—in Nigeria itself.

Nigeria is one of the few African nations where a white man can travel about freely alone, and indeed be received in many areas with sincere friendliness. If the nations of the free world follow a thoughtful policy in regard to independent Nigeria, they will have friends here in future, friends on whom they can count.

18

SYLVANUS OLYMPIO OF TOGOLAND

From Clerk to Liberator of the Homeland

※

Togoland stands in the political shadow of the other African nations. Like Cameroon, it had the unhappy fate of being partitioned after World War I, which brought many disadvantages to both countries. But thanks to a man who appeared at just the right hour, its destiny changed. In contrast to Cameroon, whose birth resulted in a blood bath, Togoland got off to a good start when it became the twelfth independent African state on April 27, 1960.

Togoland, a German colony from 1885 until it was occupied by French and British colonial troops in 1914, was partitioned by the Versailles Treaty. Under a Class B League of Nations mandate, the British administered its western section; France its eastern section. In 1946, France and Great Britain placed their zones under UN trusteeship. In 1956, British Togoland voted for integration with the Gold Coast and is now part of the Republic of Ghana as the province of Trans-Volta–Togoland (pop. 440,000; 13,041 sq. miles). The old division of the country created bitterness among its people, and a strong nationalist movement developed in French Togoland (capital: Lomé, pop. 40,000; pop. 1,100,000; 21,235 sq. miles). Its leader was Sylvanus Olympio, whose life mirrors the history of this youthful nation.

Many of the new leaders in Africa don't know the day of their birth, and some aren't certain of the year. That doesn't hold true for the "Liberator of Togoland." Sylvanus Epiphanio Olympio was born at 9 P.M., Saturday, September 6, 1902. From the day of his birth, everything about this man seemed to be right—order, clarity, integrity. These qualities make him very appealing, and are reflected in his face. It is the face of a man who has known suffering. He is not arrogant, but direct, realistic, modest, and moreover, humble.

His mother was Fidès Afe; his father, Epiphanio Elpidio Olympio. His mother was a good-hearted, deeply religious woman. His father was an industrious, dependable, solid man with an excellent position as a sales employee in the trading firm of F. & A. Swanzy. I met elderly people in Lomé who told me that Olympio was a well-behaved boy, who early distinguished himself from others by his exemplary character. As a boy, he found a hope chest, in which he carefully guarded his toys and schoolbooks. "Sylvanus was already a cultured man as a boy," I was told. "It sounds easy to say that today, now that he's become something, but it's true: everyone who knew the family said that the son would one day do something great."

His parents were baptized by Roman Catholic missionaries, and Olympio went to a German Catholic school in Lomé. When the Germans left the country, there were no German schools left. The British replaced the Germans for a time—and Olympio went to an English school. He learned English quickly; at sixteen he won a prize with an excellent English essay that was published in a book called *Our Days on the Gold Coast.*

After the country was definitely partitioned and given new boundaries, the English, and their schools, departed, to be replaced by the French. For the third time, Olympio's language changed. "I cursed about it at the time," he told me. "But now I'm glad it happened. My German is a little rusty now, but I still understand it quite well. The English I learned in school has been a great help to me. And my father, although it cost him a lot of money, sent me to England to complete my studies. I received a commercial degree from the University of London."

Back in Togoland, Sylvanus Olympio got a job in the sales department of one of the leading West African firms, the United

Africa Company (a subsidiary of Unilever). Because of his language ability, he was sent to Nigeria, where he worked at UAC
headquarters. Later, he was transferred to the Gold Coast, today's
Ghana. In 1938, in his birthplace, Lomé, he became the first
African director of the UAC. Never before had a native Togo-
lander reached such a high office in the concern which controlled
sixty per cent of Togoland's business.

His profession was deeply satisfying to him. But, as he traveled
about, he heard of the innumerable problems of his people, and
became interested in politics. He realized that his travels abroad
would enable him to give excellent counsel to his countrymen.
With friends who held opinions similar to his own, Olympio
founded the *Comite de l'Unité Togolaise* (CUT) in 1941, which
came out against Pétain. Because of this, Olympio and a number of
other Africans and Europeans from Togoland were sent to an internment camp in Dahomey in 1942.

During his internment, Olympio thought a great deal about
Togoland's future, and became an anti-colonialist. To achieve his
goal of freeing Togoland from colonialism, he developed a systematic program for the political education of the Togolese. In
1946, he became president of the first representative assembly, in
which the CUT held the majority of seats. Olympio demanded full
independence and came into conflict with the French authorities.
Here began the persecution of Olympio and his party. In 1951,
his party lost its majority, but he retained his mandate as president.

He himself told me: "Although I was a businessman, my
friends and opponents saw in me only a politician. I was forced
to become more deeply involved in politics, whether I wanted to
or not. I was confronted with our country's bitterest problem; its
partition. I realized its consequences. Our boundaries are like
those of Cameroon—and really like those of all African countries
—drawn up by whites. The boundaries drawn by the Germans
were at least half-way reasonable; they at least preserved the unity
of the Ewe people. But the Ewe were split up after the First World
War. Just as in Cameroon, land holdings were cut up, and whole
families torn apart. This could only lead to dissatisfaction, rebel-

lion, and bring with it a great deal of poverty and suffering. Riots resulted from it. A civil war threatened. My party, the CUT, allied itself with the All-Ewe Conference, which wanted to reunite all of the Ewe tribes. Together, we wanted to call into being a revolutionary movement. We established units in every part of the country. The people were enthusiastic. Men and women joined our fight, and supported us with money. Only the French mandate administration, represented by Governor Digo, was skeptical, to put it mildly. The French, of course, had their collaborators; Africans paid by Europeans, who named me as public enemy number one. But they underestimated us. The more they fought us, the stronger we became, and realized more than ever before what we had to do. They began to arrest our officials, and some of them died violent deaths. But we loved our country more than life itself. And the youth was on our side. A youth group—*Juvento*—formed out of the CUT. They were a great help in our struggle for *Ablode,* as freedom, independence is called in the Ewe language."

The fight against Olympio and his close associates became more severe. Reprisals of all kinds were undertaken. Many deserted Olympio out of fear for their lives or possessions. But Olympio and his remaining loyal supporters fought on that much harder. They were no longer interested in discussions. They put all their eggs in one basket, and attacked the French administration wherever—and whenever—they could. But Olympio was clever enough to carry on his fight within the laws of the colonial administration. The French soon realized that they had to get rid of him. It was as though they believed that his disappearance would automatically result in the disappearance of all political problems.

The French governor won the United Africa Company over. It transferred Olympio to UAC headquarters in Paris. Olympio: "At the beginning, I didn't realize anything was wrong. I thought I had been sent to Paris to negotiate normal company business. Then it suddenly became very clear to me that they wanted to keep me in Paris—forcibly really—so that I could no longer take part in the political struggles in Togoland. I was buried in work. I had risen to a fairly high position, and was earning a relatively high salary. I lived frugally, and used this money for my political activities. Finally, the board of the UAC in Paris told me that I had to choose between the UAC and politics. It was either one or the other. It didn't take me very long to decide for politics. During these rather painful discussions I came to realize what my vocation was. It was a moment of truth! I realized that my real task in life was to free my country from colonialism. I resigned as a director of the UAC in Togoland, and went to work as an unpaid politician."

Olympio returned to Togoland. F. A. Dycke, who wrote a small pamphlet called *Sylvanus E. Olympio, Libérateur du Togo,* compared him at this time with Moses leading the Jews out of captivity. This may strike Americans and Europeans as a little farfetched, but one must look at the situation through African eyes. Olympio was in fact regarded as another Moses. He renounced all personal ambitions, and appeared as a priest and prophet.

Up to then, Olympio had only ascended the lowest rungs of the political ladder, but he was about to climb higher. In 1951, he represented Togoland at the UN in Paris. The interests of the Togolese had never been presented so clearly to world opinion. When he returned to Lomé from Paris, he was greeted deliriously by fifty thousand people. Such a demonstration had never been seen before in this country. Here he was called for the first time, the "Liberator of Togo," the "Liberator of the Homeland."

But the mandate administration had not yet given up its fight against him by a long shot. New intrigues and plots arose. Like all nationalist parties in Africa, Olympio's suffered from a lack of funds. He no longer had his salary as a director, and could not finance the party himself. His supporters would now have to make some sacrifices.

Salaries and wages were put at Olympio's disposal. The people responded like a loyal family backing a favorite son in achieving his life's dream: *Ablode!* Freedom, independence!

The government did not hesitate to employ every means to bring Olympio down. He was charged with not having paid taxes on monies he had earned overseas. He was penalized five million colonial francs (around $24,000) and deprived of his civil rights for five years. But the people of Togoland knew that this was only a bald-faced political trick.

In 1955, the French administration called for new elections. The administration accused the nationalists of voting irregularities and falsifying ballots. A new attempt to downgrade Olympio! His party's answer: "We will boycott the elections!" The nationalists boycotted the cabinet formed after the elections.

After the referendum of October 28, 1956, Togoland was given internal autonomy. But the nationalists were not interested in this. They regarded an autonomous republic, associated with the French Union of the time, as "a new farce." Nikolas Grunizky, son of a Pole and a Togolese mother, and since 1951 Togoland's representative in the French National Assembly, became head of the new government. He made a new attempt to side-track Olympio by offering him a cabinet post. Olympio declined: "This government is composed of Africans and Europeans who are working for colonialism and imperialism at the expense of Togoland. They speak of compromise, but it's really a new kind of betrayal. We of the CUT want nothing to do with it."

The situation went from bad to worse. From 1956 to 1958, Togoland lived through a bloody time. Terrorism of all kinds spread, and the country was on the brink of rebellion. When a neutral European spoke in the capital or in the villages with two Togolese, he was regarded as a conspirator breaking the law against assembly. The good-hearted Togolese, who had never before displayed anti-white feelings, now began to see an enemy in every white man. The boycott of French goods was extended to include American and European goods. Everything connected with the white man was branded imperialist—the thing that had to be killed before it killed the Togolese. A storm of agitation swept through the country. A demonstration against the government took place on May 1, 1957. A resolution was passed demanding dissolution of the Assembly and new elections under United Nations supervision. On this day, the nationalists cooperated for the first time with the trade unions. A few months later the *Union des Syndicats* called for a three-day general strike in which even the market women took part.

At the end of 1957, the nationalists, represented by Olympio and the *Parti du Progres* of the Grunizky administration, appeared before the United Nations in New York, which decided for general elections under UN supervision.

Sylvanus Olympio now took a decisive course of action. Fighting at his side was, among others, Anani Santos, later minister of justice and labor in Olympio's first cabinet. Until the elections were held, there was much unrest in Togoland. An underground movement developed; the political barometer indicated an approaching storm. Olympio alone was able to maintain order. "I don't know how I was able to do it. My opponents had the funds and every material advantage to propagandize for themselves and their interests. But Grunizky knew that he was fighting a losing battle and I knew it, too. I never lost faith in our eventual triumph. And we did win. On April 27, 1958, the government party was defeated. My party, the CUT, won 32 seats out of 36, a clear majority. Grunizky and his *Parti du Progres* won only ten seats. The time of tyranny in Togoland was over. I myself could not be elected, since I had no civil rights. But this would soon be changed."

On May 1, 1958 the atmosphere was quite different from what it had been during the demonstrations of the previous May Day. The church bells rang and the people broke out in a frenzy of joy. Thousands gathered before Olympio's house in the early hours of dawn crying: *"Ablode!* Freedom. . . . Independence!"

Olympio appeared only once. He saluted his countrymen, wiped the tears from his eyes, and said: "I thank you." Then he went back to work. On this day, Olympio looked like a shadow of his former self—thin, overworked, on the brink of physical ruin. His brother, Dr. Pietro Olympio, Lomé's leading doctor, had to place him under his care to cure his nervous exhaustion. It's true that Olympio had helpers, but the principal burden had been on his shoulders. He formed his cabinet as the first native Togolese prime minister. In accordance with the United Nations General Assembly resolution of December 1959, the French trust territory of Togoland became fully independent on April 27, 1960 as the Republic of Togo.

I talked to Sylvanus Olympio several times in Togoland. This man seems to like everybody. Simplicity was born in him. When we left his study to go into a brighter room so that I could photograph him, he turned the fan off. "We must save money," he said with a laugh. My car was being repaired, and I hinted that I would appreciate the temporary use of a government car. The prime minister tried—in vain; there were none available. Probably no other African nation has so few official vehicles as Togoland. Olympio himself often travels long distances on foot, or rides a bicycle. He doesn't do this to impress, but because he thinks it is right. He is not only a fanatical nationalist, but a man who knows the value of a dollar; he learned a lot during his business career.

"I'm against pretense and ostentation," he told me. "I had a rough struggle, but when one looks back on it, one can see that I was always a moderate. And I'm proud of that. We could have gotten our full independence sooner. De Gaulle wanted to give it to us two years before we did receive it. I asked him: 'Do you want to get us into trouble, *mon general?* We need time for the transition. We want to have everything ready for freedom.' I told de Gaulle that, despite our political differences, we have always felt friendly toward France. We don't want to lose the friendship of France. On the contrary, when Frenchmen come here as guests we will receive them with open arms."

Olympio: "Certainly, the French made a lot of mistakes. They oppressed us, but because of that we awakened and started to fight for our freedom."

Olympio is of the opinion that Togoland, like Islam, is not a fertile ground for Communism. Christianity has a strong hold. But the boundaries? As before, these are his principal anxiety. Although Togoland is—like other African countries—an expression of cultural associations, a kind of national feeling has developed, in contrast to Cameroon. In Cameroon, when you ask people their nationality, they will name their tribe or province. In Togoland, they answer: "I am Togolese." Olympio's policies have strengthened this feeling of belonging to a homogeneous unit.

That is why it is all the more pressing that Ghana return the former British Togoland to the Republic of Togo. But Kwame Nkrumah has no intention of doing this by any stretch of the imagination. When foreign visitors raise the question, he evades the issue. Olympio, on the other hand, thinks of nothing else. "We can't remain a divided people. Germany doesn't like its present division. But East Germany is dominated by a foreign power, while the people in British Togoland are Africans, our blood brothers."

The Ewe are continually holding assemblies in which the reunification of all the Ewe tribes is discussed. Nkrumah has repeatedly said that he is against such a re-unification. Today it is rumored that he will make an attempt to turn the tribal solidarity of the Ewe in the Republic of Togo into an Irredentist movement. In January 1960, Nkrumah appealed to Olympio to approve a union of Togoland with Ghana. Olympio refused, and the finance minister of Ghana, K. A. Gbedemah, accused tiny Togoland of threatening its larger neighbor. Olympio replied that this was "the best joke of the century," and charged Nkrumah with "Hitlerian expansionism." There seems to be little hope that Ghana and the Republic of Togo will come to any agreement about boundaries in the near future.

Olympio has said he would like to transform Togoland into the "model democratic state of Africa." Its beginnings as an independent state were more favorable than the other African countries. Togoland does not have a one-crop agricultural system and can feed its population. Nevertheless, there are economic difficulties. Typical of Olympio is this statement: "We won't spend our money on sending delegations to international conferences, but for the development of our economy. Togo will remain in the Franc Zone and continue its association with European economic communities. We will also be the first West African state to receive technical assistance from West Germany." It is also worth noting that Olympio proposed his former opponent, Nikolas Grunizky, who still leads the *Parti du Progres,* as opposition leader in the Togolese national assembly. However, on March 1, 1961, the government of Togo put an electoral law through Parliament giving the country a one-party legislature. The new system made it impossible for minority groups to get into Parliament. Parties or individuals wishing to contest a parliamentary election must produce a list of 51 candidates, one for each of the country's constituencies.

If a party gains a simple majority it will get all of its 51 members into Parliament even though some have been defeated in their own constituencies.

On Independence Day, Olympio expressed his thanks to the nations which had formerly administered Togoland; "to Germany, first for having brought us to modern life, and to France which did not fail in her traditions of liberalism and generosity in her forty years in Togo." He stressed the benefits that France had brought to the economic and social development of the country, and praised de Gaulle as "one of the first to understand that Africa had to change."

In Togo, as in no other African land, the West has an opportunity to show what it can do in influencing an independent African state to its own advantage. The Republic of Togo has been called "the lie detector for Western policy in Africa."

19

KWAME NKRUMAH OF GHANA

From the Primeval Forest to "Messiah"
of His People

❋

The president of Ghana (91,843 sq. miles; pop. about 4,763,000), the former British Gold Coast Colony that is now an independent republic within the Commonwealth, is one of the most brilliant and controversial of the new leaders in Africa. He was born in a mud-hut West African village, once had to sleep overnight on a Harlem-to-Brooklyn subway train, and eleven years ago was an inmate of the Fort James Prison in Accra. Today his full name is President Osagyefo (Great Man, Who Assembles the Army) Kukudurini (Man of Courage, Unfrightened, Brave) Katamanto (Man Whose Words Are Irrevocable, And Who Protects the People) Kasapieko (Man of Final Words, Who Says Things Only Once) Oyeadieyie (Man of Action, Who Does Things Right) Nufeno (Strongest of All, Who Surpasses Everybody) Dr. Kwame Nkrumah, Liberator and Founder of Ghana.

The first four expressions derive from the Twi dialect of Akan; the next to last from the Asante dialect of Akan; and the last from the Gã language. It is another indication of Kwame Nkrumah's cleverness to let himself be given names from several of the Gold Coast dialects; in this way every Ghanian can address him by a suitably praiseworthy title. But then cleverness, intelligence, drive, and histrionic skill, have been the hallmarks of Nkrumah's remarkable career.

The date of Kwame Nkrumah's birth was a subject of conjecture for a long time. It was once given out as September 18, 1909; with 1912 also being mentioned. Nkrumah himself told me that he doesn't know exactly when he was born, but that "to create order in his career" he finally settled on September 21, 1909.

His father was a goldsmith in the village of Nkroful in Nzima in the extreme southwest of the Gold Coast. His mother, whom I met shortly before her death, was a "mammy trader" in local markets. She ran Nkrumah's household before his marriage, but never appeared in public. Kwame means Saturday—children in those days were often named after the day of their birth.

Nkrumah attended Roman Catholic mission elementary schools for eight years, was baptized a Roman Catholic, and then spent a half-year as a pupil teacher at Half Assini. He was an outstanding student, and in 1926 was sent to Accra (pop. 170,000) to be trained as a teacher at Prince of Wales College (at that time a division of Achimota College). In 1930, he passed the examination qualifying him as a teacher, and took up several posts: primary school teacher at the Roman Catholic Junior School at Elmina for a year; head teacher at the Roman Catholic Junior School at Axim for two years; and finally the first Gold Coast teacher appointed to the Roman Catholic Seminary at Amissano, the first institution set up to train a native clergy. Nkrumah was always very popular with his fellow students and pupils, because he was a talented athlete of "almost religious zeal" and took part successfully in theatrical presentations.

In his youth, Nkrumah was considerably influenced by two men: Dr. J. E. Kwegyir Aggrey (also Banda's model), assistant vice-principal and the first African member of the staff of Prince of Wales College; and Dr. Nnamdi Azikiwe, a leading Gold Coast revolutionary who became governor-general of Eastern Nigeria.

In 1935 Nkrumah went to the United States, where he studied economics and sociology at Lincoln University, near Oxford, Pennsylvania. In 1939, he won a B.A. from this institution, which was founded in 1854 and was the first in the United States to give higher education to Negroes. In 1942, he graduated from the Lincoln Theological Seminary with a Bachelor of Theology degree, and in the same year received a Master of Science degree in education from the University of Pennsylvania. In 1943, he won a Master of Arts degree in philosophy from the University of Pennsylvania.

While writing his Ph.D. thesis on "logical positivism," he was a full instructor at Lincoln in philosophy, first year Greek, and Negro history. (He never found time to complete his doctoral thesis, but when he visited the United States in 1951, Lincoln awarded him its honorary Doctor of Laws degree, from which derives his title of Doctor.)

An uncle paid for his trip to the United States, but once there he had to support himself. He worked as a checker in the Sun Shipbuilding Yard at Chester, Pa., and as a waiter on coastal ships. "I was a poor steward," he told me. "Often seasick." He also earned some money as a preacher at Protestant Negro churches in Philadelphia and New York. (In Africa, he had seriously thought of becoming a Roman Catholic priest. "I wanted to be a member of the Jesuit Order and the idea lingered with me for a whole year." In America, however, he became a 32nd-degree Mason.)

While at the University of Pennsylvania, he organized the African Students' Association of America and Canada, and became its president. This was the start of his political activities in the United States; he also began to take an intense interest in West African political questions, "to think in nationalist terms," and to make contacts with influential American Negroes. In 1945, he left the United States to study at the London School of Economics and to read law at Gray's Inn. He was taking an increasing interest in politics.

From 1945 to 1947, he was general secretary of the West African National Secretariat, which had been founded to propagate the idea of a united Africa. He was also general secretary of the Pan-African Congress and published a monthly paper called *The New African,* whose first issue in March 1946, preached "African unity and nationalism and attacked imperialism and the unjust laws of the colonies." It created a sensation back in the Gold Coast. Nkrumah's other works are: *Education and Nationalism in West Africa* (1943); *Towards Colonial Freedom* (1946); *What I Mean By Positive Action* (1950); and *Ghana, The Autobiography of Kwame Nkrumah* (1957).

Although still living in England, Nkrumah had become a well-known personality in his homeland. His ideas for the founding of a union of West African republics were widely discussed. Desire for self-government had awakened in the Gold Coast during the war. Dr. Joseph Boakye Danquah (b. Dec. 21, 1895 in Bepons, Province of Kwahu, Ghana) had founded the United Gold Coast Convention (UGCC) on December 29, 1947, the Gold Coast's first nationalist party. Danquah offered the post of general secretary of the UGCC to Nkrumah, not thinking that in so doing he had recruited a formidable opponent. In 1947, after an absence of twelve years, Kwame Nkrumah returned to his homeland.

Nkrumah helped Danquah organize and build up the UGCC. A fascinating speaker, he knew how to pack auditoriums, and became the party's leading spokesman as he traveled the length and breadth of the country. As he remarks in his autobiography: "during those days all my worldly goods—two suits, two pairs of shoes, and a few underclothes—could be easily stored in one small suitcase."

But Nkrumah and Danquah were too different in temperament ever to get on well together. Nkrumah broke away, and on June 12, 1949 founded his own party, the Convention People's Party, which drew its support from the revolutionary youth who considered the UGCC too moderate and middle-class. Always a brilliant propagandist, Nkrumah kept founding newspapers, most of which quickly failed. His first, however, the Accra *Evening News,* survived and is today still the most important voice of the CPP and the administration.

In the elections of 1951, Nkrumah's party won 35 of the 38 seats in the Legislative Assembly and he became the undisputed leader of the Gold Coast nationalists. Nkrumah developed this six-point program for his party:

(1) To fight relentlessly by all constitutional means for the achievement of full "self-government NOW" for the chiefs and people of the Gold Coast.

(2) To serve as the vigorous conscious political vanguard for removing all forms of oppression and for the establishment of a democratic government.

(3) To secure and maintain the complete unity of the chiefs and people of the Colony, Ashanti, Northern Territories, and Trans-Volta.

(4) To work in the interest of the trade union movement in the country for better conditions of employment.

(5) To work for a proper reconstruction of a better Gold Coast in which the people shall have the right to live and govern themselves as free people.

(6) To assist and facilitate in any way possible the realization of a united and self-governing West Africa.

At the time of his party's sweeping electoral victory, Kwame Nkrumah was in jail. Already in 1948, he had been banned from the Northern Territories, after a series of disturbances in February had resulted in twenty-nine dead and over 200 wounded. In connection with this, Nkrumah was branded a "Communist conspirator." He himself said that he stood for Positive Action ("I described Positive Action as the adoption of all legitimate and constitutional means by which we could attack the forces of imperialism in this country. The weapons were legitimate political agitation, newspaper and educational campaigns and, as a last resort, the constitutional application of strikes, boycotts, and noncooperation based on the principle of absolute non-violence, as used by Gandhi in India").

In 1949, the CCP had demanded immediate self-government, and inspired a series of strikes and boycotts along the lines of Positive Action. In January 1950, Nkrumah, and his associates, were arrested and sentenced to three years in prison. The British governor-general regarded Nkrumah as the instigator of the il-

legal general strikes. But after his party received 95 per cent of
the votes in the elections of February 8, 1951, he was pardoned
by the governor-general, Sir Charles Noble Arden-Clarke, and
asked to form a government as leader of government business.
After his release, Nkrumah said that he was walking out of jail
and into the Legislative Assembly without the slightest feelings
of bitterness towards Great Britain.

In 1952, the constitution was revised and Nkrumah received
the newly-created post of prime minister; he was the first African
to achieve that rank in a British colony, second only to that of the
governor-general's. As prime minister, he visited the United
States and England again, and recruited engineers, technicians,
teachers, doctors, and scientists to help in his program to build up
the country. His greatest project is harnessing the Volta River,
and constructing a modern hydroelectric power station there that
will serve as a base for the development of modern industry. When
Ghana became independent, Nkrumah proposed a five-year plan
to improve agriculture, build roads and harbors, and raise the living standards of the people.

July 10, 1953 was a day of great significance for Kwame
Nkrumah and his homeland. In the Assembly, he moved on a
motion of constitutional reform—his independence motion which
is known among the people as "The Motion of Destiny." This
was one of Nkrumah's most important speeches. He loves to
quote famous men, and at the beginning of "The Motion of
Destiny" he quoted Edmund Burke:

"It is our business carefully to cultivate in our minds, to rear to
the most perfect vigor and maturity, every sort of generous and
honest feeling that belongs to our nature. To bring the dispositions
that are lovely in private life into the service and conduct of the
commonwealth, so to be patriots as not to forget we are gentlemen."

After quoting Aristotle, he went on to speak of the right of
peoples to self-government, which he called a fundamental prin-

ciple. In connection with this, he quoted "a great political and social scientist":

"To negotiate with forces that are hostile on matters of principle means to sacrifice principle itself. Principle is indivisible. It is either wholly kept or wholly sacrificed. The slightest concession on matters of principle infers the abandonment of the principle."

Nkrumah did not identify the source of this quotation, but I accidentally discovered who it was. Nkrumah presented me with a copy of one of his earlier works, *Towards Colonial Freedom,* and in it I found these words of the German social democrat Wilhelm Liebknecht.

Nkrumah's motion was accepted, and general elections were held on July 15, 1954. His CCP won seventy-two of the 104 seats in the Assembly. Next day, the governor-general asked him, as leader of the majority party, to form a new government. With one exception, Nkrumah appointed members of his own party.

We will go into Nkrumah's opposition later on. But here, a few words about the Ashanti problem are called for. The Kingdom of Ashanti, lying astride the interior plateau, has about one million inhabitants with their own language and their own tribal culture, to which they stubbornly cling. The British had to fight seven wars before subduing the Ashanti in March 1901, and they now stood in the way of Nkrumah's reforms. Prof. Dr. K. A. Busia, for a long time one of the leaders of the opposition before he went into exile in Holland in July 1959, wrote an important book called *The Position of the Chief in the Modern Political System of Ashanti.* Among other things, he had this to say:

"The most noticeable thing that struck me when I began my inquiries in Kumasi in 1942 was the considerable intrigue that went on regarding constitutional disputes that came before the Confederacy Council. Bribes were given and received in all such cases. It was so common that everybody knew about it, and everybody talked about it.

"When there is a constitutional dispute, both the chief concerned and his opponents, 'malcontents' as they are called, give bribes to the chiefs, registrars, secretaries, *Akyeame* (spokesmen), and others connected with the council to enlist their support. These sums of money are called 'presents.'

"Besides those who are officially connected with the courts, there are some residents in Kumasi who collect money from the parties to a constitutional dispute which they promise to take to one or another of the chiefs known to be sitting on the case, or to the *Asantehene*. These men make a living in this way, as besides the money they receive from others, they are paid for their services. Some influential chiefs have 'agents' who are known to have access to them, and who collect 'presents' for them in this way.

"I received and checked up information on a number of such cases.

". . . The commoners are not consulted by the chiefs and elders, and they are not given a chance of expressing their views on the matters discussed. The educated commoners feel that they should be represented on the council. One of them, a trader in Kumasi, put the popular view in this way: 'Every day we see the chiefs going to the council. We have no say in what they discuss. When they come out they give us laws to obey. Most of these are in their own interest!' . . .

"It is not only the literate commoners who feel that the council is not sufficiently representative. An illiterate cocoa-farmer, sixty miles from Kumasi, put what is a general criticism most clearly when he said: 'All I know of the Confederacy Council is that whenever the chief comes back from Kumasi he brings a new law. We must not hold funeral celebrations. We must not plant cocoa. We must pay a levy. When you ask why, they say, "The Council says so," or "The *Asantehene* ruled it." Today we have too many masters, the district commissioners, the chief, the *Asantehene*, and they all make laws for us!' . . ."

Nkrumah, however, succeeded in winning over the Ashanti. In his autobiography, he writes: "It was the emergence of the CCP in Ashanti that publicly exposed these practices, and not unnaturally those who have made their living this way feel that the CCP is their greatest enemy. But it is precisely because of what the Ashanti suffered under this autocracy that the CCP got such a

firm footing there when it first started. If any man in the whole
of the country understands now the meanings of the word 'freedom' it is an Ashanti."

On Nkrumah's forty-seventh birthday, the governor-general
sent for him and told him that the Gold Coast Colony would receive its full independence on March 6, 1957. When Nkrumah
announced this news in the Assembly, he was able to say that his
country would be free on the one hundred and thirteenth anniversary of the Bond of 1844, which led to Britain's political
domination of the Gold Coast.

In a speech on Independence Day, Nkrumah declared that he
would pursue an active foreign policy, whose fundamental principles would be "Honor, Peace, and Friendship." From that day,
Nkrumah devoted himself more to foreign affairs than any other
African statesman. In January 1957, he called into being the first
All-African Trade Union Conference in Accra, and in June 1957
he took part for the first time in the Conference of Commonwealth
Prime Ministers in London, where he met Nehru, whom he later
visited in India. Queen Elizabeth and the Duke of Edinburgh received him at Buckingham Palace. In March 1958, he visited
eleven African countries for the purpose of strengthening their
mutual cooperation, especially south of the Sahara. A month before
he had called together in Ghana the first conference of chiefs of
the independent African states, whose visits he returned. A new
journey to the United States followed, where he was the guest of
President Eisenhower, and later the guest of Prime Minister
Diefenbaker of Canada. In December 1958, Nkrumah opened the
first All-African People's Conference in Accra, which was soon
followed by similar conferences.

During this conference he announced the union with Guinea,
which had voted against joining the Franco-African Community
in September 1958. Nkrumah said that the "Union of Independent
African States" was open to any state interested in joining it.

In March 1960, Ghana decided to become an independent republic on July 1, but to remain a member of the Commonwealth.
From April 19 to 26 the electorate was asked to vote on a new

draft constitution and to choose a president for the new republic. The draft constitution contained the following provisions:

(1) The head of state and holder of executive power would be an elected president responsible to the people; control of the armed forces and the civil service would be vested in him.

(2) The Parliament would be a sovereign legislature, consisting of the president and the National Assembly; the president would have a power to veto legislation and to dissolve the Parliament.

(3) A president would be elected whenever there was a general election by a method which would insure that he would normally be the leader of the party which was successful in the general election.

(4) There would be a cabinet appointed by the president from members of Parliament to assist the president in the exercise of his functions.

(5) The systems of courts and the security of tenure of judges would continue along present lines.

(6) Ghana would be a sovereign unitary republic with power to surrender any part of her sovereignty to a union of African States.

This constitution laid the groundwork for a strong presidential regime. The president would now possess all of the powers formerly divided between the prime minister and the governor-general. The governor-general formerly had some important authority, for example, the right of veto. He hardly ever used it, but it could now be employed decisively by the president. Upon acceptance of the constitution, Queen Elizabeth would be obliged to renounce her title "Queen of Ghana."

On March 6, broadcasting from Accra, Kwame Nkrumah described the constitution as "fashioned to fit in with our historical experience and designed to meet our own needs." He observed that Africans could not be "truly great, happy or prosperous" if they remained divided into small states, and declared: "So deep is our faith in African unity that we have declared our preparedness to surrender the sovereignty of Ghana in whole or in part in the interest of a union of African states and territories."

The new constitution was approved by an overwhelming majority. According to official figures, fifty-four per cent of the people took part in the plebiscite: 1,000,692 voted for the constitution, and 131,393 against. Nkrumah was elected president with a similar majority. The opposition United Party—a new union of all Ghanian opposition groups (founded 1957/58) disputed the presidential election with a petition to the Supreme Court. Danquah accused Nkrumah of falsifying the ballots, intimidating voters, and misusing state funds through the administration party. The reaction of the British press was divided. The *News Chronicle* commented: "The personal rule of a single man is a very dangerous example." *The Daily Telegraph:* "Ghana's new constitution would be a fair and useful instrument for one of Plato's Philosopher-Kings. It could be just as well-suited for an African Cromwell." *Sunday Express:* "In Ghana today under Nkrumah a merciless, compulsory dictatorship is being established by the whip."

In December 1957, Kwame Nkrumah married Fathia Halen Ritzk, a student at Cairo University. The couple live in the 300-year-old, Danish-built Christianborg Castle in the Osu district of Accra. Nkrumah's marriage to an Egyptian angered the Ghanians at first. When asked about his marriage plans earlier, he had always maintained that he did not need a wife. "Every woman on the Gold Coast is my bride. Don't all women love me? And I love them." When it became known that he had not chosen a Negress as a bride, the people were disappointed. "In the meantime, they've grown used to the idea," several leaders of the Ghana women's movement assured me.

The author must here get into the area of pure speculation. Nkrumah plainly belongs to those Africans in whom religion, progress, and tradition are still at odds. He is unquestionably an intellectual in the Western sense. Why then does he sometimes have recourse to magic, sorcery, and secret studies? Is it because he is a split personality, like so many geniuses of world history?

It is said about Nkrumah that he let himself be advised for years by a "Holy Man," a Marabout, not only in personal but in political matters. Since the "Holy One's" death he visits his grave, to meditate and to establish contact with him. The dead man's son assists him. The Marabout advised Nkrumah to marry an Egyptian, as Africa needed contact with Islam. The spirit of the "Holy One" even specified the woman, and this is the one Nkrumah married. When I mentioned this to Ghanians, I received the distinct impression that Nkrumah does consult a "Holy Man," or at least his successor, his son.

What does Kwame Nkrumah really believe in? He has described himself as a "non-denominational" Christian and a Marxian socialist, and says that he has not been able to discover any fundamental difference between the basic principles of the two. Years ago, his party published an oath of allegiance (I believe in Kwame Nkrumah, the manly leader of Ghana, founder of the Ghana schools and colleges, and of the dynamic Convention People's Party . . .) that bears an uncomfortable resemblance to the Apostles' Creed.

The Accra *Evening News,* which was founded by Nkrumah and carries his photograph next to its title, published a poem written about him by a young Ghanian. I will quote a few stanzas from it, as an example not only of how Nkrumah is regarded as a Messiah, but of the sort of honor and adulation that the new leaders in Africa receive from a section of their people. In Ghana this sort of homage has assumed an unusual character. Nkrumah must agree with it, for otherwise such eulogies would not appear in his own newspaper.

> "O, revered, beloved son of Africa;
> O, great redeemer of Africa,
> Thy wisdom has wrought things many and wonderful.
> Thou seemest a Saviour come from God.

O, before we were in darkness;
But thy beam did give us light. . . .

"O great thinker; great sage of today;
O, thou humble man, who was destined
To spring from the depths of obscurity
To redeem us, a repressed people,
Suffering, sorrowful, hypochondriac.
O, we accord thee our sincere gratitude. . . .

"At Lincoln University, in America,
O, a miserable, studious life lived thou,
O, a humble, penurious soul
Yearning after hidden knowledge.
Thy lofty aspirations have brought us all and sundry
The joy of freedom. . . .

"Thou whose name is enshrined in Africa
Now we are assured that, with thee,
No unhappy divisions and dissensions
Will tear asunder our cherished continent.
O, humble Africa is grateful to you
Thou votary of her freedom and unity. . . .

"O, our fountain of love and happiness, we do hope,
When thou hast fulfilled thy mission in life,
Enshrouded with honour and glory,
Filled with bliss and contentment,
Thy dignity and attainments,
Shalt thou depart us
A great saviour
Into the joy of the Lord.

"O, that God might grant us in Africa
Some Dantes, Psalmists, Spencers,
Miltons, Shakespeares or Tennysons
To write melodious, eulogistic lines
Befitting for a great monument thou hast achieved,
O, a monument stronger than brass.
O, men may come and men may go,
But thy fame shall endure forever."

In the market square of Accra, I was offered post cards that depicted two figures: Kwame Nkrumah and Jesus Christ. One of the cards showed Christ handing the Keys to the Kingdom of Paradise to Kwame Nkrumah. The *Evening News* carried a series of articles describing "the Messiah's seven days in the wilderness"—a reference to his holiday visit to the Cape Coast. An accompanying photograph portrayed Nkrumah in the hour of transfiguration; the caption said that the hero's whole being was at that moment going out to the groaning and dying Africans in the Union of South Africa. In the same party newspaper, I read that an Indian had had a vision of Kwame Nkrumah walking on water.

I asked the Ghana minister of information if this sort of thing struck him as odd. He replied that he saw nothing wrong with it, and was delighted that the *Evening News* is now read throughout Ghana. I almost had the feeling that "Nkrumahism" is a new kind of philosophy designed to replace Christianity in Ghana.

I have known Kwame Nkrumah personally for many years. He is an outstanding diplomat, has a fascinating manner, and knows it, this young man from the primeval forest who carved out such a fabulous career.

After we had seen each other again at a garden party during my last visit to Accra, he invited me to his office, formerly that of the British governor-general. Nkrumah was criticized on all sides for having moved into this feudal castle with its colonial associations. He has also been criticized for permitting bronze statues of himself to be erected, letting streets and institutions be named after him, and because his likeness has replaced the Queen's on Ghana's postage stamps. But he could hardly have done otherwise. Africans need symbols perhaps more urgently than do the peoples of older societies.

The castle appeared more beautiful and well-kept to me than ever. At the gates, Negro soldiers in spotless, colorful uniforms saluted. An extraordinarily courteous adjutant met me and escorted me through the patio to the prime minister's wing. Christianborg Castle offers a wonderful view of Accra and the palm-fringed

Pepper Coast. Slave traders had once done business here. Nkrumah surely knows this, and it must fill him with pride to realize that the slaves have now become masters.

I chatted for a while with his English private secretary, Mrs. Erica Powell. Punctually, at the agreed upon time, the doors of his large study opened, and Kwame Nkrumah greeted me, dressed in white tennis clothes and a blue-and-white striped Ghanian shawl. We sat on the sofa. Even though he now occupied a much more powerful position than he had when last we met, he still seemed full of youthful energy and unworried.

I complimented him for the way the castle had been decorated on his orders, and especially for his own study. "Oh, this is all simple necessity, you know," he said. "Ask yourself, can I live more modestly than the governor-general? Or government leaders in other countries? I am for equality in everything!"

The talk came round to the All-African People's Conference, which he had organized. Was he satisfied with how it had gone? "Very satisfied," he said. "Just think, for the first time in African history delegates from almost every African country came together and talked to one another in a friendly atmosphere. We'll never achieve a United States of Africa without personal contacts."

I asked: "Do you still dream of that—just as you did when you were a college student?" Nkrumah replied: "It is my only dream. And I will bring it to reality. Our union with independent Guinea is just a beginning. Other nations will join us. I know that Europeans fear pan-Africanism as, so to speak, being directed against Europe. They needn't fear it. For us it is a necessary step to insure our existence. We small African states can't survive alone. We need unity. This is directed against no one in the world."

It was just at this time that Nkrumah had met once again with Islamic statesmen, and with them given out joint policy declarations. I asked him if he feared the strong influence of the Moslem lands. He said: "No, I have no fear of Islam. We Africans have several religions. In Ghana, for example, we're mostly Christian and will remain so."

I said: "I've heard that Nasser has asked you to break off relations with Israel."

Nkrumah shrugged his shoulders and laughed. "I don't know anything about that. I go my own way. Economic and technical cooperation with Israel is very welcome to me. We understand each other, Jews and Negroes. We were both oppressed for a long time, and now have our own independent states."

"And Red imperialism?" I asked. "The first time I heard Your Excellency speak officially in Accra, you clearly drew back from Communism. But your opposition accuses you not only of still being a Marxist, but of having intimate contacts with Moscow. It can't be denied that George Padmore, one of your foreign policy advisers and one of the chief organizers of this All-African Congress, is under Communist influence. The opposition also says that you personally invited the Russian expert on African affairs, Professor Potekhin, that he came to the Congress with an important group of observers, and that he has returned to Ghana many times recently to work both as a scholar and a propagandist. And you yourself publicized your trip to Moscow and announced that Khrushchev had accepted your invitation to visit Ghana."

It was obvious to me that Nkrumah was not going to go into all of my allusions point by point. But I did expect a general answer from him. It ran as follows: "As always, we renounce every form of colonialism and imperialism, no matter which side of the Iron Curtain it comes from. We will always fight against it, no matter where it comes from, and let me stress that I realize that it must not necessarily come from Europe. We have only one motto at this Congress, and for all time: 'Africa for the Africans!' Africa must fulfill its destiny in its own way. It is often said today that I regard Africa as a projection of Europe. I don't—and I don't regard it as a projection of Asia, either. Africa is a continent in itself, and the Africans have their own special personality. Everyone should leave their hands off Africa, everyone. Africa belongs only to the Africans!"

Nkrumah had become passionate. I kept quiet for a while, and let my eyes wander over his study, to the *objets d'art*, the photographs of famous personalities with personal inscriptions, the tasteful flower arrangements, and finally to his books. He followed my gaze, and suddenly caught my hand. "I wish that all of you in the West would please believe that I have the highest ethical motives. Certainly, I'm a statesman and a politician, but principally I consider myself as a teacher, as the first teacher of my people, who deserve a better fate than they've had up to now. That's what I have lived for up to now, and that is what I will continue to work for."

"Your people love you," I said, and explained why a foreigner always felt at ease in Ghana. Nevertheless, since my last visit, I had noticed a new undercurrent of anti-European, anti-white feeling—even in the ranks of his immediate followers. In the first hours of my visit to Accra, I had a few experiences that led me to believe that racial feeling was developing against us whites. And it was not only members of the Opposition who told me that Nkrumah had become more anti-European than he had been earlier.

"As long as I live," replied Kwame Nkrumah, "there will be no racialism here. I'm colorblind, interested only in people, the color of their skins is of no interest to me. Although people don't always treat me the same way," he added softly, with a slightly bitter undertone. "People of all races must work together to fight against racial madness. My axiom number one remains: 'I believe in the indivisible worth of all men.' "

This was a reassuring talk. I made no secret of my admiration for him in Accra. But not everyone shared this admiration. I sensed a definite criticism of Nkrumah, even though it was guarded. It is very dangerous to belong to the Opposition in Ghana today. That is why it is so necessary to try to understand the Opposition's point of view. President Eisenhower said that in dealing with the Russians, he was faced with a people whose actions were often hard to understand, and were often downright incomprehensible. The same thought could be applied to many Africans.

In his autobiography, Kwame Nkrumah wrote: "It has always

been my conviction that after any political revolution, non-violent or violent, the new government should, immediately on coming into power, clear out from the civil service all its old leaders. My own experience taught me that by failing to do so, a revolutionary government risks its own destruction."

And concerning the UGCC, the party which called him back from England, he had this to say: "The leaders of the opposition parties have always vied with one another for leadership and it was because of this that so many parties have emerged in the country. However, because these parties felt unable individually to stand up against the disciplined CCP, they amalgamated, and being unable to accept the leadership of one man, the amalgamation has become weaker and weaker. Other colonial territories are afflicted by this disease. A middle-class elite, without the battering-ram of the illiterate masses, can never hope to smash the forces of colonialism. Such a thing can be achieved only by a united people organized in a disciplined political party and led by that party."

Ever since Nkrumah founded his own party, he has had violent struggles with the Opposition. As he was on the point of winning the struggle for independence, the Opposition went so far as to advise the British government not to grant independence, because the country was not yet ready for parliamentry democracy. Dr. K. A. Busia, then the official leader of the Opposition, is supposed to have fought Nkrumah and his party in London. According to Nkrumah's autobiography, Dr. Busia said: "We still need you (the British) on the Gold Coast. Your experiment there is not yet complete. Sometimes I wonder why you seem in such a hurry to wash your hands of us." Busia told me that this was a slanderous allegation, that he had led an Opposition delegation to London merely to discuss a federation of the Gold Coast with Great Britain and to discuss a "Bill of Rights."

In the summer of 1959, Dr. Busia (b. 1913) flew with his family to Holland, where he accepted the chair of sociology at the Institute for Social Studies in The Hague, and recently has given lectures on cultural anthropology at the University of Leiden. On his arrival in Europe, Dr. Busia said that the administration in

Ghana was out to destroy the Opposition. He told me: "From the day of independence, Nkrumah has banned all regional parties. About one hundred members of the Opposition are in jail, their families live in poverty, and their children have had to leave school, as the Opposition leaders—just like their parties—are without funds. Every hope for democracy in Ghana is lost. Nkrumah has destroyed the basis for it."

Dr. Joseph Boakye Danquah, doyen of Ghanian politicians, remained behind, and is president of the United Party, as the Opposition party now calls itself. He is a lawyer by profession and enjoys an excellent reputation as a university professor and philosopher. After the war he was the undisputed leader of the Gold Coast nationalists, and was jailed along with Nkrumah for a short time after the riots of 1948. He has never forgiven Nkrumah for leaving the UGCC and founding his own party. When Nkrumah was studying in the United States in the mid-thirties, Danquah was already an influential figure in Gold Cost politics. In 1931, he founded the *West African Times,* which later became *The Times of West Africa.* He was often in London, long before Nkrumah had ever been heard of, discussing independence for the Gold Coast. In 1949, he was a member of the Coussey Committee, a royal commission sent out from London to investigate the troubled situation, which recommended a new constitution with popular elections. It was at this point that Danquah and Nkrumah parted company. Born in 1896, Danquah represents the older generation of Ghanian leaders who were educated in England, while Nkrumah received his training in the United States.

Although Danquah and his party have nothing approaching the well-organized propaganda machine at Nkrumah's disposal, he did not do too badly in the voting for the new constitution; in Accra he received almost half as many votes as Nkrumah himself. The executive council of Danquah's United Party protested vigorously against the new constitution proposed and pushed through by Nkrumah. They labeled it "despotic and autocratic." The constitution did not redound to the honor of Africa in general or Ghana in particular, because it was "worse than the worst colonial constitution of the nineteenth century." The constitution contained unsatisfactory guarantees for freedom. The personal assurances of the president that he would give up many of the powers vested in him by the constitution when he took office were only "a pitiful substitute" for these guarantees.

When Prime Minister Macmillan, during his African journey of 1960, arrived at the airport in Accra and reviewed the honor guard, he commented to Ghana's minister of the interior that these soldiers looked "ready to go into action." Nkrumah has in fact created a small army, and intends to enlarge it. The English who are training it, the Finance Ministry, and Ghana's neighbors have lately begun to have second thoughts about this army. Later, we will read a declaration about this army by Dr. Houphouet-Boigny, president of the Ivory Coast; its existence also disturbs Sylvanus Olympio, prime minister of the Republic of Togo.

By the end of 1959, Nkrumah's army was composed of one brigade, and three battalions equipped with modern weapons, tanks, etc. Nkrumah soon intends to have three brigades, and to push through a "Ghanaization" of the army, although he has been warned against it (India and Pakistan were wise to retain the British model). At present, 200 British officers and enlisted men are assigned to the Ghana Military Mission; Nkrumah eventually intends to dismiss them all. He wants to create his own military academy, where officers and men from other newly independent African states, like Nigeria and Sierra Leone, can be trained. British officers are still assigned to Ghana's navy, which consists of two mine sweepers and a yacht, although it is planned to purchase more ships. The Ghana Air Force consists of one training plane, and its instructors are Indians and Israelis; it, too, will be enlarged.

Today, Ghana's soldiers may be only "an object of pride," but they could one day play an entirely different role. One observes that Nkrumah has inspired other African states to form their own armies. Members of his party explain that the army is only an extension of the police force, which is strong and well trained. The Opposition claims that the purpose of Nkrumah's army is to strengthen the one-party system and his personal power. Supporters of Nkrumah reply that an army could become "a source of opposition and revolt." Nkrumah himself has explained that a nation like his needs its own army, for defense as well as for attack.

At present, Ghana's only military ally is Guinea; they have a mutual defense treaty. While Nkrumah's army may not yet have any decisive striking power, the mere existence of an African army is another example of the radical changes that are sweeping the continent. It is also possible that, through it, Nkrumah intends to hold onto his role as the spokesman for Africa. When rioting broke out in the Belgian Congo in July 1960, he immediately offered his troops to the new regime to restore order. That he was in a position to do this must have given him great satisfaction.

Lord Beaverbrook observed not long ago that there are undeveloped countries to whom the gift of independence is like the gift of a razor to a child. This can't be said of Ghana. The country has developed quickly and even those who distrust Nkrumah cannot deny him their respect as an able politician and statesman. I once heard this said in Ghana: "In today's Africa the white man can do everything but rule, and the black man can do nothing but rule." Certainly, the elite class is small, and Ghana—like all African countries—is still a long way from true democracy. Benevolent dictators are for the most part in power. But whites should ask themselves if they aren't to blame for this development. Responsible Africans have declared that parliamentary democracy on the British model is foreign to the African nature, and cannot grow there. They have also said that it was colonialism that first awakened the spirit of opposition in the oppressed peoples. In Africa, remote villages often vote a man into power who doesn't necessarily exercise day-to-day authority there. The real authority remains in the hands of the traditional authorities on the spot, and there arises a conflict between the democratically elected central administration and the provincial villages, whose ancient tribal structures are destroyed.

One observes such a conflict going on in Ghana today. Nkrumah's ruling majority party wants to represent the democratic system of the West; the Opposition, regionalism and tradition. Certainly, Nkrumah wants to preserve democratic methods, but in so doing he himself is burying democracy. He also suffers from the fact that in his country, as in most of those in Africa, there are only a small number of trained and qualified people.

A democratic state demands a lot of its citizens. Few Africans know what it demands. Soon after he returned to his homeland and founded the first Ghana College, Nkrumah advised its young students: "Think! Study hard! Work with sustained effort. As never before we want thinkers—thinkers of great thoughts. We want doers—doers of great deeds. Of what use is your education if you cannot help your country in her hour of need?" Nations like Ghana stand today at a crossroads. One road sign reads: "Authoritarian Regime"; the other, "Anarchy." And yet America and Europe needed a long time and had to make many sacrifices to at least draw near the ideal of pure democracy.

However that may be, Kwame Nkrumah occupies a leading place among the new leaders of the once dark continent. Emerging as perhaps the most prominent spokesman of black Africa, Nkrumah made a stirring impression on the world at the United Nations General Assembly sessions in the fall of 1960 and again in the spring of 1961 when he went to the United States to meet with President Kennedy and again to address the General Assembly on the Congo crisis. "Africans and Africans only can solve the Congo crisis," he said.

As Nkrumah received his honorary Doctor of Laws degree from Lincoln University in 1951, he recounts in his autobiography that this thought came to him: "Truly, it is not the heights to which a man climbs that matter, but the depths from which he came."

20

FÉLIX HOUPHOUET-BOIGNY OF THE IVORY COAST

A Doctor Heals His People

⁂

The life of Kwame Nkrumah shows how quickly a young man of primitive origins can develop into a statesman of international importance. It also shows how a cultured, educated man, experienced in the affairs of world politics, cannot completely divorce himself from his African background. This is true nearly everywhere on the continent. Nkrumah's neighbor, Dr. Félix Houphouet-Boigny, prime minister of the Republic of the Ivory Coast, is a sophisticated modern man, infused with the culture and civilization of France, but he, too, still finds himself being influenced by the ways of his ancestors.

A small incident to illustrate what I mean. Dr. Houphouet-Boigny received a plot of land on the Ivory Coast as a gift, and at the same time French friends gave him the money to build a modern house on it. Construction work began, in which a close relative of the prime minister took part, but he died shortly thereafter of mysterious causes. The workers became restless. A Ju-Ju man was asked if the sudden death had a specific cause. He is supposed to have replied: "Yes, it is a punishment of God. The master of the house accepted French, and not African, support. It is a house of treason, of disloyalty, and a curse lies upon it. It is not wise to continue its construction. Whoever takes part in this work is damned." Result? The workers quit, and to this day no one dares visit the building site. The half-finished house is being grown over by jungle. Houphouet-Boigny argued, with all the resources of Western logic, in vain. No one knew what he was talking about, no one believed him.

The Ivory Coast is the richest of the eight territories which once comprised *Afrique Occidentale Française.* French West Africa (Senegal, Mauritania, French Sudan, Niger, Dahomey, Upper Volta, Guinea, Ivory Coast) was an immense federation of 1,718,768 square miles, eight times larger than France itself, ten times the size of California. Nearly 19 million people lived there, among them only 63,000 non-Africans; nine million were Moslems, one million Christian, the rest pagans.

In June 1956, the French government passed the *loi-cadre* (skeleton law, or enabling act), which gave virtual internal self-government to the *Assemblées Territoriales,* the local elected territorial assemblies of the individual federated states, though the chief executives were still appointed by Paris and responsible to the French governor-general in Dakar. In September 1958, General de Gaulle submitted his new constitution for the Fifth French Republic. The territories, by voting *oui* or *non* for the constitution, could have the choice of becoming French departments, continuing their semi-autonomous relationship with France within the *loi-cadre,* complete independence from France, or autonomy within the framework of the fraternal association of a federal French-African Community. All of the territories, with the exception of Guinea, voted for the latter course.

In all of these developments, Dr. Félix Houphouet-Boigny has played a pivotal role. He is a determined personality, thick-set and full of energy, short and vain, a politician and statesman who talks a lot about democracy, but, like many of the new leaders in Africa, a rather autocratic ruler. He is an African, but always dresses in elegant European clothes. He is a Roman Catholic, but this doesn't prevent him from granting the validity of judgements handed down by Ju-Ju men. One thing distinguishes him from his colleagues: while most young African intellectuals made contacts with trade unionists and Marxists in French cultural circles, Houphouet-Boigny did not. He came from a village, and the village remains his chief interest. One could almost describe him as a kind of peasant leader.

His conservatism derives from his tribal background. He is a supporter of de Gaulle, and would like to maintain close ties with France. He mistrusts those who demand the severing of all links with Europe, prefers evolution to revolution, and is critical of Nkrumah, Sékou Touré of Guinea, and Léopold Senghor of Senegal. He loves to take on his colleagues in debates and speeches, with no holds barred. He has surrounded himself with a staff of excellent European aides, and has a Frenchman as a minister in his cabinet. But it would be wrong to label him a collaborator or a Quisling. His slogan is not "Africa without Europe," but "Africa with Europe."

The first trade treaty between the native chiefs of the Ivory Coast and the *Compagnie d'Afrique* was signed in 1700. The real colonial domination of the French began in 1832; in 1893, the Ivory Coast (pop. 2,482,000; 124,500 sq. miles) became a self-governing colony; formerly it had been part of Senegal. Félix Houphouet-Boigny was born on October 18, 1905 in Yamoussoukro, Dimbokro District.

He comes from a family of chiefs; at the age of five he became a chief himself. His uncle, Kouassi N'Go, chief of the Akoué tribe, was murdered by a fanatic named Allangba, who had never forgiven the Houphouet-Boigny family for having helped the French to extend their rule to this district in 1909. According to the matriarchal tribal custom, the nephew became heir. Houphouet-Boigny's father died while he was still under age, and his mother carried out his duties as chief.

He began his schooling rather late. During the early days of the French occupation, the chiefs hesitated to send their own children to the white schools, which were attended only by the children of slaves. The Houphouet-Boigny's duly despatched three slave children, but they failed, and the young Félix was forced to go to a

French school because of a shortage of pupils. He first attended the village school in Yamoussoukro, then an advanced school in Bingerville. He enjoyed his studies, and decided to continue them. His family sent him to the *École Normale William Ponty,* on Gorée, an island off the coast of Dakar which had formerly been used for slave trading. From here he went to the *École de Medicine* in Dakar. He successfully completed his studies in 1925, received the *Diplôme de Médicine Africain,* and worked until 1940 in the public health service of the French colonial administration.

In 1932, the Akoué tribe asked Houphouet-Boigny to take over his duties as their chief. He declined in favor of his younger brother, who died seven years later. Whether he wanted to or not, the young African doctor was obliged to take office as a cantonal chief in December 1939. There were no more brothers who could relieve him of his obligation, but he grew to enjoy the job. He discharged his traditional duties, and took on new ones. He did not simply rule and collect taxes, but concerned himself with the cultivation of coffee and toiled as a doctor. As an educated man in the midst of a largely primitive people, he soon created a position of great power for himself. He enjoyed the loyalty of everyone, and received honors and adulation that were almost of a religious character.

In 1932, he began his campaign to assist the Abengourou tribe, whose cocoa harvests were being bought at an unjustly low price. He regards this campaign as the start of his struggle for better social conditions for the African. When he became chief, he doubled his efforts on behalf of the cocoa growers and traders.

Another important step in his career was his founding of the *Syndicat Agricole Africain* of the Ivory Coast in 1944. With this syndicate, the first of its kind in Africa, he prevented twenty thousand small planters from being drafted for forced labor. He founded cooperatives and succeeded in raising wages. Agricultural workers had formerly received 3.50 colonial francs a day; thanks to Houphouet-Boigny's efforts, they received twenty. The French colonial administration became suspicious of him, but could not prevent him from being elected as the Ivory Coast's deputy to the French National Assembly, where he remained until 1959.

His first legislative action in Paris was against forced labor; together with his colleagues he worked out a law which was accepted without debate in April 1946, and became known as the *loi Houphouet-Boigny*. In 1945, he founded the *Parti Democratique de la Côte d'Ivoire* (PDCI), whose honorary president he still is. But he had come to the conclusion that the territories of French West Africa had the same problems, and could only solve them in a united front. He dreamed of a powerful collective movement, whose creator he in fact later became. In October 1946, the *Rassemblement Démocratique Africain* (RDA) was founded, on Houphouet-Boigny's initiative and under his presidency, at Bamoko, capital of French Sudan, in the presence of eight hundred delegates.

In those post-war days, Communists were members of the French government. They were the only ones to support the RDA, and it had strong ties with the left wing. Houphouet-Boigny was at that time suspected of being pro-Communist. From 1947 to 1952, reprisals of all kinds were taken against the RDA. But Houphouet-Boigny gradually broke with the Communists, and began to pursue a liberal democratic course. The majority of his supporters followed him, with the exception of a small group in Niger and Senegal, and the leaders of French Cameroon, who continued their leftist course under Félix-Roland Moumié.

It became increasingly clear to Houphouet-Boigny that the colonial administration did not represent all of France. During his lengthy visits to Paris, he met Frenchmen who were sympathetic to African nationalism, and he wanted to cooperate with them. In October 1951, he gave a speech to a mass rally in Abidjan in which he announced that he wanted commitments with no other country but France. His speech had wide repercussions, and in the years that followed, the RDA became what it had wanted to be when it was founded: a great collective movement of Africans sympathetic to France. By 1956, the RDA had become the most powerful political force not only on the Ivory Coast, but in all French West Africa and French Equatorial Africa.

On November 18, 1956, Houphouet-Boigny was elected the first African mayor of Abidjan (pop. 127,000), capital of the Ivory Coast. On March 31, 1957, general elections, within the framework of the *loi-cadre,* were held, from which the RDA emerged as undisputed victor. It was a triumph for Houphouet-Boigny. He became president of the territorial assembly of the Ivory Coast, and soon afterwards president of the *Grand Conseil* of French West Africa in Dakar, where the RDA had also won a majority.

From 1956, Houphouet-Boigny had been a minister in every French government. He resigned as minister of state in the French cabinet following his election as prime minister of the Ivory Coast on May 1, 1959.

Houphouet-Boigny was one of the creators of the *loi-cadre,* and took part at the same time in planning a law for the development of the *Organisation Communes* of the Sahara regions, because of his conviction that the development of the numerous untapped natural resources of the Sahara could bring prosperity to all African countries. As de Gaulle's principal adviser on African affairs, he helped work out the new constitution of 1958 with its offer of membership in a Franco-African Community. His thesis: "Underdeveloped countries like ours cannot develop their natural resources alone. Therefore it is necessary that they integrate themselves into a large economic and political community."

In the spring of 1959, on Houphouet-Boigny's initiative, the *Conseil de l'Entente* was formed as the supreme organ of the Sahel-Bénin Union, consisting of the Ivory Coast, Upper Volta, Niger, and Dahomey. The union agreed to coordinate their legislation in the fields of justice, labor, communications, finance, public service and health; form a Customs Union; and coordinate their tax legislation. It would be open to all French West African states "which believe in the future of the Community."

However, when the Mali Federation, in the spring of 1960, sought complete independence and separate UN membership, which would give them a new status within the Community, Houphouet-Boigny reacted quickly. He had been the leading advocate of a closely-knit federal community, but on June 3, 1960, the heads of government of the *Conseil de l'Entente* member states met with General de Gaulle and requested full independnce for their countries. On June 5, in a press conference, Houphouet-Boigny said: "The remodelled Community was worked out without our participation, and contrary to our wishes for a federal organization. . . . We are asking for our independence in order to be able subsequently to determine our relations with the Community in absolute clarity."

The French were disappointed, but on June 12, 1960, signed agreements to give full independence with the Community to Dahomey, Niger, Upper Volta, and the Ivory Coast. At midnight on August 6–7, Prime Minister Houphouet-Boigny proclaimed the full independence of the Ivory Coast to the National Assembly. He praised de Gaulle and said: "We are saying *au revoir,* not farewell, to France." Though still maintaining close ties with France in defense, cultural, economic, and technical spheres, the *Conseil de l'Entente* states now have a loose association with France that is more like a commonwealth status than the original form of a federal community which Houphouet-Boigny once vigorously espoused. Possibly this *volte face* was an indication of Houphouet-Boigny's ability to scent the winds of change and sustain his leadership in West Africa, both in the Ivory Coast and throughout the former colonial territories.

Houphouet-Boigny has a great deal of common sense. It is a pleasure to listen to him in private, or to follow one of his public speeches. He doesn't mince words, even when he's dealing with such ticklish questions as defense. Speaking at the Géo Andre Stadium in Abidjan on September 7, 1958, he said:

"The organization of our communal defense is France's concern. I say this advisedly, for what kind of a burden would it place on our shoulders, what would we have to pay for it in taxes? It would cost at least a thousand million francs [the Ivory Coast's annual national budget hardly reaches ten million francs]. Concerning our defense, people say: 'Look, Ghana's national defense is not the same as England's.' Agreed! But do you believe, my brothers, that in the time of which we are speaking, Ghana's four battalions which have already cost our good friend Nkrumah millions (and who knows, now that his appetite is whetted, he may want an airplane, an old submarine, an old destroyer tomorrow?) that these battalions and these millions that our good friend Nkrumah has poured into a military organization serve any useful purpose except his own false prestige?"

Houphouet-Boigny still follows a policy of strong cooperation with Europe. Because of this he is uneasy, suspicious of nationalist fanatics like Sékou Touré and Kwame Nkrumah. Or, consummate politician that he is, is he afraid that they may one day drive him to the wall?

In speaking of his party's program at Adzope, Ivory Coast, Houphouet-Boigny had this to say: "The final goal of our policies —and I have repeatedly said this to my friend Sékou Touré when he was still a member of the RDA and trusted me completely—is to make the African richer, better equipped in skills and productivity. But here Sékou Touré stubbornly opposed me—the goal of his policies was the African nation. This worthy descendant of the Samory, this dedicated trade unionist, knows what he wants. I have received two letters from him since he left us. I don't like to make public letters that have been addressed to me privately, especially when they come from former friends. I did not reply to Sékou Touré. Why not? For one thing, because he hasn't changed, and neither have I. Sékou Touré, and he is convinced that he is right, wants to draw all of Africa into nominal independence. The sight of me, a man to whom he once gave his trust and whom he still respects, makes him despair, because he knows that I am just as stubborn as he is and have decided to hold firm to a recognizable truth, until I am convinced that I am wrong. I believe in the French Community, he doesn't. . . .

"I made a bet with Kwame Nkrumah during his visit to Abidjan two years ago that applies to Guinea as much as to him. I said: 'When those states which choose to pursue a course different from ours have succeeded better than we in raising the living standards of their people, then you have won our bet.' . . . We will cause no trouble of any kind for Guinea or Ghana, but we will not cease to remind them that this contest must take place in a spirit of healthy, dynamic competition, and that they must abandon intrigues and murderous plots to overthrow us. . . ."

On September 4, 1959, speaking at a special congress of the RDA in Abidjan, Houphouet-Boigny said. "At present, Africa is divided by two currents. The first is powerful and passionate . . . it is a stream called 'African unity,' or 'pan-Africanism,' which defines neither its ends nor its means, and brands everyone a traitor who desires the real and rapid emancipation of the African people within a great community which includes the highly-developed peoples of the earth. . . . The 'traitors' are accused of 'Balkanization,' of being dutiful slaves in the pay of the colonialists, gravediggers of African dignity and African pride.

"The other stream is ours. Our limited know-how foresees the realization of true unity in the framework of a great political grouping by reconciliation, friendship, and brotherhood and the same appreciation of the true interests of the African masses."

His opponents dismiss Houphouet-Boigny as "a new breed of collaborator." But Europe should be grateful for his efforts at mediation. What would become of the Western world—and of Africa itself—were it not for men like him? There is no doubt that Houphouet-Boigny's roots are in Africa . . . like those of Ahmadou Ahidjo, Sylvanus Olympio, Léopold Senghor, or Sékou Touré, to name just a few of the new leaders in French Africa. Perhaps he sees better than do the others the storm clouds that are closing in over Africa from every side. Not long ago, in a speech at Abidjan, he said:

"Believe me and share with me my confidence and above all my unshakeable faith in our eventual success. France, Europe, the whole Western world cannot afford to turn aside our offer of brotherly cooperation, because this makes possible the crossing over of all Africa into the camp of the free peoples. There are those who would like to cordon off this Africa, which is so rich in potential, so thinly populated, in a deceptive, so-called positive, neutrality, which, if it is successful, will sooner or later make Africa the easy prey of the overpopulated lands who will penetrate into Africa with the help of their confederates who are against nature. Then Africa will definitely lose its personality, its soul, its originality. The responsible men of Africa and of the Western world must be aware of this deadly danger from now on, because Africa is a decisive factor in maintaining the balance of power in the world today."

21

WILLIAM V. S. TUBMAN OF LIBERIA

President of Africa's First Negro Republic

✳

When Kwame Nkrumah returned to Africa in 1947 after twelve years in England and the United States, he made a short stop in Monrovia, the capital of the Republic of Liberia. He described his reactions in his autobiography:

"That was the first time I had ever seen Africans who were heads of state, and I was greatly impressed and encouraged. In those days we looked upon Liberia as the symbol of African redemption, as it was the only independent state, in spite of the fact that nobody ever said anything good about the country. To be like Liberia, in fact, was then considered to be the worst thing that could befall any country. I must say that in 1947 I could see the foundation for such sayings. I was not impressed at all with what I saw of Monrovia. However, when I visited the country again five years later the place had changed so greatly that I could hardly recognize it. President Tubman had certainly lost no time in introducing many long overdue administrative, economic, and social reforms, all of which have contributed to the advancement of the Republic."

Who is this man who succeeded in giving Liberia (pop. 2,000,000; 43,000 sq. miles) a new look after it had been withering on the vine for decades? What has been the accomplishment of William V. S. Tubman, and how does Liberia differ from all the other states of Africa?

Liberia was founded by American slaves who returned to Africa and established the first sovereign, independent Negro republic on the continent. Founded at the beginning of the nineteenth century, Liberia often gives the impression that it hasn't changed much since then. That is why it is so open to caricature, why it seems so backward, so unique in comparison to the other African nations. By their manner and behaviour men like Félix Houphouet-Boigny and Léopold Sédar Senghor are today "Frenchmen"; Kwame Nkrumah and Tom Mboya, "Anglo-Americans." It's true that they wear national costumes at celebrations, but in their personal appearance and in the styles of their homes and offices they are influenced by contemporary France and England. They have French, American or English advisors.

It's all very different in Liberia. In the capital, Monrovia (pop. 40,000), one sees at the smallest social gatherings old-fashioned frock coats and cutaways, highly polished top hats or cocked hats. The people love to wear wax flowers in their buttonholes or to keep them in their rooms. The ancient arts have disappeared, and creators of a new art—of which there are many in the other Negro lands—can be counted on the fingers of one's hands. An American Negro, whom I met in Monrovia, told me: "Sometimes I have the feeling here of being transported back in time to the Old South. They have mammies here, and Uncle Toms, and have even copied the architecture of the Southern states. And they love ceremony, just as we once did. The twentieth century has yet to break through here." And there is a lot of truth in that.

My first audience with President Tubman took place in Monrovia, one weekday at twelve noon. It was a hot, sticky day, and I had a bad siege of malaria. Because of my poor physical condition I had put on a light tropical suit. But my friend, Roland Tombekai Dempster, professor of world literature at the University of Monrovia, who was to present me to the president, became angry when he picked me up; my suit was impossible. I asked if I might change to a white tropical tuxedo. "That's the uniform of a colonialist," Dempster said. Because I had been warned in advance, I had packed a dark tuxedo (which I never found use for anyplace else in Africa). I forced myself into it, sweating as though I were in a steam bath, and in this condition had my first talk with the president of Liberia, who was himself wearing an old-fashioned dark cutaway, with a vest! At the president's New Year's reception even the representatives of business firms are required to appear in gray top hats.

President Tubman himself—a middle-sized, energetic man with horn-rimmed glasses—had offered me a chair at the university named after him, and I considered spending a few years in Monrovia. Because of this we talked of educational matters. Many times I visited the university, was the guest of its rector, an American Negro who had formerly been the head of a Negro university in the United States, gave a few lectures to the students and held discussions with them. I finally decided not to teach there, because I had to admit that Kwame Nkrumah was right when he told me that doctoral candidates in Monrovia had reached the level of high school graduates in Ghana.

One day, President Tubman was given an honorary doctor's degree by his university (he also has an honorary doctorate from Wilberforce College in Ohio). He invited me to the ceremonies. I asked him if he really couldn't do something about modernizing the scholarship levels. "No," he replied. "I prefer the ways of our fathers." Later, as at all parties in Monrovia, a lot of whisky was served and the president himself smoked his usual fat cigar while striking a Churchillian pose. Suddenly he jumped up and began to sing, in a deep voice, "Sometimes I feel like a motherless child." He seemed to me to be himself a motherless child, a helpless child, exposed too early to a strange world not too friendly toward him. I understood why the Liberians are called "orphaned settlers."

The Portuguese, who dropped anchor off several parts of the West African coast in the 15th century, also landed on the Pepper Coast, as it was called at the time. Perhaps the French were there even before the Portuguese to carry on trade with the natives. It is hard to reconstruct what really happened, for the ruling class of Liberia puts no value on it. They want the country's history to begin with those freed American slaves who were transported here by the American Colonization Society (founded 1816). Landings began in 1818, and the first large contingent of transported slaves arrived on January 7, 1822—now celebrated as "The Day of the Pioneers." There were clashes between the natives and the immigrants, won by the latter thanks to their better arms. The United States wished the new country peace and progress, but all efforts to help failed because of indolence and corruption. The differences between the natives and the newly arrived freed slaves arose because the latter had no intention of treating the former like equals. They felt themselves to be privileged settlers—not very different from white settlers—and kept their distance from "the natives of the hinterland." Pridefully, in order not to be confused with anyone else, they called themselves Americo-Liberians. Naturally, the original inhabitants rebelled, just as the other Africans rebelled against their oppressors. It was in vain. Today the Americo-Liberians number about 25,000, and we see once again the spectacle of a tiny minority dominating a huge majority. The original inhabitants are divided into numerous tribes, the Kru, Mandingo, Gissi, Gola, etc.

Liberia (Land of the Free) became an independent republic in 1847, after the American Colonization Society withdrew. In the years that followed American influence in Liberia was—and is—strong. It is sometimes maliciously referred to as "an American colony," or "the Firestone State," since the American rubber company plantations are by far the country's leading industry. There are many American Negroes who have bad things to say about Liberia. Most educated Africans inwardly despise the country, since it seems to betray everything the modern Negro stands for. The poor condition of the first Negro republic, in comparison to most of the former French and British colonies, almost makes it an advertisement for the benefits of imperialism! The ruling class has done little for the great mass of its own people.

Liberian intellectuals, on the other hand, reply that the United States and Europe have not given enough help to the country. "We were held between life and death, and vegetated because of it. Only when the whites began to build mines and plantations that brought them profits, did they begin to make capital investments."

The president of Liberia is fighting to change these conditions with toughness and energy. But will he himself reap the harvest of his efforts? Probably only coming generations. Tubman is still too much a man of the old school, full of the complexes that stem from the slavery of his ancestors. From the standpoint of many Africans, Liberia is a reactionary country. Until recently, Tubman had few friends among the young African politicians and statesmen. At African congresses, Liberian delegates take a back seat to those from Nigeria, Ghana, Guinea, the Ivory Coast, or Senegal. One always hears Africans say that the intellectual level of the Liberians is lower than that of the other African peoples. As an example, among other things, the Liberian newspapers are pointed to; they are in fact rather primitive, while excellent periodicals of every kind appear in the former French and British colonies.

There is something tragic about all this, because Liberia was the first independent Negro republic in Africa. Today, it should be a model for all the newly-independent states. The contrary is true: Liberia, independent for over a century, has been surpassed by countries which have become independent in the last few years. The sentimental pathos which runs through all Liberian official pronouncements and meetings deceives no one. Here are a few sections from a speech by President Tubman, "The Birth of a Free People":

"History reveals that all nations great and small have passed through a period of oppression and suppression on the long and arduous journey to self-government and independence. . . . Yet by dint of perseverance, courage and tenacity of purpose they have surmounted all obstacles and laid the foundations which neither time nor circumstance has been able to uproot.

"Liberia too has had her share of problems. But like other nations she too has been able to solve them one by one. Her early settlers were the descendants of hardy men and women who had been carried away from their families, loved ones and friends to strange and distant lands. . . . But never for one moment were they dissuaded from their lofty ambition which was to return to Africa. . . . Time in its inevitable march moved the hearts of great American philanthropists, stirred them to action, and they embarked upon a programme of repatriation, collected and pooled their financial resources, provided means of transportation and sent out our fathers to fend for themselves on a continent that was being rapidly partitioned by colonizing powers.

"After twenty-five years of harrowing experiences, on July 26, 1847, they boldly declared themselves a free, sovereign and independent state by the name and style of the Republic of Liberia; and handed down to us our immortal Declaration of Independence. In that memorable document they said: 'In coming to the shores of Africa, we indulged the pleasing hope that we should be permitted to exercise and improve those faculties which impart to man his dignity, to nourish in our hearts the flame of honorable ambition, to cherish and indulge those aspirations which a Beneficent Creator hath implanted in every human heart, and to evince to all who despise, ridicule and oppress our race that we possess with them a common nature, are with them susceptible of equal refinement, and capable of equal advancement in all that adorns and dignifies man.' In addition, they fired our zeal with a national motto. . . . That motto: 'The Love of Liberty Brought Us Here' rings as true today as it did more than a century ago."

William Vacanarat Shadrach Tubman, the eighteenth president of Liberia, is—like all the presidents before him—an Americo-Liberian. He was born on November 29, 1895 in the coastal town of Harper City, Maryland County, in southeast Liberia. His father, Alexander Tubman, was speaker of the Liberian House of Representatives, a Methodist minister, and a descendant of the first settlers, who came from Georgia. His mother, Elizabeth Rebecca Barnes, did not emigrate from Georgia until 1872.

Tubman attended government schools, and then the Cape Palmas Seminary, a Methodist institution, until 1913. Later he was a teacher and took private instruction in law. After passing his bar exam, he became an attorney in his birthplace, Harper City. In his official biography, it says: "His character and generosity were so great, that when his clients were not able to pay, he took their cases for nothing."

Tubman became a judge of the superior court and "collector of internal revenue for Maryland County." By 1919 he was a district attorney, and in 1923 became the youngest senator in the National Legislature. After fifteen years of service he became an associate justice of the Liberian Supreme Court. "The military career of the president was just as outstanding as his civil career. He rose through the ranks from simple soldier to colonel."

As an active Methodist, Tubman visited several church conferences in the United States and Europe as well. Later he travelled frequently to Europe and the United States. In 1943 he was elected president for the first time; for the second time in 1951; for the third time in 1955; and in May 1959 he was elected for another four-year term, polling 168,000 votes against twenty-four for his only opponent. He will probably hold the job for life. Nothing much happens in Liberia in which he does not have a hand. He is the Supreme Master of the Old Freemasons of Liberia, and of other Free Mason sects. Bridges, houses, institutes bear his name. He has been married several times. His present wife, Antoinette, born a Padmore, is a granddaughter of an earlier president, Arthur Barclay; the Tubmans have five children; one of his sons entered Harvard in 1954. The president frequently carries a pistol, and likes to amuse himself by shooting it off like a cowboy.

In recent years, President Tubman has displayed a great deal of cleverness in improving Liberia's international relations. In economic matters, he follows an "Open Door Policy," and is pleased when his country is called "the Switzerland of Africa." Liberia is one of the founding members of the United Nations, and takes part in many important UN conferences.

In an article published in the year book, *Afrika Heute,* called

My Policy, Tubman emphasized that he and the people of Liberia identified themselves irrevocably with the free peoples of the world, and that they could never be lured from this conviction. He said that whoever clasped the enemies of democracy to his breast risked the loss of religious freedom and individual liberty. He described the United States as Liberia's best and staunchest ally, and added that it was part of his program to make Liberia attractive to U.S. capital, and investors from the other friendly nations with free economic systems.

Tubman has been accused of denying to Liberians that freedom which he has set as one of his goals. In Liberia, the leaders seem to be more sensitive to this criticism than they are in the Soviet Union. At least in Russia a certain humorous way of looking at things has recently been observed—even though it is frequently bitter. Liberia is a bleak, humorless country—as though every joke violates Negro honor.

No opposition is tolerated in Liberia; the smallest criticism of the actions of the president and his administration is styled "revolutionary," and severely punished. The strongest opponents are barred from the country, or are in jail. One is continually hearing of political murders committed by The True Whig Party, Tubman's party, which—with a few short interruptions—has been in power for almost ninety years.

Tubman's most important antagonist, Dihdwo Twe, former district commissioner and member of the Legislature, had to flee the country after he had accused Tubman—in an essay in the Monrovia newspaper *The Listener* in the summer of 1951—of running an unscrupulous, one-man dictatorship. The newspaper was confiscated, but copies of the article circulated throughout the country. It is said that Twe was to be murdered. Twe himself wanted a trial, in order to bring his charges to light, but the administration feared this and therefore the "rebel" was marked down for liquidation.

Disguised as a fisherman, Twe fled through the jungle to Sierra Leone, although the whole Liberian Frontier Force was sent to look for him. The Kru tribe protected him—Twe is not an

Americo-Liberian. He had already lived in exile once, back in the twenties, but was amnestied. At that time he had helped the League of Nations to uncover the Liberian slave trading scandal. (He had been able to prove that the Liberians were selling slaves on the Spanish island of Fernando Po. Because of this President King had to give up his office; his vice-president, Allen N. Yancy, was clearly implicated in the slave trading.) Since then, Twe has been regarded by the Americo-Liberians as a traitor. Before his flight, Twe wrote the president a letter about the necessity for electoral reforms. Tubman replied: "For the present time, my reply to your note is that you are inherently a traitor to your country, a consummate liar, a senile visionary, a sophisticated bigot, and an uncompromising egotist, the truth of which you will be made to realize."

Dihdwo Twe now lives in exile with his wife in Freetown, capital of Sierra Leone, under the protection of the Human Rights Commission of the UN. As a young man, he had traveled to the United States, where he lived in a hotel with Mark Twain and advised him on African affairs while Twain was writing a series of articles about the horrors of the Belgian Congo of Leopold II.

I came to know Dihdwo Twe in Freetown. Now in his seventies, he gave me a thorough report on his fruitless struggle to create an opposition party in Liberia—"which is necessary for every democratic state." His Reformation Party was permitted only a short life, as was the opposition newspaper *The Friend*. The publication of our talk got the sympathetic old man into new difficulties. Curiously enough, as I was writing this chapter, I received a troubled, anxious letter from him. Therefore I will not repeat his thorough criticism of the helpless state of the opposition in Liberia. Dihdwo Twe's fate shows once again how sensitive Tubman is, and how much pressure he can bring to bear on even those Liberians who are living in exile. "Yet I love my country as much as does President Tubman," Twe repeated many times.

In one of my earlier books, *The Restless Continent,* I wrote: "Perhaps in all fairness the authoritarian regimes of Nkrumah and Tubman should be measured by different standards than those of the governments of the older European states. Perhaps they have no choice but to act the way they do. In respect to Ghana and Liberia, one must wonder what would happen if these decisive men weren't around. The tasks confronting them are really extraordinary, and not to be judged by European standards."

Nevertheless, one must continually note that the African dictators are walking a dangerous path. The day may come when they betray the democratic freedom for which they themselves fought. Then they will justify those who contend that the Africans are still a long way from being able to govern themselves; that they are immature and will need the strong hand of experienced Europeans for decades to come. For some of the African countries this may well be true; Liberia is a leading example. There are only about two thousand whites in the country (including about one thousand Americans and two hundred Germans and Dutch). Fifteen hundred Lebanese carry on most of the small trade.

Because of the transported slaves from America, the official and commercial language of Liberia is English, its constitution is modeled on the United States', and so is its flag (red, white, and blue, with one star and eleven stripes). Until 1955, the only bank in Liberia was American, and most of the large business enterprises are American. Liberia was the first country to benefit from President Truman's Point Four program, and during World War II the Americans built two large air bases on its territory.

The United States still has extensive commitments in Liberia, but recently other states have made investments. Sixty-three nations sent representatives to the festivities celebrating President Tubman's third inauguration. Twenty-five delegates from the Soviet Union appeared; twelve from North America; the Vatican dispatched three monsignors; Israel was represented by its foreign minister; and experts came from Red China and Japan, Great Britain, Czechoslovakia, Spain, Germany, Lebanon, Holland, Yugoslavia, Bulgaria, and even Korea. Without doubt, President

Tubman has given a new and wider base to Liberia's foreign relations.

He has recently taken an increased interest in making contacts with the other African countries. This is the most interesting change in the country's policies. Tubman realizes the importance of African consciousness today, that he must make contact with his African neighbors in order one day not to be isolated by them, for he may well need them more than America or Europe. He has no need of contemporary African nationalism; for Liberia, like Ethiopia, did not experience colonialism and imperialism. The radical change that has come over Tubman can be measured by a speech he gave at his third inauguration; he mentioned his northern neighbor, Sékou Touré, president of Guinea, as a model leader for an African nation.

Tubman is hesitant about political cooperation with the other African nations. He stresses that conditions within the individual states are still too dissimilar. It is still too early to tell which countries can best be combined politically, socially, and economically. Tubman is a supporter of the plan for a common market between Liberia and the newly-independent states of West Africa. But each individual state must be left to decide whether it wants to join or not. The first step towards strengthening internal African relations is "regional and not continental, economic and not political."

In August 1959, Tubman was host in Monrovia to a conference of representatives from nine African states: Ethiopia, Guinea, Ghana, Libya, Morocco, the Sudan, Tunisia, the United Arab Republic, and Liberia. The conference, at its opening session, unanimously agreed to admit representatives of the Algerian rebel government as a delegation with full rights. The conference passed a number of resolutions. It assured the Algerian rebels its full support, sharply condemned France's use of colored troops in Algeria and its proposal to test atom bombs in the Sahara, and promised Nyasaland its moral support. In his opening speech Tubman stressed that the African states were called upon "to help reduce the tensions and divisions in the world." Colonialism was not limited to Africa alone, but all races had "gone through periods in their history that were real ordeals by fire."

In respect to Algeria, Tubman underscored his view that the war there could endanger world peace. The recognition of the Provisional Government of the Algerian Republic by the African states was fully justified. Tubman sarply criticized the *apartheid* policies of the Union of South Africa, and proposed a conference that would take positive measures against "this despicable betrayal of Mankind." In 1958, Tubman had already put through a law in the Liberian Congress that made racial discrimination a crime in Liberia. It was principally directed against whites, and made any person or firm found guilty of racial discrimination liable to fines, expulsion, prison, or the withdrawal of concessions. This law earned the eighteenth president of Liberia a great deal of applause in Africa, and his measures were soon taken as a model by many African peoples.

Yet, he still has merciless critics throughout the world. Especially in America, his actions are continually analyzed—and skeptically judged. Perhaps Americans feel themselves particularly responsible for their "black step-children." Recently an American wrote a sharp criticism on conditions in Liberia. Professor W. Alphaeus Hunton, an African expert who was for years head of the Council on African Affairs, wrote a candid chapter about Liberia in his *Decision in Africa—Sources of Current Conflict.* Since Hunton is a Negro, and his book had a preface by one of the most important and influential American Negro intellectuals, Dr. W. E. du Bois, who called it an admirable contribution to African aspirations for freedom, there can be no suspicion that it was written by an anti-African author.

Hunton recalls that while Tubman draws a yearly salary of only twenty-five thousand dollars, he has a share in many business enterprises, owns many homes and a feudal country estate. *The New York Times* reported a leading Liberian official as saying that the Point Four program had principally benefited the ruling class and especially Mr. Tubman's rubber plantations in the eastern province. Aside from the plantations owned by Tubman and his family, there are 750 independent rubber producers among the Americo-Liberian elite. During Tubman's administration the elite has been given every office, large or small, in the country. Hunton reports that though the leading families of Liberia are prosperous, the same can't be said for the workers; they have received no wage increases, in contrast to those who are in the good graces of the government.

Under Tubman's regime, numerous paramount and clan chiefs have received large coffee, cocoa, palm oil, and rubber plantations; they own de luxe automobiles and homes in the capital. On April 23, 1953, one of the few numbers of the opposition newspaper, *The Friend,* to appear reported: "Yes, some Liberians have become rich through taxing the people, while the average man is hardly able to exist, and yet taxes keep going up. For some of these 'Blessed Ones' it is only natural to build ten-, fifteen-, twenty-, thirty-, or fifty-thousand-dollar houses. . . . We won't mind paying taxes when there is no favoritism, no protection of the selfish, no wastefulness by the foolish, no discrimination, no illegal wealth, and no drain on our national treasury."

Alphaeus Hunton wonders who rules the country—and for whose benefit. He does not think that Tubman's long and successive regimes mean political stability, and notes that the government harassed the few who dared to present themselves as rival candidates for the presidency in the last two elections. He credits Tubman with extending voting rights to all adult citizens of the country, even when the balloting itself comes under suspicion. And he also credits him with introducing representatives from the tribes and the hinterland provinces into the House of Representatives—although not yet in the Senate—and appointing personalities from the Grebo, Vai, and other native tribes to high government posts for the first time in the country's history. But he wonders if this adds up to real progress toward political democracy for Liberia—and thinks that the reforms introduced in the neighboring former English and French colonies will make it impossible for the True Whig Party to remain the source of all political authority in Liberia. He thinks that if the archaic, authoritarian

control of the True Whig Party is not replaced by local and national self-government, there can probably never be a "New Deal"
for Liberia. According to Hunton, this West African Republic
will only become a free and independent nation when the people—
the whole people—govern the land in the interests of all.

Although Liberia has made more progress under Tubman than
under any other president, there is still a lot of room for improvement. Liberia will probably need more time than other countries to
modernize itself, as the other Negro nations have done—or are
doing. It is paradoxical that Liberia, despite the freedom it has
enjoyed since its founding, has lagged behind those countries
which had to go through the colonial phase. The Southern Rhodesian, Ndabaningi Sithole, in *African Nationalism,* wrote that the
positive contributions of colonialism should not be underestimated.
Nationalism is the legitimate child of colonialism. One even meets
Liberians who admit that their country would be farther along if
the whites hadn't left it to its own devices for a hundred years.
To that extent, Liberia's role in African history is unique.

22

SÉKOU TOURÉ OF GUINEA

The Boldest African Nationalist

⁂

Sékou Touré appears to be the most daring of the new leaders in Africa. One recalls the situation of August 1958. De Gaulle traveled through Madagascar and Africa, drumming up support for his new constitution and its offer of membership in the Franco-African Community. Military men and statesmen in practically every country welcomed him with praise and enthusiasm. It's true that in Dakar he saw some clenched fists, and heard some boos, but eventually the people voted *oui*.

In Guinea, things went differently. It is difficult to pinpoint what really happened. What is certain is that de Gaulle flew into Conakry on August 25th to address the people and carry on negotiations. He was accompanied by the governor of the time, Pierre Messmer, now French minister of defense. Sékou Touré is supposed to have sent de Gaulle the draft of a proposed speech which outlined his political views, but Messmer is said to have advised the general not be bothered reading it: "It's unnecessary, the fellow's all right."

Sékou Touré never learned that de Gaulle had neglected to read his speech, and came to the conclusion that it had his approval. In addressing de Gaulle, Sékou Touré said something along these lines: Guinea intends to remain within the French Community for about six years, and then to become fully independent, but, even as a member of the French Community, Guinea demands the complete withdrawal of colonial control over its government and economy. The residents of the Conakry heartily applauded their favorite son. De Gaulle, on the other hand, was not just "surprised" at these "pre-conditions"; he was enraged and let fly with some very cutting remarks. He canceled a private dinner to which he had been invited by Touré, and let it be known that if Guinea wanted complete independence "it can have it right now, as far as I'm concerned." There was no more room for an exchange of views; Sékou Touré was now the one who was surprised and enraged. He took up the challenge and mobilized the people against de Gaulle and his new constitution with the slogan: "We prefer poverty in liberty to riches in slavery." On September 28, 1958, 97.12 per cent of the electorate voted against de Gaulle, and the country became immediately independent; the new state was proclaimed on October 2, 1958.

A chance still existed of reaching some kind of reasonable accord with France. But the shock in Paris was so great, and de Gaulle so poorly advised, that he ordered the withdrawal of all French functionaries. Only about fifteen of 4,000 were left two weeks later. Cash registers were emptied, and the weapons of the police, the library of the Ministry of Justice, the furniture of the governor's palace were stripped and shipped back to France. Some Frenchmen went so far as to tear out telephone wires and electrical fixtures; fruit trees were cut, gardens decimated, walls torn down, obscene curses scrawled on buildings, and a ship bringing five thousand tons of rice re-routed. Guinea suddenly found itself on the brink of catastrophe; in any case, there was a real political and economic vacuum for months. A number of sensible Frenchmen warned Paris of the consequences of this; they were ignored.

The break between Guinea and France was not really necessary, and, one can say this today with the wisdom of hindsight, not desired by Sékou Touré. Future biographers of de Gaulle may well describe his visit to Conakry as a dark day in an otherwise bright African journey.

Sékou Touré had the inscription changed on a French war memorial in Conakry; today it reads: "From the Republic of Guinea to the martyrs of colonialism." The German journalist

Marion Countess Donhoff has written that "if the day should ever come when Communism takes root in Africa, this inscription should be changed to read: 'To our dear friend General de Gaulle from a grateful Soviet Union.' Because what happened here, out of a reaction of stubbornness and pure pride, could lead a whole continent to a fate for which the French chief of state can be held principally responsible, and that is also the opinion of many Frenchmen." And that of many experts in the whole Western world.

French, Portuguese, and British merchants opened trading posts on the coast of Guinea in the 15th century, but it was not until the 19th century that the French explored the interior. French domination began in 1882; in 1890, Conakry (present population 52,500) was named as capital. In 1920, Guinea, which is about the size of West Germany or Oregon (pop. 2,600,000; 95,000 sq. miles), received the status of a colony. Its development paralleled those of the other seven territories of French West Africa, and like them, Guinea received its internal autonomy in 1957 through the *loi-cadre*. But Guinea's destiny soon changed, and the cause of it was a young nationalist named Sékou Touré.

Who is this man who defied de Gaulle? A Marxist (he was given a Lenin Peace Award in April 1961), a former labor leader half de Gaulle's age, a self-taught, self-made man brimming with daring, self-confidence, and above all, strong will power. Not for nothing is Sékou Touré nicknamed *Silli* (The Elephant), or *Monsieur Guinea*.

Sékou Touré stems from the Malinké tribe and was born on January 9, 1922 in Faranah, Guinea. He is a descendant of a famous warrior family; he claims as his grandfather the legendary chief Almany Samory Touré, who fought the French until he was captured in 1898. Sékou Touré's parents were poor peasant farmers who had six other children. Touré attended a school of Koranic studies (his family was Moslem, as are most Guineans) and then a French public school. As soon as he learned to read, he became a zealous browser in libraries and read his way through numerous encyclopedias. He obtained his high school education through correspondence courses, *par correspondance,* as he describes it.

In 1940, he became a clerk with the Niger Français Company, then a post office official and a trade unionist. He had already set himself apart from others by his extraordinary capacity for work and received his nickname, "The Elephant." (One of his first remarks as president: "Africans must work harder, because the underdeveloped countries only capital is human energy.") He made people around him feel uneasy. It was said of him: "He's an impossible man, always up to something, always stirring up things, always dissatisfied with what's been done."

In 1945, he was the general secretary of the *Syndicat du Personnel des PTT* (Posts, Telegraphs, and Telephones), then general secretary of the Treasury Employees Union. From 1950 on, he held the same post with the *Comité de Coordination des Syndicats C.G.T.* (General Confederation of Workers) in French West Africa and Togoland. In 1956, he became president of the *Confédération Générale des Travailleurs d'Afrique Noire.* In this capacity, he created a single African union independent of all the French federations, the *Union Générale des Travailleurs d'Afrique Noirs* (UGTAN).

The French trade unions of the time were under strong Communist influence, and the Communists began to take note of Sékou Touré. They were particularly impressed by his oratorical talents: he could give fascinating speeches in French, Malinké, or Souso. He traveled through Europe and is said to have studied the trade union movements in Poland, Czechoslovakia, and the Soviet Union, although he has lately denied this. In any case, he returned to Guinea as a convinced Marxist, founded the first trade union in Guinea, and organized a strike in 1953. From those days of struggle derives a saying one often hears in Guinea today: "Sékou Touré can kill with words."

In 1946, in Bamoko, capital of French Sudan, the *Rassemblement* (rally) *Démocratique Africain* (RDA) was founded. Sékou

Touré and Houphouet-Boigny were among the founders of this large African people's movement, which originally cooperated with the Communists, and did not break with them until 1950. Touré's political rise began with the RDA. After he had become a territorial counselor in Beyla, Guinea, in 1953, he was elected mayor of Conakry in November 1955, and took his seat as Guinea's deputy to the French National Assembly in 1956. After the elections of 1957 within the *loi-cadre* he became prime minister of Guinea. He detached himself (provisionally?) from those Marxists who maintained close contacts with Moscow. Sékou Touré regarded the *loi-cadre* as a real step forward. Guinea could be further developed within its framework, but Touré regarded it as a transitory solution. Then came his clash with de Gaulle. The Eastern bloc took quick advantage of the opening by sending cultural and economic missions and signing agreements. A special foreign trade office was even fitted out for the Eastern bloc states.

Above all, the prime minister of Ghana lost no time in seizing his chance. Dr. Nkrumah granted a loan of 28 million dollars to Guinea, and he and Touré announced a union between their two countries. Their joint statement, issued on November 23, 1958, read: "Inspired by the example of the 13 American colonies, the tendencies of the countries of Europe, Asia and the Middle East to organize in a rational manner, and the declaration of the Accra conference, we, the Prime Ministers of Ghana and Guinea, on behalf of our respective Governments and subject to the ratification of our respective National Assemblies, have agreed to constitute our two States as the nucleus of a Union of West African States. . . ."

This union created a sensation. The French were angry at "this new trick of the *enfant terrible* from Guinea." The British resigned themselves more quickly to this "marriage of convenience." Nkrumah proclaimed the ratification of the Union at the All-African People's Conference in Accra in December 1958, to the applause of the representatives of the African peoples. Some, however, sat on their hands. They sensed what could come of this union: "Nkrumah wants to make himself the *Führer* of pan-

Africanism." The president of Senegal said: "Crazy Ghana doesn't interest us." The Nigerians and the Liberians also wanted no part of Touré's and Nkrumah's union.

I met Sékou Touré many years ago during a trip to Conakry. But when I first saw him at a nationalist meeting he impressed me as little as had Tom Mboya. Therefore I was all the more anxious to see what kind of impression he would make now that he was president. As I began my tenth journey through Africa, Guinea had just become independent. In Dakar I heard disturbing reports about conditions there, about the arrests of whites and a "rebellion against all whites." This hardly filled me with joy at the prospect of going to Guinea. But I went nevertheless, and was one of the first Europeans to visit independent Guinea.

I expressed a desire to talk to the president. One morning, as I was returning to my hotel, I was told that Touré would receive me at 4:30 P.M. But in the afternoon, the chief of the cabinet confided to me that an unforeseen meeting of the cabinet council was being called. It was questionable, under these conditions, if the president could find time to keep his appointment. But I should come to the *Présidence* anyway. And Sékou Touré did find the time. He left the meeting for an hour, because, as he said: "I didn't want a foreign visitor to come over here for nothing." I mention this small incident because it seems to me to be typical of the man. He has been accused of not having any manners, of being a roughneck. That is certainly not true. I came to know him as a polite, natural, and sympathetic African.

In view of what had been going on for the past few weeks, it seemed natural to speak of racial problems first. Was he advocating an anti-white policy on racist grounds? He gave me, on the same floor where the cabinet council was in session, a private lecture on the racial problem:

"People are not born with racial prejudices. For example, children have none. Racial questions are questions of education. The Africans learned racism from the European. Is it any wonder that they now think in terms of race—after all they've gone through under colonialism? You whites shouldn't get so excited. I say to you: whoever thinks and acts like a racist in this country is finished as far as I'm concerned. Everyone has his own race, like his religion. Whatever it is, doesn't interest me. Only people interest me—whatever their skin color. That is the example that I want to set for Guinea. To me, every white, no matter what position he holds, is just as welcome as every Negro. Men of good will are the ones that our young state needs above all others. Up to now we've had independence only on paper. It's now a question of making it work. That's why we haven't celebrated our independence for the time being. We'll do that later. I don't know if you recall what I said to my people on Independence Day: "We've come this far . . . now let's get to work."

When Guinea became independent and the French functionaries left, the other Western powers, to show their solidarity with France, preserved their distance. As they held back assistance, the Eastern countries quickly got the upper hand. One example: Touré wanted police weapons from the United States, in order to maintain peace and order. The Americans hesitated for months, without even replying. Finally, a Polish ship arrived, with weapons and ammunition from Czechoslovakia.

There is no doubt that the Communist countries were waiting to set up a base of operations in Guinea. In the first weeks of the new state's existence, delegations from Russia, China and all the satellite countries appeared. I asked Touré why he signed agreements with these countries. He replied: "They offered me these agreements, I went over them very carefully and signed them. Now we're receiving scholarly material that we urgently need, and can send our students abroad."

What will be his role among those African politicians who are oriented toward the East? What does the Soviet Union, which, as a start, lent him 140 million rubles, expect of him? It is said that the Soviet Union believes that Guinea can be made into "a model state for a future Communist-oriented Pan-African Union." The Kremlin seems to hope that this model state will permit no Western military bases on its territory and will remain militarily neutral. Many times, Sékou Touré has made clear avowals of his Marxism, but he is categorized as a "revisionist" and seems ideologically closest to Marshal Tito. As indications of Guinea's Marxism, the following are noted: Touré's radical anti-colonialism; the one-party system; the pyramid of bureaucracies throughout the country; the integration of the trade unions into the party; the puritanical style and the theoretical planning behind Guinea's three-year economic development plan, that at the moment is receiving important support from East Germany.

During a visit to Morocco, Touré said: "Without being Communists, we believe that the analytical qualities of Marxism and the organization of the people are methods especially well-suited for our country." He often speaks of "democratic Marxian centralism." Every citizen is suited for leadership. "We want to guide history and not to be guided by it. In this way we will draw out the best of our people's economic and human resources." He seemed to betray Titoist tendencies when he spoke about foreign assistance: "From the moment when we can determine the conditions under which foreign investments are made in Guinea, their goals will become our goals."

Sékou Touré has set up a government import-export agency, the *Comptoir Guinéen* to replace the earlier "normal capitalistic trade." Guinea has important mineral deposits, and its deposits of bauxite (from which aluminum is produced) are among the world's largest. Guinea's largest economic enterprise is a bauxite plant, which, as before, is operated by French engineers along pure capitalist lines. The politburo in Conakry nevertheless has reached an agreement whereby the firm must pay taxes on the export of bauxite.

Sékou Touré is also called an African Tito because, like the Yugoslavian marshal, he does not recognize "Stalin as a god, and Khrushchev as a prophet." The parallel has also been drawn because both men fear "Balkanization." There is no question but that

Touré is for an African Union. During his visit to Moscow, he said: "We know nothing of East and West, only of imperialists and anti-imperialists." The Soviet Union welcomes this neutral course. Touré was given a stormy welcome in Moscow. He was more spirited than usual as he thanked the Soviet Union for its moral, material, and diplomatic assistance, and it sounded like a call for further aid when he described Guinea as "a springboard for the struggles of all African peoples." He said to President Voroshilov: "Guinea is a small country, but we have raised high the banner of freedom and know no fear."

After Guinea's adventure turned into a success, in so far as its independence was quickly recognized by most of the states in the world, Sékou Touré's interests perhaps went out to playing a role of leadership outside of Guinea itself. Therefore the union with Ghana. In the meantime he is supposed to have come to regard Nkrumah as too capitalist-orientated. Does Touré want to become the undisputed leader of the African socialist states? Some experts believe that the Soviet Union doesn't regard Touré as important enough to give him assistance in founding the first Communist-oriented state in Africa—Guinea is too small. More useful for the Soviet Union's interests would have been a man like Félix-Roland Moumie, the recently poisoned Opposition leader in Cameroon. But the late Moumie had only a government-in-exile at his disposal—while Touré has a nation. Therefore, for the moment, the Soviets are supporting Touré, even though he is provisionally playing the role of an African Tito.

The opinion is often expressed that the Communist course of Guinea can't be taken seriously enough. The events of March 1960 pointed this up. Guinea left the Franc Zone and created its own currency. Touré: "It is guaranteed by the natural resources of our country, and the human energy of our people."

In Africa, it is said that Touré, who combines in his own person the offices of head of state, president, foreign and defense minister, has no freedom of choice left, that he is a figure being pushed

around Moscow's chessboard. Western observers regard Guinea as
the bridgehead for Communism into Africa. In return for its
economic aid, Touré must dance to Moscow's tune. The situation
is all the more unfavorable for the West because Touré's closest
associates are all radicals. In this connection are cited his brother,
Ismail Touré; Diallo Saifoulaye, party general secretary and president of Parliament; and Keita N'Famara, organization secretary
and chief of planning. These influential key officials are all orthodox Marxist-Leninists. It must be emphasized that they got the
upper hand while the West hesitated to give its assistance. The
politburo works closely with the political police.

Sékou Touré himself went to Moscow, after visiting West Germany, Washington, and London, to carry on negotiations with
Khrushchev. Moscow, like Peking, offered him experts. When the
economic crisis in Guinea worsened, Touré accepted these offers.
Today one sees in Conakry numerous Communist technicians from
all the Eastern countries. They have specific jobs to do, but also are
busy as political functionaries. They judge their professional problems by their "political content." No area is excepted from this.
Russia is not only giving assistance in numerous industrial projects,
but is also building a huge sports stadium in Conakry, and
Hungarians are training Guinean sports teams. The Red Chinese
are on hand, developing agricultural collectives on the style of the
"people's communes." Soviet agricultural experts are supporting
them, and *kolkhoz'* on the Russian model are beginning to appear.
Czech officers are reorganizing the army, and Guinean officers are
being trained in Czechoslovakia.

In addition, the Soviet Union has despatched its leading Oriental expert as ambassador to Conakry: Daniel S. Solod, former
chief of the Near East section of the Foreign Ministry in Moscow,
a man who is known for successfully building key positions for
Communist action. All of the Eastern countries are flooding Guinea
with propaganda material—books, brochures, newspapers, and
training films. In the schools, political instruction on the Russian
model is given.

Imports from the Communist bloc now total more than three-fourths of Guinea's imports, and they have extended credits of 102 million dollars, which, in view of Guinea's size and limited resources, is a huge sum. Guinea's economy is now largely dependent on the Red bloc.

On January 15, 1961, Sékou Touré became Guinea's first elected president (up to then he had served as president through a vote of the National Assembly). He won 99.9 per cent of the votes cast, and no other candidate used the right granted by the Constitution to enter the election against him. In a speech on January 29, he declared that Africa would not give up its fight for independence until the continent had been freed "of all foreign influence and every foreign army," and ridiculed those African leaders who were trying to compromise with the former colonial powers instead of seeking "total independence."

The Guinean army put on a parade after the speech. They carried Czech rifles, displayed Soviet and Czech-made artillery and anti-aircraft batteries, and rode in heavy Soviet-built armored cars.

Despite the obvious gains that the Communist bloc has made in Guinea, it is difficult to judge whether Sékou Touré has passed the point of no return on the road to Communism, or whether he can sustain his declared intention to remain neutral. In any case, he tries to promote understanding for his "democratic country" in the West. Perhaps a sign of his indecisiveness is that he always comes back to the old relationship with France. A Western diplomat in Conakry told me that Touré has developed a "love-hate" complex towards France.

The President seems to feel the need to report personally on the youthful history of Guinea. He likes to use slogans in connection with this. "We are not rug dealers," he likes to say, or: "Dignity is more important than money." Not without betraying a certain hypersensitivity, he is always telling the West: "An African statesman is not a naked boy begging from rich capitalists."

In October–December 1959, Sékou Touré visited the United Kingdom, West Germany, the Soviet Union, Czechoslovakia,

Morocco, and the United States. After leaving Washington on October 28, he and his party toured the United States, including visits to Chapel Hill, North Carolina; Chicago; Los Angeles; Omal, Ohio; and New York City.

On October 26, Sékou Touré was President Eisenhower's guest at a state dinner in the White House. During an exchange of toasts, he said:

"No one can claim for himself the right to speak for all of Africa. But each man has the right, and the pride, to be able to attempt to express the hopes and the aspirations of the peoples of Africa. And the only ambition which fills us is that of making understood the aspirations and the hopes of Africa. . . .

". . . And when we come here, we come not as the messengers of the sufferings of our people but rather as the messengers of the future hopes of our people. Our present difficulties do exist. They are realities which we must face, but we feel that our courage will enable us to overcome them. And we are confident of the relations that will exist between our countries. We know that we came here in the first place to express our thanks for the kind invitation of the United States Government inviting us here, to express our confidence that the future will be built on the strong and close relationships which will exist between our peoples. . . .

"There are those who do not see the future of Africa the way we in Guinea see it, and they may believe that the policy of Guinea is a different one from that which is publicly expressed every day by those who are in charge—who lead the people of Guinea. If there is one small country in the world around whom more legends have been created than any other since 1958, we can say that that country is Guinea. But we thank God that we have acceded to full sovereignty over our own people under worthy conditions. And the pride and consciousness we feel of the part we must play does not allow us to have an attitude of disloyalty toward any party, because the ambition which fills us is to rehabilitate and rekindle the civilization of Africa. And these civilizations of Africa are in no wise in conflict with or in contradiction to the civilizations and cultures of other countries but will come as a valuable contribution and join with the contributions made by other peoples, so that the whole world may profit thereby. . . .

"We ask you therefore, not to judge us or think of us in terms of what we were—or even of what we are—but rather to think of us in terms of history and what we will be tomorrow. . . ."

Sékou Touré is always ready to admit that Guinea has many problems. The country is made up of many different tribes, who speak more than twenty different languages. This is one of the problems that must be solved; it does no good to ignore internal disunion. At first, there was opposition to the reforms, but in two, three, or five years, the people will get used to them. The Guineans want to be responsible for their own affairs. One can always give his brother good advice, but he will still prefer to make his own mistakes. This is the African psychology and another reason for the existence of the Guinean nationalists. The Africans of today are looking for justice and equal rights.

In a speech to the Royal Institute of International Affairs in London, in November 1959, Sékou Touré said: "Here are a few examples of what we have been able to accomplish since we became independent. First, we freed ourselves from the old customs in our villages. The tribal chiefs had used them to serve their own purposes, and they no longer had any useful function. The people were no longer free. We influenced the people against the chiefs. We created the system of elected councils, and formed the villages around them. A third of the seats on the village councils are reserved for women, and many villages have women mayors. We created district councils, for which the whole electorate votes—anyone who is over twenty-one has the right to vote in Guinea. A district is normally made up of two or three hundred villages. The peasant farmers have six of the ten seats, so that they have twenty-four seats in a district council with forty seats. The educated have no advantage over the uneducated. Before independence, there were twelve political parties in Guinea. Now there is only one: *Le Parti Démocratique de Guinée* (PDG). Anyone who says that I am a dictator because we have only one party and no opposition doesn't understand what we are trying to accomplish. The party is not a goal, but a method to achieve the goal of human freedom.

"Certainly, we received at first a great deal of criticism and rejection from abroad. People said that our system couldn't work. But it does work, and it is democratic. In the villages everyone is equal, the majority decides, and this has inspired confidence. The intellectuals have no special privileges. All problems are discussed, so that everyone can come to feel that he belongs to a single nation and that Guinea belongs to us. . . .

"Our constitution permits complete freedom for the existence of Opposition parties. However, in the last elections, 91 per cent of the people voted for the PDG. The Opposition received only five or six per cent of the votes, and decided to join our party. This meant reconciliation, and two of their leaders received responsible posts. Actually, the Opposition's point of view can be expressed much better within the party than from outside it. . . ."

Nevertheless, Sékou Touré admitted in May 1960, that the People's Court had condemned nineteen people to death and twenty-one to fifteen years' hard labor in connection with a "counterrevolutionary plot." The president demanded the creation of a watchdog committee; he had received assurances from African and Asian states that this could be mobilized in twenty-four hours, in case of an imperialist attack, in order to help Guinea.

Like all the new leaders in Africa, Sékou Touré can be viewed in the light of "the African personality," the consciousness of everything specifically African. In Conakry, I discussed this with Alioune Diop, who lives in Paris, publishes the newspaper *Présence Africaine,* and is the organizer of the International Conference of Negro Authors and Artists. Naturally, the Negro intellectuals pay close attention to Touré's speeches and actions. Alioune Diop: "Our culture must do more than stimulate us, it must determine our future path. Experience has shown that we have always solved our problems without difficulty, when we have approached them from an authentically African point of view."

President Touré himself on this point: "The meaning of the concepts Independence and Unity, which is repeatedly distorted in its interpretation, is for the African as follows: a healthy and clear comprehension of compelling historical forces, of what Freedom, Peace, and Unity signify. And this is to be contrasted to the unnatural and therefore impossible so-called communities of European-African composition of those few politicians who proceed from the thought that 'Africa will never achieve unity.' "

Diallo Abdoulaye, Guinea's diplomatic representative to Ghana, has explained: "For the apostles of this new imperium, the Franco-African Community was possible, the Belgian Congo capable of healthy life, and Angola an extension of Europe for Portugal as well as Africa. The only thing that was missing was the specific African personality." In Sékou Touré's opinion, these associations of geographical, cultural, economic and racial realities represent an "incomparable impudence," which would be unnecessary to refute if they didn't more or less consciously follow the theory of racial superiority, on the basis of which the colonialists had "for centuries on end justified their oppressions in Africa."

Touré: "In contrast to the several paths proposed out of arrogance or degeneracy, we propose to follow an African path, that of the restoration of the personality, that of the building up of this continent in the interests of all mankind. . . . The goals of the different areas are complementary. This actual unity leads to prospects for development that are related to total emancipation. Let us recall certain figures: with eight per cent of the world's population, Africa produced in 1950 (according to the Soviet Union) 54 per cent of the world's gold, 46 per cent of its chrome, 60 per cent of its manganese—in 1954 alone the so-called Belgian Congo produced 60 per cent of the world's diamonds. Therein lie the real possibilities for the opening up and development of Africa. But Africa needs freedom to be able to exploit its natural

resources for the benefit of its people. . . . In ten years I hope
that Africa will have achieved its unconditional independence."
The chief goal of Sékou Touré's policy of neutralism is "harmony between the different groups of the whole world." He rejects
the division of the world into Eastern and Western blocs—which
doesn't prevent him from making every attempt to deepen his
contacts with the Eastern countries.

From April 11 to 15, 1960, a second Afro-Asian Solidarity
Conference was held in Conakry. The first had been held in Cairo
in December 1957. Both conferences were inspired by "the spirit
of Bandung." The resolutions of the Conakry conference reflect
what is going on in Africa and Asia today. Certainly, there were
differences of opinion, and it was evident that many young African nationalists are skeptical about the influence of the Eastern
bloc. But for the moment they welcome every chance to attack
colonialism and imperialism—and with it the West. Delegates from
68 African and Asian groups, parties, and unions came to the
discussions. The largest representation was from the nations of
Negro Africa. The second largest bloc came from Asia, the third
from the Arab countries, and the fourth from the Soviet Union,
Red China, Vietnam, North Korea, and the Mongolian People's
Republic.

The conference decided to adopt a new name: *Organisation de
Solidarité des Peuples Afro-Asiatiques* (OSPAA). The permanent
secretariat was composed of delegates from the following countries: Cameroon, Ghana, French Sudan, Iraq, Syria, Soviet Union,
Red China, India, Indonesia, and Japan. Egypt provided the general secretary, who was to be advised by functionaries from the
Soviet Union, Red China, India, Japan, Iraq, and Indonesia, as
well as delegates from the provisional government of Algeria,
Ghana, Guinea, the former Belgian Congo, Uganda, and the provisional government of Cameroon. There is Afro-Asian parity in
the executive. Although neutral countries belong to the organization, Communist influence has the upper hand.

The conference passed resolutions condemning French nuclear tests in the Sahara, the *apartheid* policies of the Union of South Africa, the U.S.–Japanese security treaty, French policy in Algeria, and decided to recognize the provisional government of the Algerian Republic and grant the Algerian rebels more support.

As host to the conference, Sékou Touré declared: "People would like to draw us into the division of the world at all costs, but we are striving for peaceful co-existence and positive neutrality; only in this way can world tensions be reduced. We are of the opinion that the leadership of the affairs of the Afro-Asian peoples should be left to those peoples without limitations and without interference." He went on to say that the delegates to the conference represented a world of hunger, misery and disregard, a world denied every human right by imperialism. "As the representatives of a hundred million people we feel completely justified in regarding ourselves as equally responsible for the management of universal questions and in taking an active part in those decisions that affect all mankind."

It has become the custom to speak of Sékou Touré's touchiness. All Africans today are hypersensitive. They have become so because the interest that the West has shown in the underdeveloped countries has been—and still is—primarily political and economic. Technical and economic aid is usually not motivated by the pure desire to help. Too often those who give it ask themselves: "What's in it for me?" Business is still the primary concern. It is especially necessary to change this. The German business journal *Handesblatt* summed it up: "Human relations are more important than business relations. Foreign aid should first of all be applied on the human level. Too little attention has been paid to this in the press of business."

If this point of view had been expressed earlier, and put into action, everything that has happened in Guinea might have been avoided. It is possible to regard Sékou Touré, too, as an African who has been disappointed on the human level. One recalls his shocking confession that he felt more at home with his French friends than with his own older brothers who had never been to school. His protest against de Gaulle can also be viewed in this light. The misunderstanding between Sékou Touré and de Gaulle will go down in African history as a classic case of misunderstanding between Africans and Europeans, and it is all the more tragic because de Gaulle has tried to help the African more than any other Frenchman.

The other path that existed, and still exists, has been followed by the last of our new leaders in Africa: the remarkable Léopold Sédar Senghor, president of Senegal.

23

LÉOPOLD SÉDAR SENGHOR OF SENEGAL

*The Poet-Philosopher as
          Politician and Statesman*

❋

Until now, we have concentrated on the political aspects of Africa, and culture has gotten rather short shrift. It is therefore fitting that the last of our new leaders in Africa should be primarily a man of learning and culture. Professor Léopold Sédar Senghor, president of the Republic of Senegal, is perhaps Africa's foremost intellectual. Everyone who meets him, esteems this slight, ascetic man. There is something unusual about him, something that sets him apart from the other Africans we have dealt with: he gives one the feeling that he is not an African at all, although he is a Negro. His thought patterns and way of feeling are European—or perhaps it would be better to say universal.

It is possible to place Africans in three rough categories. The first type thinks, feels, and acts like an African—whether among Africans or Europeans. With the best will in the world, they cannot surmount their African origins, and remain to the European decidedly foreign. The second type is represented by most of the men in this book. When they are among Africans, or give speeches to their people, they think, feel, and act wholly African. When they are among Europeans, they act like Europeans. When a European (often unnoticed) observes them among other Africans, he is struck by the transformation and thinks: Africans are hard to understand, unfathomable, even hypocritical, and not to be trusted. In most cases, this would be a false interpretation, especially since Africans are such good tacticians. The third is embodied by Léopold Sédar Senghor—the citizen of the world, a type one meets with increasing frequency in artistic and intellectual circles.

I have talked with Prof. Senghor many times. In Dakar, I came to know his brother, who is trying to formalize the African's cultural heritage, and his second wife, a Frenchwoman. The three of us chatted about Senghor's marriage. "I'm color blind," he said. "I looked for a wife not on the basis of her skin color, but on whether or not I could love her and she could return my love. This is the woman of my heart, and it's only an accident that she is white. She could have been red or yellow or green," he added with a laugh. "We were in love, so we got married."

Léopold Sédar Senghor was born on October 9, 1906 in the coastal town of Joal, Senegal. His family were of the Mandingo tribe. His father was a rich landowner, who became prosperous through the growing and exporting of peanuts. Born a Roman Catholic, Senghor wanted to become a priest. He began his studies with the Fathers of the Holy Spirit, and later attended the Catholic Liebermann Seminary in Dakar, but gradually lost his enthusiasm for a religious vocation. In 1926, he won his baccalaureate degree *summa cum laude*.

Because of his extraordinary talent, his professors saw to it that he received a scholarship to the *Lycée Louis-le-Grand* in Paris. His enthusiasm for Paris, and his passion for poetry, art, and the theatre hindered his scholarly pursuits, but he did pass the examination for admission to the school of philosophy at the *École Normale Supériere*. He wrote an important work on Baudelaire's exoticism and became the first African Negro to win the coveted diploma of *agrégé de l'Université*.

Until 1940, Senghor devoted himself almost exclusively to the teaching of literature, first at the *lycée* in Tours, then at the *Lycée Marcellin Berthelot* in Paris, where the war caught him by surprise. He was drafted into an infantry battalion of colonial troops, became a prisoner-of-war when France surrendered, and was interned until 1942. He organized a resistance group in the internment camp, and when this was discovered by the Germans, they put him in a penal battalion. In 1943, he was permitted to resume teaching at the *Lycée Berthelot*, but continued his resistance work and took a greater interest in politics.

From 1945 to 1959, Senghor was deputy for Senegal to the French Constituent Assemblies and the National Assembly. He was a member of the Socialist Party until 1948, when, with Mamadou Dia, he founded the *Bloc Démocratique Sénégalais*. Despite his political activities, he was appointed professor of Negro-African Languages and Civilization in Paris. From 1948 on, he taught at the *École Nationale d'Administration,* but was politically active in Paris and Dakar.

In 1949, Senghor joined the Group for Overseas Independence and was its president until 1955. On February 23, 1952, Premier Edgar Fauré appointed him secretary of state in the French cabinet, and in 1956 he was elected mayor of Thies, Senegal. Still dissatisfied with the success of his political efforts, Senghor and a number of other leading federalists founded the *Parti du Regroupment Africain* on July 25–27, 1958.

At this time, the African leaders in French West Africa were divided into two camps: those who, like Senghor and Sékou Touré wanted to remain within a unified federal structure, and those led by Houphouet-Boigny who preferred to see each individual territory establish its own relationship with France. In the vote on the new constitution, Senegal, and all of the other territories of French West Africa, with the exception of Guinea, voted to join the French Community.

An important development took place within the new French Community on January 17, 1959, when the union of a new federal state of Mali was announced, comprising the republics of Senegal, Sudan, Dahomey, and Upper Volta, and named after a flourishing empire that had covered much of the territory of West Africa from the 11th to the 17th centuries.

On March 24, 1959, a congress of federalists from Senegal,

Sudan, Upper Volta and Niger met in Dakar, and founded the
Parti de la Fédération Africaine, which would embrace all of the
small conflicting parties in these territories. Senghor was elected
president of the PFA, and said that the party wanted to build a
Negro-African civilization in West Africa, but did not desire immediate independence, and regarded the French Community as the
ideal framework and means for an association with France.

But when the Mali Federation came into official being on April
4, 1959 it comprised only Senegal (pop. 2,260,000; 76,000 sq.
miles; capital, Dakar, pop. 230,000) and the Republic of Sudan,
formerly the French Sudan (468,000 sq. miles; pop. 3,700,000;
capital, Bamako, pop. 100,000.) Senghor was elected president of
the Federal Assembly at Dakar, and Modibo Keita of Sudan was
elected prime minister of the Federation.

Despite what had been said, the directing committee of the
PFA unanimously decided on Sept. 24, 1959 to seek complete
independence for the Mali Federation, within the framework of a
confederal association with France. In presenting Mali's views to
General de Gaulle on November 26, Senghor said that "it is not
a question of rupture or of secession; it is a matter of independence
within the framework, not of an administrative community, but of
a contractual community."

Shortly after midnight on June 19–20, 1960, Senghor proclaimed the independence of Mali to the Federal Assembly in
Dakar. He praised France, which, he said "despite the errors . . .
of colonization . . . has never completely denied the inheritance
of the great revolution of 1789." The new agreements provided
for Mali's continued membership in the French Community, and
cooperation with France in foreign policy, defense, and other areas.

But trouble quickly arose for the Mali Federation. On August
20, 1960, the Legislative Assembly of Senegal, in an atmosphere
of near violence and counter-threats, proclaimed the independence
of Senegal as an independent republic, and the Mali Federation
ceased to exist. De Gaulle tried to arbitrate—in vain. What was
the reason for the sudden end of the Mali Federation? Personal
rivalry between Senghor and Modibo Keita, of the Sudan, the

ambitious prime minister of the Federation, and the difficulties of understanding between the quite different races of both lands, the trading folk of Senegal and the more backward inhabitants of the Sudanese steppes. In any case, African unity suffered a crushing blow.

Senghor was elected president of Senegal on September 5, 1960, and the French government formally recognized the new republic on September 11. Senghor received a message from de Gaulle, in which the general described his election as "the best pledge of friendly and fruitful relations between Senegal and France within our community." Senghor replied that Senegal would always remain loyal to her ties of friendship and cooperation with France.

In sketching Senghor's life, one must not forget to mention his truly remarkable literary works. He began to write as a youth, but did not publish his first collection of African poems until 1945, *Chants d'Ombre,* which made him a lion of the Paris literary salons. There followed *Hosties Noires, Chants pour Naett,* and *Éthiopiques.* In 1948, he published an excellent anthology of African Negro and Madagascan verse, which inspired Sartre's famous essay *Orphée Noire.* This anthology has become the most important collection of contemporary Negro poetry, and has made Negro authors known to a wide public. Senghor collaborates on many important French journals, publishes the newspaper *L'Unité* in Dakar, and has written many essays and political tracts.

Senghor is working hard to combat the economic poverty of independent Senegal. He has started an ambitious development program, and announced austerity measures. The government would like to avoid raising taxes by rigorously paring the costs of government. The number of civil servants, which had been already reduced, was cut back another fifteen per cent. Senghor belongs to those Africans who believe that socialism is the only path for the future development of the African peoples. He is striving for a special kind of socialism, a "democratic socialism that will embrace even spiritual values."

What is the eventual goal of a philosopher and statesman like Léopold Sédar Senghor? "The nation is the first reality of the twentieth century," he has said. But from the individual nations, a powerful federation must arise in West Africa embracing all the former French colonies. "They will turn to the ideal of socialism, 'an open socialism.' From this perspective they will remodel themselves into federated states. These states will have as a goal the advancement of their peoples by raising their living standards and cultural levels. The ways and means to achieve this will be a strong democracy and a planned economy."

The second reality of the twentieth century, according to Senghor, is the interdependence of races and continents, of nations. Senghor's thoughts always return to independence, but: "Let us be logical and have the courage of our convictions. We thought and still think that true authority, through which sovereignty is exercised, is dependent for all nations today on genuine alliances and coalitions. We thought and still think that the French Community is an alliance that is the ideal framework and means of achieving genuine cooperation, because the constitution of 1958 intended it to be a dynamic community. The whole world seeks French technicians. Whereas the great nations of Europe and America allot only one per cent of their national budgets to the underdeveloped countries, France allots two per cent. And, finally, the French people have always spoken out for the emancipation of the colored peoples. It was Frenchmen who supplied the most important and decisive anti-colonial literature."

Nevertheless, Senghor would like to transform the French Community, which recent events have already modified from its original form, into a "multi-nation federation." Today even the anti-federalists are coming around to this view, and, for that reason, Guinea and Arab North Africa should not be left to go it alone. "In the old régime, they were part of us. They are our African neighbors. Their intellectuals were educated in the French pattern. While we await developments within the French Community which will permit us to establish political ties with them, we can, under the protective leadership of the Community, create economic and cultural ties. There is no question here of ignoring our African neighbors, especially those who speak English. But let's be frank: they shouldn't ask us to sever our links with the French Community while they remain within the Commonwealth. Horizontal, inter-African unity is being increasingly established, in that, as a beginning, we are establishing cultural and economic ties, while the vertical unity between us and our mother countries is changing, without being broken. We cannot secure peace by a war of the races or a war of the continents. Man remains our chief concern; he is our measure in all things."

The new leaders in Africa are still ready to co-operate with Europe. Under the sign of this readiness the future should read: Co-operation between the technically and economically highly-developed countries and the nations which are still underdeveloped. On its success depends not only the future of Africa, but the future of Europe, and perhaps the world.

Perhaps the spirit of emerging Africa has been given its finest expression in the words of the Senegalese national anthem, composed by its poet-president, Léopold Sédar Senghor, product of two cultures, whose words are the white man's but whose imagery is purely African:

> We will make your great plan our own,
> And protect the chicks from the raids of the kite,
> Making of them, from East to West, from North
>   to South,
> An upstanding and united people without
>   divisions,
> But a people turned to face the winds of all the
>   world. . . .

24

MUCH STILL REMAINS TO BE DONE

*

Now that the reader has made the acquaintance of a number of the new leaders of Africa, the old question poses itself once again, *"Quo Vadis, Africa?"*

And what can the white who counsels the African in cultural, technical, and economic matters do to help him—and really all peoples of the earth? The most important prerequisite for all cooperation in Africa—and everywhere in the world—is at last to create better relations between people. That has been lacking for centuries.

Many Africans of good will have been left in recent years without answers to the many diverse questions they have put to the West. Instead of answers, there has been silence. Instead of doors being opened to the African, they have been closed. Because of this many Africans have become our enemies, and we whites—Europeans and Americans—are still going on making more and more enemies in Africa. An end must be put to this! Not tomorrow, but today—immediately. There is no more time to lose.

We can find partners in establishing these better relations— and this must be done without exceptions—among all Africans with whom we come into contact. Our partners in Africa are by no means only to be found among presidents and leaders of governments, party workers, teachers, and manual laborers, but in every individual African. It was always one of the great mistakes of the whites to believe that they should behave differently towards highly placed Africans than towards those who lead a primitive, simple life close to the earth in an isolated jungle village. The primitives of Africa have just as much of a soul as the *Evolués* in the large cities. They are not "soulless savages" or "soulless animals" as they were often portrayed in derogatory writings of an earlier era. Yes, some of them are even unspoiled by modern civilization and therefore more sensitive than the harried, tense, and overwrought Africans in the large cities.

In caravan camps or in oases in the deserts of the Sahara, or in villages in the jungle or primeval forests, I continually encountered people of the purest manners and morals and was often ashamed when they offered me their friendship and hospitality and in so doing revealed goodness, kindness, humility, and sincerity in the most sublime form—ashamed because I hadn't expected it. Anyone who has lived in Africa free of prejudices will be able to testify that one frequently finds more humanity among the Africans than among Europeans and Americans.

It is really important that no white, wherever he lives, make himself guilty of racial defamation or discrimination. It is necessary to emphasize that in this area there can be no distinctions. Whoever considers himself superior to one group is no better than one who considers himself above all groups.

It is also impossible to say: "I have nothing against the Jews; I am against the racial clashes in Little Rock, but I do agree with *apartheid* in South Africa, because . . ." When one makes distinctions, compromises, one is opening the door—however slightly—to those men who despise Mankind. As many people repeat what certain unscrupulous men say, the danger is too great of the poison of racism continuing to spread.

God created the races and there is no divine command that one race should subjugate another. To cite de Beaumont: "The stupidest nobility is the aristocracy of the skin." One must accept the races as a fact, like the earth, the sun, the moon and the stars, like the equinox or the seasons. One should rejoice at the great variety of God's human garden.

The summons to religious tolerance should obviously not be

ignored. There are many religions on this earth, enough so that a European from a Christian background above all must take a firm stand for religious tolerance. We are reminded of the necessity for this every day in Europe and America.

Yes, why do we frequently deny that there are other religions, some of them older than Christianity and in which millions of people believe, and which have just as much right to exist as Christianity? In this connection, Jacob Burckhardt described religion as: "the expression of the eternal and imperishable metaphysical needs of human nature. . . ."

The failings cited have still another consequence: lack of tolerance in cultural matters. That is logical. Whoever doesn't tolerate other races and religions also cannot countenance their cultures and civilizations, recognize their existence or rights to equality. Each race and religion has its own view of the world and its own conception of God.

That is also based on the will of the Creator—under whatever name He may be worshipped. Differences in cultures and civilizations constitute the diversity of our world. Why do so many hesitate to accept this? It should give us strength, should make us powerful, fill us with joy and happiness, humility and gratitude, also in relation to the divine, the creative—and indeed without regard to whether this richness is of divine, mythical or human origin.

Just as there are many mansions in God's house for many races and religions, so is there enough room for many diverse forms of cultures and civilizations. From them derive all those tensions that are continually displayed by new cultures and civilizations. When a people isolates itself, not only economically, but by pursuing a policy of cultural autarchy (self-sufficiency), it will fail. Autarchy is a synonym for sterility, for infertility.

The whites must at last come to see in each human being the image of God. If they don't, they will be themselves hastening their own downfall. Whites overlook the fact that biology alone is against them. The colored peoples are propagating more quickly than the white and are already awaiting the disappearance from this earth of the white race. Nearly every African country has a rapidly rising birth rate and a rapidly declining death rate. Let us recall the words of the Nigerian nationalist leader Nnamdi Azikiwe: "Before we reach the year 2000 the United States will be almost destroyed, Europe in any case completely destroyed. By whom? Naturally by black Africa!" Let us recall Elijah Muhammad, founder of the extremist Black Moslem movement. This Negro has already won hundreds of thousands of colored people to his cause in the United States, and Arthur Schlesinger Jr. and Melville J. Herscovits are justified in continually sounding warnings about him.

In any case the colored peoples are now declaring a racial struggle against the whites that is obviously tied up with the racial policies of the whites and contains an extremely bitter ultimatum. The whites must make peace with the colored peoples not only for humanist and Christian reasons, but because wisdom, self-preservation demands it. As the number of independent African countries grows, so does the power of the Afro-Asian bloc, for example in the United Nations. Whites are becoming increasingly dependent on the favor of the underdeveloped countries. That is why it is so urgent that we extend cultural, economic and political assistance to them under the proper conditions. Only then can we count on their friendship in future.

Yes, the whites' most pressing task is truly this: at last to create better, more worthy relations between themselves and the Africans and really among all peoples, without regard to their skin color, race, religion, culture or civilization. No one has the right to say: that's no concern of mine. It affects everyone. And only when everyone finally contributes to the leveling of the mountain of false or long betrayed traditions that confine our current way of life, and apply the lessons of history to the present, can the necessary change take place. The Tuaregs of the Sahara teach that hearts can draw closer, even when the tents stand far apart.

INDEX

ABAKO, 147, 148, 149, 150, 152, 156, 157
Abbas, Ferhat, 17–24
Abbud, Ibrahim, 49, 50, 51–54
Abdoulaye, Diallo, 287
Abubakar Tafawa Balewa, Alhaji, 193–199, 204, 209, 214
African National Congress (ANC), 93, 94, 111, 114, 115, 116, 117, 120, 121, 123
African Democratic Rally (RDA), 170, 176, 179–180
Afrikanders, 104, 108 ,109, 127
Afro-Asian Solidarity Conferences, 288
Aggrey, J. E. Kwegyir, 96, 228
Ahidjo, Ahmadou, 179–186, 187, 189, 190–191, 257
Ahmadu Bello, Alhaji, 211–214
Akintola, Samuel Ladoke, 207–211
Algeria, 17–24, 30, 34, 103, 186, 269, 270
All African People's Conference, 4, 33, 61, 64, 75, 94–95, 96, 111, 130, 151, 210, 235, 241, 242, 277
Americo-Liberians, 262, 267, 271
Anglican Church, 124, 126, 132
Angola, 149, 155, 160, 287
Apartheid, 4, 88, 94, 95, 101ff., 106–107, 109ff., 114, 116ff., 120, 122, 125ff., 136, 270
Arab League, 14, 33, 42
Asians, 66, 70, 71, 79, 81, 85, 87, 88, 103, 129
Association des Ancièns Élèves des Pères de Scheut (ADAEPS), 145, 146
Awolowo, Obafemi, 193, 203–207, 208, 209, 211, 212, 215
Azikiwe, Nnamdi (Benjamin), 193, 199, 202–203, 205, 206, 211, 215, 228

Banda, Hastings Kamutzu, 78, 88, 93–100, 200
Baudouin, King, 143, 144, 158, 159, 163
Bloc Démocratique Sénégalais, 293

Boers, 101, 102, 134
Boer War, 102, 119
Bolikango, Jean, 145–146, 157–158
Bourguiba, Habib, 17, 25–30, 34, 36, 43
Brussels Congo Conference, 154–155, 162, 165
Buddha, 150
Bunche, Ralph, 164
Busia, K. A., 4, 233–234, 244–245

Cameroons, 176–191, 217, 219, 225
    British, 176, 177, 183, 186, 188–189
    French, 170, 176, 177, 184, 186–188, 189, 253
Cameroon Congress Party, 188, 233, 234, 244
Cameroon National Democratic Party, 188–189
Catroux, George, 18–19
Central African Party (CAP), 93
Central African Republic, 168, 174
Chad, 168, 174
Choureau, Etchika, 15
Churchill, Winston S., 38, 97
Circle of *Evolués,* 152, 156
Colons, 9, 22, 24
Coloureds, 108, 114, 116, 133 *(see also Mulattoes)*
Comité de l'Unité Togolaise (CUT), 219, 220, 222, 223
Communes, 282
Confédération des Associations des Katangaaises (CONAKAT), 157, 162
Congo, 43, 138–175
    Belgian, 138–140, 168, 174, 191, 192, 247, 267, 287
    French, 149, 158n., 160, 170
    Kingdom of the Lower, 149
    Portuguese Lower, 149
    Republic of the, 158–167, 168–175, 179
    United States of the, 161
Convention People's Party, 230, 238
Coptic Christian Church, 56
Council of Commissioners-General, 166

302